Psychology in Progress

General editor: Peter Herriot

The Pathology
and
Psychology
of Cognition

Psychology in Progress

Already available

The Pathology
and
Psychology
of Cognition

edited by
ANDREW BURTON

METHUEN

London and New York

First published in 1982 by
Methuen & Co. Ltd
11 New Fetter Lane, London EC4P 4EE

Published in the USA by
Methuen & Co.
in association with Methuen, Inc.
733 Third Avenue, New York, NY 10017

British Library Cataloguing in Publication Data

The Pathology and psychology of cognition. —
(Psychology in progress)
1. Cognition disorders
I. Burton, Andrew II. Series
616.89   RC553.C64

ISBN 0-416-30810-4
ISBN 0-416-30820-1 Pbk

Library of Congress Cataloging in Publication Data

The Pathology and psychology of cognition.
(Psychology in progress)
Includes index.
1. Cognition. 2. Cognition disorders.
3. Human information processing.
I. Burton, Andrew. II. Series. [DNLM: 1. Cognition.
2. Cognition disorders. BF 311 P297]
BF311.P315 1982   153   82-12526
ISBN 0-416-30810-4
ISBN 0-416-30820-1 (pbk.)

35,167

Contents

Notes on the contributors

D. E. Blackman is Professor and Head of the Department of Psychology at University College Cardiff, and was President of the British Psychological Society for 1981/2. His main experimental research interests are in operant conditioning, with particular reference to the effects of drugs on operant behaviour, but he is also interested in all aspects of contemporary behaviourism, and in psychology and law. He has published numerous research papers and has written one book, *Operant Conditioning: an Experimental Analysis of Behaviour* (Methuen, 1974) and has edited another with J. P. Sanger, *Contemporary Research in Behavioral Pharmacology* (Plenum Press, 1978).

Anthony W. H. Buffery is Senior Lecturer in Psychology at Melbourne University and Honorary Neuropsychologist at the Austin Hospital and the Royal Children's Hospital, Melbourne. He graduated from Hull University and has studied and taught at the Universities of Cambridge, Oxford, McGill and London, he was also a Prize Research Fellow and Full Fellow of Corpus Christi College, Cambridge. His research interests are developmental neuropsychology, and techniques for brain rehabilitation and humour.

Andrew Burton is Senior Lecturer in Psychology at the North East

London Polytechnic. He received his Ph. D. from London University in 1974 and has published (jointly) two books on the psychology of thinking: *Thinking: Its Nature and Development* (Wiley, 1974) and *Thinking in Perspective* (Methuen, 1978).

David R. Hemsley is Senior Lecturer in the Department of Psychology at London University, an honorary principal clinical psychologist to the Bethlem Royal and Maudsley Hospital, and a Fellow of the British Psychological Society. He graduated from Magdalene College, Cambridge in 1968 having studied psychology as part of the Natural Sciences Tripos and subsequently trained as a clinical psychologist at the Institute of Psychiatry, London University. The author of numerous journal articles on a wide range of topics, his special interest is in cognitive disturbance in schizophrenia.

Ruth Lesser is Head of the Sub-Department of Speech, and Senior Lecturer, at Newcastle University, with an attachment as honorary speech therapist to the Newcastle Health Authority. She graduated in English from London University in 1951; after working in features editing, advertising and child-rearing, she took a degree in Speech at Newcastle University, became Ridley Fellow in Psychology there and completed her Ph. D. on acquired disorders of verbal comprehension.

Ray Meddis is Senior Lecturer at the Department of Human Sciences, University of Technology, Loughborough. He has been involved in sleep research since 1967, with a particular emphasis on clarifying issues surrounding the function of sleep. More recently he has concentrated on the statistical comparison of sleep in different mammalian species. He also has an interest in non-parametric statistics and speech perception. His publications include *The Sleep Instinct* (Routledge & Kegan Paul, 1977) which broadly summarizes his theoretical standpoint.

Susanna Millar is a Research Officer at the Department of Experimental Psychology, University of Oxford. She has published many research papers and articles on cognitive development and sensory handicap, and is currently working on children's utilization of information from touch and movement.

Jules Davidoff is at present investigating disorders of visual perception at the Neuropsychology Unit at the Radcliffe Infirmary, Oxford. He studied psychology at University College, London and has lectured at the Universities of Swansea, London, Edinburgh and Ghana.

Keith Phillips is Lecturer in Psychology at North East London Polytechnic, teaching physiological psychology and the experimental analysis of behaviour. He graduated from Cambridge University in 1972 having studied psychology within the Natural Sciences Tripos, and obtained a doctorate in 1976 following research on psychopharmacology from Hull University. He was subsequently appointed Research Fellow at Hull on a project investigating cardiovascular psychophysiology. His research interests include cardiovascular psychophysiology, bioenergetics of learning, and optimality analyses of response allocation.

Shuli Reich is Senior Psychologist in the Neurology Department at The London Hospital. She received her doctorate in psychology in 1975 from University College London; since then she has been involved in teaching behavioural sciences to medical and speech-therapy students. Her current research interests include the relationship between language and thought in aphasia and schizophrenia. She has published papers on psycholinguistic and cognitive processes in normal adults, patients with organic brain damage and patients with psychiatric disorders.

John T. E. Richardson is a Lecturer in psychology at Brunel University. He graduated in philosophy and psychology at Oxford University in 1970, and carried out research for his D. Phil. in the Laboratory of Experimental Psychology at Sussex University. He then spent two years at the Churchill Hospital and the Radcliffe Infirmary in Oxford, investigating cognitive dysfunction in neurological and neurosurgical patients. He has published numerous research papers in the field of cognitive psychology, as well as books on Wittgenstein's philosophy of language and on the role of mental imagery in human memory.

J. D. Sanger is Senior Section Leader in charge of the central nervous system research section in the Pharmacology Department of Reckitt and Colman's Pharmaceutical Division in Kingston-upon-Hull. After obtaining a first degree in psychology and physiology from Nottingham University he carried out research and obtained a Ph. D. from the Pharmacology Department of University College London. Since then he has worked as an ICI Research Fellow in the University of Birmingham and as a Lecturer in Psychology in University College Cardiff. At present his research concerns analyses of the ways in which behaviour is altered by drugs and the relevance of such work for developing new and more effective psychoactive drugs.

Foreword

Andrew Burton has succeeded in pulling together a vast range of experimental data and ideas with his team of authors. We learn here about normal human memory, sleep, perception and behaviour and still more about when and why things go wrong. Each chapter is concise and clear, and there are useful references to key original papers which should be of great help to students and their teachers, as well as to those who have perhaps had some of these problems thrust upon them.

This is not a mere catalogue of what is known experimentally and clinically: here there are assessments of evidence and underlying assumptions which only occasionally surface as 'theoretical models'. These are the most difficult to discuss, particularly as there still is no generally accepted philosophy of science. One suspects indeed that as we learn more of information processing and cognitive dysfunction in the human nervous system so we shall also gain insight into how science itself functions, and sometimes leads us astray with its 'clinical' dysfunctions. Conversely, as we understand the information processing in science and medicine so we may gain understanding of information processing in general. However this may be, Andrew Burton's achievement will surely be appreciated by psychologists, and especially those who are concerned with understanding and helping people with problems - and who hasn't got problems?

Richard L. Gregory

Introduction

'From error to error one discovers the truth.' (Freud)

A distinguished professor of anatomy at the University of Vienna addresses his students with the following words: 'In the case of the female genitals, in spite of many temptations - I beg your pardon, *experiments*'. This calamitous slip of the tongue (the substitution of *Versuchungen* for *Versuche*) is one of the many delightful gaffes recounted in Freud's *The Psychopathology of Everyday Life* (1901). Freud held that such blunders were often very revealing and he made extensive use of similar examples to illustrate various principles of unconscious motivation which were central to his psychodynamic psychology. Hidden motives, he believed, could temporarily suppress conscious intentions and lead to a variety of errors; through bungled actions, slips of the tongue and selective forgetting one sees processes at work which normally remain hidden.

To Freud's catalogue one could add the recent study of 'absent-mindedness' reported by Reason (1979), though of course the framework used to interpret these observations is very different. Such reports are more than intellectual curiosities. In psychology situations and tasks likely to produce errors are often deliberately selected for use in experiments. In fact much of the familiar literature of cognitive psychology is concerned with the behaviour of subjects performing various laboratory tasks at or beyond their limits. From the behaviour of systems under stress we hope to make inferences about what those systems are and how they normally function. Both in everyday life and in laboratory investigations, of course, disturbances in cognitive functioning are usually transient and rarely dramatic. Profound alterations with serious and far-reaching consequences may occur, however, in mental illness or where there has been damage to the central nervous system. Sensory handicaps such as blindness and deafness can also result in significant deficits. In contrast to such 'experiments in nature' other disorganizing effects can be artificially produced through conditions such as sleep deprivation and the administration of drugs. The vast literature on all these topics underlines the importance attached to such alterations in behaviour, and this book sets out to examine these fields of research from the point of view of experimental cognitive psychology.

The book's central theme is the relationship between the normality and pathology of cognitive function. It takes as its starting point the unique opportunity afforded by groups suffering cognitive disturbances to examine models of cognitive processes in the context of populations very different from those on which the models are frequently based. In particular, two interrelated questions are considered. What is the significance of psychological dysfunction for our understanding of normally operating processes? And how useful are current models of cognitive function in the analysis of the disorders observed in the groups suffering cognitive disturbances?

The precise value of behavioural changes resulting from disordered function in shedding light on normal processing has been a matter for debate. The sensory functions lost or reduced in subjects who are deaf or blind are relatively clear. Functions disturbed as a result of brain damage, however, are much less clearly defined. Since several of the chapters in this book are concerned with these types of (neuropsychological) data, it is wise to remember Bernard's comment: 'It does not suffice to destroy an organ to understand what functions it serves.' The results of lesions are notoriously difficult to interpret. To begin with there are logical pitfalls in deciding how to localize particular functions. A car deprived of a spark plug will lose power, but it would be incorrect to conclude that power is therefore 'located' in the plugs. Similar difficulties can arise in trying to ascribe particular psychological functions to discrete areas of the brain. In many ways we are trying to understand the effects of damage to an organ whose normal mode or modes of operation we have scarcely begun to understand. In the final chapter I suggest, as an analogy, that the activities of the brain may be compared to a symphony orchestra. Particular processes (musical parts) may be performed in localized regions, but any complex psychological function is like playing a symphony: it requires the integration of many different parts. This suggests that if particular processes are abolished or suppressed by a localized lesion it may be possible to 'hear' the remaining parts more clearly. However, this is little more than a crude metaphor. If, as it is thought, some neuropsychological deficits are the result of a *disconnection* between different systems rather than being caused by the *destruction* of those systems, the analogy is difficult to apply. A related difficulty is that regional brain processes are unlikely to remain static once a lesion has been sustained. Such considerations inevitably complicate the process of interpreting the effects of brain damage in terms of localized systems. Nevertheless, as the opening chapter by Phillips argues, such problems need to be kept in perspective. In addition, a degree of independent verification for hypotheses concerning brain function comes from studies of lateralized stimulus presentation discussed by Davidoff in Chapter 2.

Neuropsychology has more than one focus of interest and is not exclusively concerned with building up a detailed picture of the precise physical location of cerebral functions. It is also concerned with the organization of information-processing systems suggested by the study of impaired functions. As Millar points out in Chapter 6, the study of abnormal populations involves more than the mere description of ways in which the performance of the impaired group 'deviates' from normals. Research will only be of lasting value if it allows us to say something about the underlying mechanisms involved. One of the theoretical aims of neuropsychology, like experimental cognitive psychology, is the fractionation or 'decoupling' of stages of processing. Thus, for example, much attention has been devoted to a detailed examination of patients in whom the capacity to form long-term memories has been severely reduced, but whose performance on tasks requiring short-term retention is unaffected (Richardson, Chapter 3). Studies of disordered cognitive functioning are of great theoretical interest therefore partly because of their ability to disentangle, to an extent not possible under laboratory conditions, processes which normally operate together. Though one cannot assume that such dissociations *prove* the existence of separate processes, these observations provide important convergent evidence to complement investigations using normal healthy subjects. Neither Oatley (1978) nor Richardson (this volume) feel that studies of memory disturbance have done *more* than this. Rather than creating fresh hypotheses, the results have generally only corroborated hypotheses previously confirmed for normals using conventional laboratory methods. On the other hand, the power of such methods to isolate types and stages of processing may be more limited than is often assumed. To quote Anderson (1976): 'It is not possible to uniquely determine cognitive structures and processes.' Some of cognitive psychology's underlying assumptions are also under attack. Allport (1980), for example, rejects the belief that the human information-processing system comprises a set of 'general-purpose' computing devices, the basis of many well-known models of pattern recognition, word storage and memory organization. Citing neuropsychological data, he argues than many human skills appear to be organized in terms of highly specialized subsystems. Arguably, therefore, the insights of neuropsychology have prompted a reappraisal of 'normal' models which in practice would probably not otherwise have occurred.

Of course, Freud's own interpretation of his observations was in line with his psychodynamic psychology. A different perspective, however, is adopted in this book, that of *information processing*, currently the major theoretical and practical framework used to study cognitive processes. A number of influences contributed to the evolution of this, including computer science, systems and communication theory, and many of the quantitative methods and laboratory procedures used generally in human experimental psychology have played an important part in its development. The principal assumption of information-processing psychology is that man can be considered as an information transmission device, and that cognitive activities can be described in terms of a series of stages through which information is guided. Though not directly observable, each stage has unique characteristics which may be isolated by using a range of selected tasks. The stages are also considered to act as components of larger systems. An important assumption is that the overall passage of information through the system is controlled by processes of selection, attention and coding. A further characteristic of information processing is the attempt to express the steps envisaged in formal models which can then be tested experimentally or perhaps by employing computer representations.

In principle, information-processing models have a great deal to contribute to the study of dysfunction. They offer both clear, unifying theoretical structures and established laboratory procedures which have been applied successfully to the analysis of cognitive tasks. In neuropsychology in particular they can also supplement psychometric techniques which are limited in their capacity to define the processes underlying cognitive abilities (Gillham, 1978). The information-processing perspective is also in sympathy with current views which reject the older image of the brain as a collection of isolated and static functions, and which emphasize instead the inter-active and flexible nature of processing in the brain. The contri-butors to this volume were therefore asked to examine their material from the point of view of information-processing psychology, and to consider in particular two questions. What has been revealed about normal processes through investigations of disturbed function? And how useful is the information-processing approach in understanding cognitive dysfunction?

In recent years various misgivings about cognitive psychology and criticisms of it in general and information processing in particular have been expressed. From outside the discipline has come the objection that the information-processing metaphor is a dehumani-zing one. Were it not for the effective counterarguments dis-cussed by Boden (1977) this criticism would limit the applications of the approach to the human problems of adjustment and recovery presented by, for example, neuropsychological patients. In addition, however, searching questions have sprung from within cognitive psychology itself. These are summarized and cogently discussed by Claxton et al. (1980). To the common complaint that the methods of cognitive psychology lack 'ecological validity', they add the frag-mented research efforts, the oversimplified conceptual frameworks, and the concern with the structure or 'architecture' of cognition at the expense of understanding how, under what circumstances and for what purposes the machinery of information processing is actually used. Learning, motivation and action are neglected, while research concentrates on identifying 'general-purpose' structures and processes in cognition or becomes inward looking, focusing either on narrowly defined laboratory phenomena or parochial methodologi-cal issues. No one familiar with the literature could possibly dispute the force of many of these arguments, several of which are echoed in the contributions to this book. At the same time, however, they must be kept in proportion. Allport (1980) discusses some tentative solutions to such problems and, more generally, there are signs that research is now being increasingly directed at applying the study of cognitive processes to real-life problems. Some of these are discussed by Baddeley (1981), and other examples include work on eyewitness testimony, the use of voice identification evidence in criminal investigations (Clifford, 1980) and memory for television news (Berry *et al.*, in press), not forgetting the work on cognitive rehabilitation discussed in Chapter 10 of this volume.

Information processing, the framework for much contemporary cognitive psychology, emerges reasonably well from the close examination it receives in this book, though not without its feathers ruffled. The reader will find no shortage of ideas in the various contributions. All the fields of research discussed demonstrate the 'decoupling' or dissociation of cognitive processes which can occur in functions which are disrupted. Less success has been achieved in the use of such effects to develop an overall integrated picture of cognitive activity, to some extent reinforcing the criticisms discussed above. We can only capture the purposive, adaptive and stimulus-seeking nature of human behaviour, and move beyond a narrowly defined and potentially mechanistic concept of information processing by embracing the dynamic and interactive nature of the process. This represents a formidable challenge to clinical neuropsychology in particular, since here we have probably the strongest evidence of the power of the human mind to organize its resources, adapt its functions and, in the face of crippling deficits, to patch together skills capable of remarkable achievements. No information-processing analysis comes close to explaining the degree of flexibility and inventiveness necessary for residual abilities to function so effectively. though arguably cognitive psychology has the potential capacity to do so.

When we examine behaviour whose normal structure and functions have been disorganized, we look into a window through which we can glimpse only a small part of the whole building. What we see are systems in disarray, stretched beyond their limits and striving to cope. The scene may be confusing and hard to decipher, but it presents cognitive psychology with some of its most urgent intellectual and practical challenges. The argument of this book is that not only does the consideration of disordered functions provide a valuable source of insights for cognitive psychology, but that the analysis of dysfunction will be enhanced through the application of the concepts and methods embodied by the information-processing perspective.

ANDREW BURTON

References

Allport, A. (1980) Patterns and actions: cognitive mechanisms are content-specific. In G. Claxton (ed.) *Cognitive Psychology: New Directions*. London: Routledge & Kegan Paul.

Anderson, J. R. (1976) *Language, Memory and Thought*. Hillsdale, NJ : Lawrence Erlbaum Associates.

Baddeley, A.D. (1981) The cognitive psychology of everyday life. *British Journal of Psychology, 72*: 257-69.

Berry, C. *et al.* (1982, in press) Memory for televised information: a problem for pure and applied psychology. *Current Psychological Reviews*.

Boden, M. (1977) *Artificial Intelligence and Natural Man*. Hassocks, Sussex: Harvester Press.

Claxton, G. (ed.) (1980) *Cognitive Psychology: New Directions*. London: Routledge & Kegan Paul.

Clifford, B. R. (1980) Voice identification by human listeners: on ear-witness reliability. *Law and Human Behaviour 4*: 373-94.

Gillham, W. E. C. (1978) Measurement constructs and psychological structure: psychometrics. In A. Burton and J. K. Radford (eds) *Thinking in Perspective*. London: Methuen.

Oatley, K. (1978) *Perceptions and Representations: The Theoretical Bases of Brain Research and Psychology*. London: Methuen.

Reason, J. (1979) Actions not as planned: the price of automatization. In G. Underwood and R. Stevens (eds) *Aspects of Consciousness*. Vol. 1. London: Academic Press.

1 Investigating psychological dysfunction: problems and prospects

Keith Phillips

Neuropsychology has long been concerned with determining relationships between psychological functions and brain structures. Its primary source of inquiry has been the study of dysfunctions of information processing in adult neurological patients. Such inquiry has three objectives: diagnosis of lesions causing particular dysfunction, elucidation of the nature of the dysfunction, and understanding of 'normal' function. The pursuit of these objectives has depended upon a particular methodological approach where knowledge of neurology is applied to the interpretation of behaviour. The tradition of relating structure to function has a long and well-documented history (e.g. Clarke and Dewhurst, 1972; Young, 1970).

The nineteenth century witnessed the introduction by Gall (1758-1828) of phrenology, which postulated that the brain comprised mental faculties localized within cerebral cortex. The strength of each faculty was determined by the size of the associated cerebral region, and that size could be detected by examination of the overlying cranium. This doctrine gained wide acceptance through its dissemination by Gall and his pupil Spurzheim (1776-1832). Its assumption of functional brain localization remained largely unchallenged until the classical experiments of Flourens (1794-1867).

By employing the techniques of ablation and electrical stimulation Flourens demonstrated that psychological functions of higher vertebrates are not localized in specific regions of cortex, but are rather products of its total action. He asserted that the cerebral cortex functions in an integrated and holistic manner, and his work was the precursor of field theories of cerebral equipotentiality. This philosophy was further advanced by Goltz (1834-1902), who on the basis of partial decortication of dogs concluded that the behaviour deficit observed was proportional to the extent of ablation.

A fresh perspective upon the debate between adherents of the narrow localization view and their opponents the field theorists emerged towards the end of the nineteenth century when clinical evidence began to accumulate, indicating focal representation of psychological functions in cerebral cortex. In 1861 Broca (1824-80) described a patient with a severe dysfunction who showed almost total impairment of motor speech (expressive aphasia) and who had damage to the posterior portion of the inferior frontal gyrus. Subsequent studies on other patients confirmed that expressive speech is associated with this area of the left hemisphere, which is now referred to as Broca's area. Some years later in 1874 Wernicke (1848-1905) described clinical cases where damage to the posterior portion of the left superior temporal gyrus gave rise to an entirely different speech deficit involving loss of ability to understand speech (receptive aphasia). There followed many reports of a similar nature indicating localized centres in the brain for cognitive processes, and by the beginning of this century neurologists had produced detailed functional maps of the cerebral cortex of man. These were similar in one respect to those of the phrenologists: they shared a view of narrow localization of function.

Despite the clinical evidence, this view has not been unchallenged. Lashley (1890-1958) undertook an ambitious research programme studying the relation between learning, retention and amount of cerebral cortex available, the latter being manipulated by lesions. His work, which represents a continuation of both the method and philosophy of Flourens and Goltz, culminated in the publication of his major work *Brain Mechanisms and Intelligence* (1929). It contained the statement of two important and influential principles – equipotentiality and mass action. The empirical support offered by Lashley for these principles is often held as evidence against the view of narrow localization of function. Zangwill's (1961) comprehensive critique of the status of these principles, however, concludes that neither equipotentiality viewed as a 'complete lack of specialization within an area (which may be the whole cortex)' (p.64) nor mass action as 'a general factor governing such parts of the cortex as are demonstrably equipotential in control of a given behaviour pattern' (p.65) are incompatible with concepts of localization. Logically the two polar views are not irreconcilable. As Lashley recognized, for some complex behavioural function there may be a limited area of cortex that is equipotential in control of that function, but different areas of cortex may support different behavioural functions. Nevertheless, in the clinical domain Zangwill admits that 'it is almost impossible to rid oneself of the concept of functional localization in attempting to make sense of the psychological sequelae of brain injury' (p.84). As Zangwill anticipated statements of localization of function have remained as important elements of explanations of psychological dysfunctions.

Miller (1980) has identified two complementary approaches to neuropsychology which he terms the anatomical and the functional. The anatomical approach is concerned with describing changes in psychological functioning that result from lesions in different regions of the brain. In interpreting those changes it attempts to draw conclusions about the functional significanc of particular structures. The functional approach, on the other hand, is concerned with elucidating the nature of dysfunctions that might occur as a result of damage to central nervous tissues; it may be considered as the experimental cognitive psychology of clinical patients, and it may proceed quite independently of any knowledge of structures involved. The latter approach is considered further in Chapter 2. The remainder of the present chapter is concerned primarily with problems encountered during the investigation of the structural bases of psychological functions. It is my intention neither to review the current status of localization controversy nor to summarize the clinical data relevant to that controversy, as excellent commentaries are already available (e.g. Walsh, 1978), but rather to consider the nature of the controversy, the issues contained within it and the prospects for future inquiry.

Two fundamental issues that must be confronted are reductionism and localization. These are clearly related and, in the context of the present discussion, demand consideration of a more general issue, namely the nature of the relationship between psychological models and neural structures. Investigation of the relation between structure and function must take account of these issues, and they are discussed briefly below.

Reductionism

Within neuropsychology reductionism may be considered the implicit belief that neural explanations may be found for behaviours, including cognitive acts, that otherwise have only psychological explanations. There has been considerable debate in psychology about the validity and utility of reductionism. Miller (1980) proposes that the debate is ill directed and ultimately sterile, as different types of explanation, some reductionist others not, may co-exist within psychology. In his considered analysis of this issue, Clark (1980) arrives at a similar conclusion. He correctly points out that reductionism is restricted to the relation between two theories in different disciplines. It does not imply that the two disciplines themselves bear the same relation. This seemingly unremarkable observation has extremely important consequences, as it helps remove the commonly held fear that, if successful, reductionism will entail the elimination of psychological explanations and their replacement by neurophysiological explanations. As Clark clearly shows, this fear is unwarranted: it derives from a particular view of reductionism that he calls 'eliminative reductionism', and which contains a particular feature, the 'implicit replacement assumption'. This assumption states that, if a theory is reduced, then the explanations of the reducing theory replace those of the reduced theory which consequently is eliminated. Clark argues that this assumption is false and that reduction without elimination is not only possible but indeed is inevitable in psychology. Whilst accepting that psychological theories may be reduced to physiological theories he maintains that psychological explanations cannot be replaced by physiological ones, the reason being the non-interchangeability of structural and functional terms. The explanations provided are of different kinds and answer different questions. Essentially a distinction exists between asking *what* a structure does and *how* it does it. Answers to the latter question demand functional explanations employing psychological concepts that cannot be replaced by terms having merely structural characteristics.

12   The pathology and psychology of cognition

Localization of function

The notion of localization of function is an important one for the idea of reductionism because, as Clark has pointed out, statements of localization of function are used to relate psychological to physiological terms. Such statements generally make assertions of the type that structure x is the neural basis of psychological function y. Often those statements are derived from observations of dysfunction following lesions to a particular structure. The logic of such inferences will be examined in some detail below, but first it is necessary to consider what is meant by the terms 'function' and 'localization'.

The term 'function' may have several different senses. That employed in the context 'psychological function' generally means 'does the job of'. Thus, memory function, for example, means the jobs performed by memory in information processing. Dysfunction means that the performance of these jobs is either absent or deficient. 'Localization' suggests that some structure does the job defined, and localization of function involves the identification of some particular structure that does the job. In this case specifying the jobs to be performed specifies what the functions are; that is to say the jobs to be performed must be specified before they are able to be localized. This means that some model of the system must be available from which the jobs to be performed may be derived before localization may proceed.

Models

Attempts to understand psychological functions such as attention, memory or perception have frequently made use of models that 'explain' how the functions are performed. The models adopted are often dependent upon knowledge and concepts from physical science, and hydraulic models, electric models and more recently computer models, for example, have been used. The value of such models is that they allow us to interpret psychological concepts in terms of known principles (Oatley, 1978). A problem with such models is that different levels of explanations may exist, as Gregory (1961) has shown. These levels may be represented as a hierarchy where in principle each level may be reduced to the next level below it. Though each level will express the organization of the system, the lower levels specify only the components of the system and do not predict how the system will function; for that, molar levels of explanation are required. In psychology molar levels of explanation are represented by the 'block-diagram' approach; this, in Gregory's words, specifies 'how a system works' (p.319) by describing the functional organization of the system.

This approach involves drawing boxes with input and output arrows. Each box is responsible for relating a set of input variables to a set of output variables, and the mechanisms within the box must account for the relationship between the variables. The formal relations between the boxes comprising the system will also be specified. Using this approach function is often defined by the job performed by a particular block in the model, in which case the identification of a neural structure which corresponds to that block allows localization of the function concerned. A familiar example is the flow chart for human memory produced by Atkinson and Shiffrin (1968). They postulate three structural features: sensory memory which holds the sensory image, short-term store (STS) and long-term store (LTS). Though cognitive psychologists have now largely rejected the existence of separate 'states' in favour of 'process' models (e.g. Craik and Lockhart, 1972), neuropsychological evidence has largely supported the STS/LTS distinction (see Shallice, 1979; and Chapter 3).

Many models of this type were developed from the information-processing theory approach which emerged in the early 1960s. Newell and Simon (1972), for example, suggested that cognitive functioning is a product of programmes executed by the brain. This computer analogy allows us to conceptualize functions by using familiar principles drawn from a physical information-processing system. The model developed is able to identify the necessary and sufficient set of component processes and the relations between them, and to account for the performance characteristics of the system.

One attraction of the information-processing approach for neuropsychology is that it offers an alternative to a static, compartmentalized view of brain functions by considering functions as dynamic information-processing capabilities. The approach, however, has suffered a decline in recent years; one reason for this as identified by Tulving and Madigan (1970) is that it generates many similar models at a rate that exceeds the rate of their refutation.

Shallice (1979) suggests that neuropsychological evidence may be useful as a means of refuting some models and thereby limiting the number of plausible models for further investigation.

Investigating models

It has been asserted by some that explanations of psychological functions may be achieved by structural models that are independent of knowledge of the brain. Weiskrantz (1973) has argued that such models may be inappropriate for two reasons. First, it is possible that two or more different structural models may be in accord with the known empirical facts. Secondly, a structural model may make correct predictions and yet still be fundamentally incorrect because it ignores the mechanism existing in the brain. For example, several models of pattern perception have been produced which predict the relations between input and behavioural output, but electrophysiological studies have shown that the 'real' nervous system has a logical structure quite different from those of the models. In this context neuropsychology may be applied as a valuable tool in the study of psychological function because it allows the investigation and validation of structural models (Luria, 1979).

Attempts to study function through observations of dysfunction suffer considerable problems, both theoretical and methodological. Major problems related to the interpretation of lesion effects include the limitations inherent in drawing inferences from treatment effects and the extent to which the organizing principles of information processing by the central nervous system may be considered fixed. Methodological problems include the nature of the lesion itself, whether it be diffuse or discrete, the duration of the deficit, the experimental analysis of the deficit, individual differences in performance and the probabilistic relation of symptoms to syndromes (see Kinsbourne, 1971). Consideration of the latter problems, though important, is beyond the scope of the present discussion, which will restrict itself to the problem of interpretation of lesion effects.

Drawing inferences from altered behaviour

It has often been argued that the effects of limited damage to the central nervous system are useful for interpreting 'normal' behavioural function. This potential use of neuropsychology depends upon drawing inferences about function based upon observations of altered performance following damage or injury to, or disease of neural structures. This pursuit, however, is fraught with dangers and should be approached without preconceptions, but, as Webster (1973) has observed, the clinician or experimenter must at some point decide what to observe, and any resulting inferences will tend to be in terms of existing conceptualizations. Gregory (1961) raised a more fundamental issue by challenging the logic of using lesion studies as a means of understanding a complex system. He has argued that it is impossible to deduce how a system works by observing the effects of interference with its parts without knowing in advance the basic design of the system. Using the example of an electronic system - a radio set - he illustrates his argument by pointing to the fallacy of deducing that, because removal of a resistor causes 'howling', the function of resistors is to suppress 'howling'. By analogy he argues that inferences about function made following lesions to neural structures may be similarly false.

The weaknesses of Gregory's argument have been clearly revealed by Weiskrantz (1968) who contends that the functioning of the brain is not deduced in a logical fashion but rather by formulating models or theories that may be tested and subsequently modified, or abandoned to be replaced by others that provide a better fit for empirical data. This pragmatic approach avoids the logical pitfalls illustrated by Gregory's analogy. Further, the nature of the system being investigated may also be important. Gregory's objections apply particularly to a device that is a serial processor of information. Consider the example below where the structures, A, B and C, each perform separate functions.

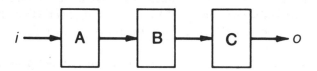

It would be impossible to infer the function of structure B simply by observing a change in the relationship between the input variable i, and the output variable, o, following lesion to B, without knowing the organization of the system. Nevertheless, lesions can be useful for investigating serial-processing systems. Weiskrantz (1974) has pointed out examples of inferences concerning serial processing by the brain that have emerged directly from lesion studies. They include the analysis of interhemispheric integration as inferred from commisural sectioning (e.g. Gazzaniga, Bogen and Sperry, 1965) and the re-interpretation of classical clinical syndromes, such as aphasia, apraxia and agnosia, as disconnection syndromes (Geschwind, 1965). Mishkin's (1979) work using non-human primates illustrates the value of disconnection lesions for investigating the functional organization of sensory systems.

Of course, the brain may not be a serial processor of information. In many ways it resembles more a parallel processing device made up of several separate processing units (Neisser, 1967). Given such a device the lesion method has far greater utility for it allows the simplification of a complex system by fractionation. Patterson (1981), for example, has shown that varieties of acquired dyslexia show orderly relations to dimensions and manipulations of reading performance, suggesting that neurological damage may impair different aspects of a complex function. Similarly, Shallice (1979) has shown how neuropsychological evidence allows fractionation of memory systems into component processes.

To a large extent the demonstration of separate functional systems depends upon a concept introduced by Teuber (1955): double dissociation of function. This requires that symptom A appears following lesion to one structure but not another, and symptom B appears following lesion of the other structure but not the former. Such dissociation is taken to demonstrate the specificity of a particular lesion. Weiskrantz (1968) has pointed out that for maximum information to be derived from this method it is necessary that the lesions be alike in all but locus and that the tasks adopted for revealing symptoms A and B are similarly alike in all but one aspect. If these constraints are observed the method is extremely useful for the analysis of complex processes by fractionating them into simpler component parts.

In reality the brain may be both serial and parallel processor in which case the interpretation of lesion effects may be extremely complex. The situation may be further confused by a hierarchical organization within the brain. As Luria has observed (1973), many psychological functions depend upon the interaction of both cortical and subcortical structures. Information processing depends upon the maintenance of a sufficient level of cortical excitation. This is regulated by the dynamic reciprocal relationship between cortex and subcortex. The general principle that information processing may take place on different levels was expressed by Hughlings Jackson and has been re-iterated by others including Craik and Bartlett (see Broadbent, 1977). Essentially, it suggested that the organization of complex psychological processes can only be viewed from their level of construction rather than their localization. If such a hierarchical organization exists where lower levels are controlled by higher but are also capable of functioning independently, then local lesions will give rise to both primary and secondary effects. A lesion in a particular locus will affect both the higher and lower levels of functioning subserved by that structure: the higher levels directly, and indirectly the lower levels that are dependent upon the higher. Interpretation of such effects will present a challenge of massive proportion to the clinical analyst.

Organizing principles

Adoption of the block-diagram approach as outlined above means that the task of localization of function is to locate and identify structures within the brain that do the jobs of the labelled boxes. This exercise can only be successful if the two systems, the neural system and the model system, are functionally isomorphic. It must be possible to map the model directly onto the neural system; each function must be localized to some particular structure or set of structures. There is sufficient clinical evidence available, however, to suggest that such direct mapping is unlikely to be achieved because the organizing principles of the cerebral cortex may be indeterminate.

The functional organization of the brain is not fixed. Luria (1973) has described reorganization occurring during normal development. More dramatic examples of reorganization occur during abnormal development, such as the congenital absence of the *corpus callosum* failing to result in detectable changes in psychological functioning (Jeeves, 1965). The importance of developmental influences upon cerebral organization is clearly seen in the dependence on the effects of hemispherectomy upon the age of the patient. Following left hemispherectomy it is generally accepted that, unlike adult patients, infants do not show major speech deficits; their language impairments are subtle and relatively insignificant (Dennis and Kohn, 1975; McFie, 1961): see Chapter 10 of this volume for a more extended discussion of such data. These considerations suggest that simple mapping of structure to function is unlikely to be possible, in which case strict localization of function may prove to be an impossible goal. A further restriction upon the achievement of that goal concerns the issue of strategies of information processing.

The notion of strategies of information processing is hardly a new one (e.g. Newell and Simon, 1972; Underwood, 1978) but it does raise important questions for neuropsychology. In his discussion of this issue Kohn (1979) has observed that, 'A basic assumption of localization is that all individuals approach a given task in the same way' (p.237). This, of course, is almost certainly not the case. Different strategies may be employed to achieve the same functional goal, which means that different neural structures may be involved in what appears to be the same function. The possibility of alternative strategies for a particular task may explain the variability shown by patients with similar lesions. An implication of this situation is that for the interpretation of clinical syndromes and the localization of their neurological bases we need to know far more of the strategies of information processing available for a given task.

The relationship, however, is not one way. As Kohn has pointed out, the relation between strategy and structure may depend upon the ability of structures to process information in particular ways. Through experience individuals may learn to recognize which strategy is most appropriate for a particular task and be able to shift input to the appropriate processing structure. Following damage to particular structures the neurological patient may have fewer strategies available and hence have to adopt non-preferred strategies or even to re-learn the principles governing information processing for some tasks. In such instances neuropsychology may provide unique insights into performance of information-processing tasks according to limited or non-preferred processing strategies, and offer a means of looking at the limits of the system.

Lesion studies are also of interest in those instances where function remains despite lesion damage. An area of particular interest is recovery of function. This phenomenon refers to the well-established empirical finding (discussed further in Chapter 10) that the initial effects of brain damage are more severe than the long-term effects (see Finger, 1978). This phenomenon is often taken to indicate that the plasticity of the central nervous tissues allows remaining neural structures to substitute for the regions destroyed. Clearly, such substitution would require reorganization of the functional capabilities of the spared tissues (see Chapter 10).

An intriguing alternative hypothesis has been offered by LeVere (1980). He points out that lesions may have one of two effects, either temporary or permanent disruptions. In the former instance recovery of function is dependent upon functional sparing of the lesioned neural structure rather than compensation by reorganization of alternative neural structures. His hypothesis assumes that neurological damage results in a shift in 'behavioural control' or in our terms, information processing to those structures not affected; this causes a shift to alternative processing mechanisms. If the shift is successful and performance goals are achieved then it may be retained, in which case compensation may be said to have occurred. If, however, the shift is unsuccessful, then provided there has been some sparing of the original structure for the function in question, there will be a shift back and re-utilization of the spared tissues, and recovery of function may be concluded. The behavioural deficit observed corresponds to the shifts to alternative processing mechanisms. If there is insufficient sparing of the original tissues recovery of function is impossible, and if alternative processing strategies are inappropriate a permanent deficit will result.

It appears, therefore, that the organizing principles of information processing need not be biologically predetermined, but rather depend upon the demands of the task and neural structures operationally available at a particular time. The availability of neural structures need not of course be limited solely by physical restrictions such as lesion damage, but by other processing demands occurring at the same time as those required for the task being investigated. It is generally the case that investigation of neurological patients looks at performance on tasks in isolation. This fails to simulate 'real-life' tasks where simultaneous and even incompatible processing demands may co-exist. With this in mind one is forced to accept Kohn's (1979) conclusion that 'Untangling the web of the relations between strategy and localization can only be accomplished through studying CNS function in human beings engaged in real behaviour' (p.245). Though this may introduce difficulties and complexities for the clinician and research scientist, it might repay rich rewards in terms of the validity and applicability of the findings.

Summary and conclusions

This chapter has attempted to draw attention to some of the considerable problems faced when investigating cognitive dysfunction. Both the logic and the methodology involved in interpreting the functional effects of lesions is complex. Both Gregory (1961) and Oatley (1978) have warned against the dangers of acceptance of lesion effects as a means of studying psychological functions. Though admitting that alterations in behaviour may be useful for investigating the brain's resistance to damage or in isolating neurologically separate subsystems by dissociation of complex functional systems, they assert that such knowledge cannot answer questions of *how* a mechanism works. Localization of function may show that some necessary though not sufficient condition is fulfilled by a particular structure, but it is unable to say what the causal mechanisms are. Oatley has further argued that a limitation to progress in the brain sciences generally has been lack of appropriate models to explain functional organization of systems. It seems to me that the information-processing approach offers a potentially powerful framework from which such models might emerge.

Adoption of this approach has the immediate and obvious advantage of considering psychological functions as dynamic processing capabilities in contrast to the static compartmentalized view implied by the narrow localization philosophy. This is more in accord with our knowledge of the plasticity of central nervous tissue and its apparent indeterminacy of function. Further, even if strict localization could be demonstrated, which, as indicated above, is unlikely, it is unable to explain the interactions required to produce the integration evidenced by organized and efficient behavioural function. Luria (1973) has proposed that functions should best be regarded as 'complex functional systems' with dynamic levels of organization in the brain, which might explain why local brain lesions are rarely accompanied by total loss of a function but rather by its disorganization. In this case discrete loci of functions are unlikely to be found and the concept of localization becomes far more imprecise.

There are, as Moscovitch (1979) points out, some similarities between the assumptions and practice of nineteenth-century localization theorists and present-day information-processing theorists, notably their attempts to fractionate complex psychological functions into simpler subsystems and to establish the relations between them. He suggests that the potential for 'cross-fertilization between the two disciplines is very high' (p.381). Both neuropsychology and information-processing theory aim to develop models that can account for the performance characteristics of psychological functions by identifying the component processes and the relations between them. It may be that the models of one discipline become reduced to those of the other, but as observed earlier this does not mean that the disciplines themselves bear the same reductionist relationship. As Shallice (1979) suggests, their relationship is more likely to be as alternative explanations for the same phenomena within different knowledge systems, each having its own distinct theoretical structures. Moscovitch (1979) concludes that 'the partnership between information-processing theory and neuropsychology has been successful and lucrative for both' (p.433). It is undeniable that analysis of dysfunction will be enhanced by application of knowledge and techniques from information-processing theory, but it should also be appreciated that neuropsychology can provide invaluable insights for information-processing theory. The integration of these insights should be mutually beneficial, and provide a theoretical framework that is capable of reflecting the complexities presented by the functional organization of the brain.

References

Atkinson, R. C. and Shiffrin, R. M. (1968) Human memory: a proposed system and its control processes. In K. W. Spence and J. T. Spence (eds) *The Psychology of Learning and Motivation: Advances in Research and Theory.* New York: Academic Press.

Broadbent, D. E. (1977) Levels, hierarchies and the locus of control. *Quarterly Journal of Experimental Psychology 29*: 181–201.

Clark, A. (1980) *Psychological Models and Neural Mechanisms.* Oxford: Clarendon Press.

Clarke, E. and Dewhurst, K. (1972) *An Illustrated History of Brain Functions.* Oxford: Sandford Publications.

Craik, F. I. M. and Lockhart, R. S. (1972) Levels of processing: a framework for memory research. *Journal of Verbal Learning and Verbal Behavior 11*: 671–84.

Dennis, M. and Kohn, B. (1975) Comprehension of syntax in infantile hemiplegics after cerebral hemidecortication. *Brain and Language 2*: 472–8.

Finger, S. (ed.) (1978) *Recovery from Brain Damage: Research and Theory*. New York: Plenum Press.

Gazzaniga, M. S., Bogen, J. E. and Sperry, R. W. (1965) Observations on visual perception after disconnection of the cerebral hemispheres in man. *Brain 88*: 221–36.

Geschwind, N. (1965) Disconnection syndromes in animals and man. *Brain 88*: 237–94, 585–644.

Gregory, R. L. (1961) The brain as an engineering problem. In W. H. Thorpe and O.L. Zangwill (eds) *Current Problems in Animal Behaviour*. Cambridge: Cambridge University Press.

Jeeves, M. A. (1965) Psychological studies of three cases of congenital agnesis of the *corpus callosum*. In A. V. de Reuck and R. Porter (eds) *Functions of the Corpus Callosum, Ciba Foundation Study Group N. 20*. London: J. & A. Churchill.

Kinsbourne, M. (1971) Cognitive deficit: experimental analysis. In J. L. McGaugh (ed.) *Psychobiology: Behaviour from a Biological Perspective*. New York: Academic Press.

Kohn, H. (1979) Current topics in neuropsychology. In K. Connolloy (ed.) *Psychology Survey No. 2*. London: George Allen & Unwin.

LeVere, T. E. (1980) Recovery of function after brain damage: a theory of the behavioural deficit. *Physiological Psychology 8* (3): 297–308.

Luria, A. R. (1973) *The Working Brain*. Harmondsworth: Penguin.

Luria, A. R. (1979) Neuropsychology of complex forms of human memory. In L-G. Nilsson (ed.) *Perspectives on Memory Research*. Hillsdale, NJ: Lawrence Erlbaum Associates.

McFie, J. (1961) The effect of hemispherectomy on intellectual functioning in cases of infantile hemiplegia. *Journal of Neurology and Neurosurgical Psychiatry 24*: 240–9.

Miller, E. (1980) Neuropsychology and the relationship between brain and behaviour. In A. J. Chapman and D. M. Jones (eds) *Models of Man*. Leicester: British Psychological Society.

Mishkin, M. (1979) Analogous neural models for tactile and visual learning. *Neuropsychologia 17*: 139–52.

Moscovitch, M. (1979) Information processing and the cerebral hemispheres. In M. S. Gazzaniga (ed.) *Handbook of Behavioural Neurobiology*. Vol. 2: *Neuropsychology*. New York: Plenum Press.

Neisser, U. (1967) *Cognitive Psychology*. New York: Appleton-Century-Crofts.

Newell, A. and Simon, H. (1972) *Human Problem Solving*. Englewood Cliffs, NJ: Prentice-Hall.

Oatley, K. (1978) *Perceptions and Representations: The Theoretical Bases of Brain Research and Psychology*. London: Methuen.

Patterson, K. E. (1981) Neuropsychological approaches to the study of reading. *British Journal of Psychology 72* (2): 151–74.

Shallice, T. (1979) Neuropsychological research and the fractionation of memory systems. In L-G. Nilsson (ed.) *Perspectives on Memory Research*. Hillsdale, NJ: Lawrence Erlbaum Associates.

Teuber, H. L. (1955) Physiological psychology. *Annual Review of*

Psychology 6: 267-94.

Tulving, E. and Madigan, S. A. (1970) Memory and verbal learning. *Annual Review of Psychology 21*: 437-84.

Underwood, G. (1978) *Strategies of Information Processing*. London: Academic Press.

Walsh, K. W. (1978) *Neuropsychology: A Clinical Approach*. Edinburgh: Churchill Livingstone.

Webster, W. G. (1973) Assumptions, conceptualizations and the search for the functions of the brain. *Physiological Psychology 1*: 346-50.

Weiskrantz, L. (1968) Treatments, inferences and brain function. In L. Weiskrantz (ed.) *Analysis of Behavioral Change*. New York: Harper & Row.

Weiskrantz, L. (1973) Problems and progress in physiological psychology. *British Journal of Psychology 64*: 511-20.

Weiskrantz, L. (1974) Brain research and parallel processing. *Physiological Psychology 2*: 53-4.

Young, R. M. (1970) *Mind, Brain and Adaptation in the Nineteenth Century: Cerebral Localisation and its Biological Context from Gall to Ferrier*. Oxford: Clarendon Press.

Zangwill, O. (1961) Lashley's concept of cerebral mass action. In W. H. Thorpe and O. L. Zangwill (eds) *Current Problems in Animal Behaviour*. Cambridge: Cambridge University Press.

2 Information processing and hemispheric function

Jules Davidoff

Introduction

Standard tests of human mental abilities such as the Wechsler Intelligence Scales are divided into two main sections, one relating to verbal skills and the other to performance (supposedly, non-verbal) skills. Even though many tests of mental ability are performed poorly after damage to either cerebral hemisphere, verbal tests are more affected by left-hemisphere (LH) and performance tests by right-hemisphere (RH) damage (Reitan, 1955). It would seem that each hemisphere is dominant for different skills. Perhaps because of the importance of speech and logical reasoning for our culture, clinicians refer to the language hemisphere as the dominant hemisphere and the other hemisphere as the non-dominant. The usual arrangement for right handers is for the LH to be dominant for language. Dominance in left handers seems to be less certain but, even for this group, more will show LH than RH dominance for language.

The use of brain-damaged patients to further investigate the psychological processes involved is complicated by methodological problems peculiar to the use of such populations. For example, one cannot always be confident that lesions are unilateral and that adequate controls have been chosen. Also, populations of brain-damaged subjects are often small and cannot be tested for long periods.

The investigation of hemispheric function in normal subjects can be carried out in most modalities. For vision, this is only possible because certain anatomical connections from the sense receptors progress solely to one hemisphere. Stimuli in the subject's left visual field (LVF) are directed to the RH and stimuli in the right visual field (RVF) to the LH. Thus, with the subject looking at a fixation point, a stimulus to one side of fixation, presented at a speed too fast for the eye to move, will be received initially by one hemisphere. In the auditory modality, despite the lack of such a clear anatomical division, there also seems to be a similar privileged contralateral access. Simultaneously presented (dichotic) sounds give a right-ear advantage (REA) if verbal, and a left-ear advantage (LEA) if non-verbal. This functional contralateral advantage (Kimura, 1961) is most clearly observed when there is competition for the hemispheric processing mechanism. Monaural stimulation is certainly less likely to produce an ear advantage. Though less often investigated, it is also possible to present stimuli for tactile manipulation to normal subjects since distal movements (e.g. finger movements) are controlled from one hemisphere. The major experimental work to be reported here will concern the visual modality, but the arguments and theoretical points raised concern the other modalities as well.

Experimental procedures with normals use either accuracy or reaction time (RT) as the measure of performance. RT studies need special methodological care as a motor response (hand or foot) is more compatible with ipsilateral input. For vocalization, which is controlled, at least for most people, from the LH, there is the possibility that this will favour stimuli initially received by the LH. A further problem with the methodology is the use of briefly presented stimuli, which must restrict the complexity of task under investigation. The use of brief stimuli may also encourage the subject to approach the task in a different manner from that which would be used under more favourable conditions.

The following sections will review work carried out with lateralized stimuli within the framework of information processing. Despite the caveats about methodology it must be the hope that sufficient work has been carried out to tell us about any cognitive processing differences that may exist between the two hemispheres. The general information-processing model distinguishes between processes of registration, coding and retrieval. Differences can be looked for at all of these stages. Most central for information processing are differences in coding. These will be looked at in greatest depth to see if assertions about processing modes which are special to one hemisphere are indeed warranted.

Registration

Visual information from a brief display is available in a rich form for only a short interval. This representation, known as an icon (Neisser, 1967), decays rapidly; extraction has to be before 100 ms to result in performance comparable to that after a delay of many seconds. Presentation of a subsequent (or prior) visual display (mask) can seriously alter our ability to extract information from the icon. The action of a mask may be to affect the quality of the initial stimulus by integrating with it (Kinsbourne and Warrington, 1962) or to interrupt visual processing (Schiller and Wiener, 1963). Turvey (1973) showed that flashes of light or visual noise affected processing through integration interference and were only effective when presented to the same eye as the target stimulus. Such peripheral masking is sensitive to the luminance and duration of the mask, but in general has little effect at intervals of more than 25 ms after stimulus offset. Masking by random patterns of elements similar to the target is effective for roughly twice that interval. Pattern masking is also effective when presented to the eye other than the target. It can, therefore, be considered central masking, as information from the eyes comes together only at the visual cortex.

The distinction between peripheral and central is considered critical by Moscovitch (1979) in determining hemispheric involvement in the processing of a brief display. His view is that it is only after recoding that the hemispheres differ and a visual-field advantage (VFA) is observed. In his terms a VFA will not be observed at registration, that is the pre-categorical stage of processing. Moscovitch presented words followed by either a peripheral (flash) or pattern mask. The interstimulus interval needed to avoid the effects of masking did not differ between the visual fields for flash masking, but it did for pattern masking, showing a superiority for the RVF. Moscovitch therefore concludes that the cerebral hemispheres are equivalent for initial registration, but differ at some later processing stage.

McKeever and Suberi (1974), using a metacontrast technique of masking a letter by surrounding it by a subsequently presented ring, found the RVFA to emerge only for interstimulus intervals of more than 20 ms. Hellige and Webster (1978) have argued the case that insufficient attention has been given to the effect of masks which occur within 20 ms of stimulus offset and propose a different explanation to Moscovitch (1979) concerning the hemispheric involvement at registration. Hellige and Webster (1979) expect stimuli presented to the LVF to be better perceived due to some undefined superior equipment that the RH possesses for dealing with degraded perceptual displays. This suggestion is supported by the finding that normal typeface exhibits an RVFA for recognition whereas elaborate typefaces show an LVFA (Bryden and Allard, 1976) and the clinical evidence of RH damage causing impairment for visually degraded letters (Faglioni et al., 1969).

The view that the RH may have a superiority for the perception of uncoded stimuli, perhaps due to a longer duration of the icon, received some support from an experiment by Cohen (1976). Her experiment made use of the paradigm of Sperling (1960). This technique allows information available in the icon, but soon lost, to be extracted. A cue (for example, an arrow pointing to one line of the display) is given soon after stimulus onset. Using these cues, it can be shown that information from any part of the display can be recalled (partial report superiority) if demanded soon enough. From her results, Cohen deduces a 20 ms LVFA for icon duration (visual persistence). However, Marzi et al. (1979) pointed out that she did not obtain the basic requirement of the Sperling paradigm of superiority for the partial report. Marzi further reports that when he did obtain it, there was no interaction with the VFA found for either letters or shapes. The rate of decay of the icon appeared equivalent for both visual fields. This experiment strongly suggests hemispheric equivalence at registration, but the case is not yet proven. The cues to report in Marzi et al. (1979) were not given till at least 300 ms after stimulus onset which they admit may be too long a delay to verify a visual persistence superiority of 20 ms.

The effect of a masking stimulus on a non-verbal stimulus is to produce an LVFA (Moscovitch et al., 1976). However, if there were an RH superiority at an earlier stage then one should also obtain an

LVFA for the non-masked stimulus. Evidence for a VFA for non-masked stimuli is reported in Davidoff (1982) where visual complexity, stimulus duration and all factors likely to degrade visual quality lead us to find considerable numbers of cases where LVFAs are found. While such VFAs for briefly presented unmasked stimuli are common, there is still some doubt as to the mechanism by which they are effected. There exists only a little evidence for an RH which is in some way better 'tuned' in a physiological sense. This comes from adaptation studies (Tei and Owen, 1980; Meyer, 1976) and evoked potentials (Ledlow et al., 1978). Without further evidence, preferably related to neural firing rates, we cannot be sure that some more central process is not activating the whole cerebral hemisphere. Indeed, Kinsbourne (1970) has suggested that all VFAs are attentional biases due to individual hemispheric arousal.

The question of the level of processing at which the hemispheric advantage may first be observed is not settled. Differences may well exist at registration as VFAs and ear advantages continue to be reported for stimuli that one would not think of as categorical. Letters and objects have a clear necessity to be recoded categorically as we need to be able to recognize many different stimuli as being examples of the same stimulus. This is not so easily seen to be the case, for example, for tones (Sidtis, 1981) for which an LEA is still found. The debate concerning the level of processing at which hemispheric advantage can be first seen will be returned to after discussing stimuli that do have to be categorized and hence recoded.

Coding

After extraction from the icon or an auditory equivalent, information has to be laid down in some permanent form. Differences in the retention of words and pictures led Paivio (1971, 1975) to postulate a dual (verbal and visual) coding model. Posner (1969) provides evidence that the two codes are independent from an experiment which asked subjects to say 'same' or 'different' to pairs of letters. When asked to perform a physical identity (PI) match (A-A or a-a), subjects rejected the negative, nominal identity (NI) match (A-a) in the same time as a pair with different names, e.g. (A-b). Thus names were not relevant to the visual coding needed for PI matching. Since hemispheric function has some relationship to the verbal/non-verbal distinction, it is tempting to map the storage of verbally coded material on to the LH and non-verbally coded material to the RH.

Imagery

The least recoded type of non-verbal storage would be imagery, and while subjects operate as though stored information was in the form of pictures (Paivio, 1975) there are those (e.g. Pylyshyn, 1973) who dispute the existence of this form of storage. The hemispheric advantage for imagery has been investigated with a rotation task devised by Shepard and Metzler (1971) who claim that the image is rotated to fit a visual template. Cohen (1975) finds an LVFA for such a task as do Kroll and Madden (1978) for some of their subjects. Seamon (1972) had subjects remember a set of words by rehearsing them or by constructing images. Response latencies to probes increased linearly with set size for rehearsal but remained constant for the imagery condition, implying parallel processing for imagery. Despite non-replication (Rothstein and Atkinson, 1975) of this effect, it has been shown that image probes produce more recall if presented to the LVF, and rehearsal probes more recall when presented to the RVF (Seamon and Gazzaniga, 1973; Metzger and Antes, 1976). Paivio and Ernest (1971) also report that subjects with high imagery ability had an LVFA for shape perception at the beginning of their study even though it was easily overridden by the verbal demand characteristics in their experiment. Thus an RH locus for imagery has been proposed.

The clinical literature provides a few examples of patients who report the loss of visual imagery. Such very rare cases (e.g. Basso *et al.*, 1980), provide evidence for this type of recoding, but do not provide evidence for an RH locus. However, imagery which is related to words does seem to involve RH processes. Jones-Gotman and Milner (1978) found that right temporal lobectomy damages the ability to associate words related by visual imagery without disrupting learning of pairs of abstract words.

Verbal v. non-verbal coding

One must distinguish between stimulus discriminability and low-level stimuli from the point of view of information processing. For example, if one is asked to discriminate between two colours of almost identical hue one is faced with a difficult discrimination, but nevertheless, in terms of information processing, one is faced with a low-level or unrecoded task. Low-level stimuli may be visually coded, though there are conditions which make this less likely. For example, identification of a colour from memory would seem to depend on having a name for the colour. This is because most people find it hard to hold a visual image for anything above a few seconds. Lantz and Stefflre (1964) found a 7-second delay was sufficient to prevent colour matching by Zuni Indians for those colours which had no names in their language. Verbal recoding of colours is therefore common and it does not surprise that LH-damaged as well as RH-damaged patients are impaired in colour-recognition tasks (Boller and Spinnler, 1967). Evidence from normal subjects when giving colour or shape judgements from memory also points to LH involvement because of the RVFAs obtained (Malone and Hannay, 1978).

There will be individual differences for choosing a verbal recoding of non-verbal stimuli. Thus, it is noteworthy that only subjects with a high vocabulary score showed an RVFA for matching rather complex forms and only then if the two stimuli were identical in orientation (Kroll and Madden, 1978). Labelling was presumably inefficient if the stimulus had to be rotated. Most people showed evidence of verbal coding within the orientation judgement task of Umilta et al. (1974). An RVFA occurred but only for the horizontal, vertical and 45° meridians. It was just these directions that were used by White (1971) when reporting LH involvement for the task. The rare reports of an RVFA rather than an LVFA for faces (Marzi and Berlucchi, 1977; Umilta et al., 1978) have also to do with some sort of verbal coding, though whether this is naming per se is still unclear.

A non-verbal recoding of a stimulus is not sufficiently established by finding an LVFA since this could apply to an uncoded stimulus. The nature of the recoding has also to be considered. Surprisingly few attempts have been made to determine this nature. The LVFA for shapes does not depend on the number of verbal associations that a shape produces (Fontenot, 1973) so one can reject verbal recoding as a cause of the VFA. Surprisingly, Dee and Fontenot (1973) found that the LVFA was also not affected by visual interference from similar shapes which the subjects were asked to remember. This would argue against a visual coding. Dee and Fontenot (1973) do not, in fact, give the recall scores for the interfering shapes so it is possible that subjects ignored the interfering task. Certainly, this experiment would bear proper replication.

Stimulus frequency

Hardyck, Tzeng and Wang (1978) also place the locus for VFAs at storage. They point out that VFAs seem dependent on a restricted set of stimuli and the use of a great many trials to create engrams either in the LH or RH. Increases of the set size of items in memory did not, however, affect the VFA for Klatzky and Atkinson (1971) or Madden, Nebes and Berg (1982), but did for Miller and Butler (1980) who emphasize the need for the subjects to realize that the set size is restricted. Discrepancy with the Hardyck model with respect to the effect of familiarity are to be found (Kimura, 1967; Ward and Ross, 1977), but the model is supported by Hellige (1982). He found that the effect of frequency on VFA did not interact with that of stimulus quality, implying that the two effects operate at different stages of information processing.

Levels of processing and hemispheric dominance

We now return to the question of whether cerebral dominance can be observed at a processing stage prior to coding or categorization. It is in this sense that we approach the relationship between level of processing and hemispheric function. Categorization of the input to the visual system is essential if we are ever to form associations to an object. It would be a horrendous waste of effort, if not impossible, to form the same association to every view an object presents to the viewer. Recognition of a need for a mechanism of stimulus equivalence has still not produced a satisfactory explanation of its nature and remains a major problem for pattern-recognition theory (Reed, 1973). Mishkin (1979) suggests a bilateral site for pattern recognition in the monkey, but in humans it is quite likely that verbal and non-verbal categorization have differential hemispheric bases. The question at issue, however, is not the need for a categorical level of processing but whether hemispheric differentiation can be observed prior to categorization.

A VFA which only occurs for higher-order processing, as Moscovitch proposes, means that there will be no VFA in a PI judgement for two simultaneously presented stimuli. This is what Moscovitch *et al.* (1976) found; concluding that two faces needed to be separated by 100 ms (unless the first is masked) or be different representations of the same face for a VFA to occur. However, the proposal that a VFA is found only for higher-order processing does not gain much support from Simion *et al.* (1980) in a direct test. They found no interaction between processing level (PI, analogue (size) or NI matches of triangles) and VFA. Indeed, it looks as if PI matches were most likely to produce an LVFA; for though not reaching significance it was the condition exhibiting an LVFA for the highest number (seven out of eight) of subjects. One would have expected, if Moscovitch (1979) was correct, higher-order tasks to have been more reliable in producing an LVFA. The counter to this argument, put forward by Strauss and Moscovitch (1981), is that different levels of processing were simultaneously required of the subject and the higher-order processing was responsible for the lower-level advantage.

Generally, a delay between stimuli is likely to produce a VFA when the non-delay condition does not do so (Dee and Fontenot, 1973). Moscovitch uses this as evidence to support his viewpoint. According to him, an abstract higher-order target is referred to in the delay condition. There is an alternative explanation of the effect of a delay. For an LVFA, the result is also compatible with an explanation from lower-level processing. Delay could result in a degraded representation of the stimulus; recognition of which is known to be related to RH function (Faglioni *et al.*, 1969).

An important difference between studies which do or do not give LVFAs for lower-level processing is the part played by stimulus characteristics. LVFAs found for non-categorical perception are related to stimulus characteristics of visual complexity (Fontenot, 1973; Hellige, 1976; Umilta *et al.*, 1980) and exposure duration (Cohen, 1972; Rizzolatti and Buchtel, 1977; Pring, 1981). This should not surprise as stimulus characteristics are important in determining a reliance on a visual rather than a nominal code. Matches based on PI can even remain superior to name matches over intervals up to 15 seconds if the stimuli are superimposed rather than spatially separated (Walker, 1978). One important consequence of lower-level superiorities depending on stimulus characteristics is that their hemispheric advantages will be less easy to show than those for categorical perception. This is because both hemispheres can process lower-level stimuli and any advantage is likely to be small.

Moscovitch's use of the term 'categorical' may also be criticized. Categorical is not used by him in its true sense of a classification by which two stimuli are both considered members of the same class.

His usage 'merely' states that 'categories can be determined by the relations among sensory features', but not 'by the presence or magnitude of any of those features'. But what is a relationship? The mere detection of a stimulus relies on the relationship between the stimulus and the background. Are there degrees of relationships, the most difficult of which produce a VFA? This is not what Moscovitch believes, rather, that a configuration can be considered to be a higher-order coding. Warrington and Taylor (1978) use a less circular definition. They find that there are some RH-damaged patients who can match two identical objects (a task not requiring categorization) but cannot match two non-identical views of the same object. Therefore, Warrington and Taylor are right to contend that the RH visual loss was categoric. It is not so obvious from the experiments of Moscovitch.

How does non-categorical perception relate to categorical hemispheric function if not as according to Moscovitch (1979)? An alternative, reductionist view of hemispheric function as exemplified by Semmes (1968) says that there can be 'no understanding of how complex mechanisms can be built up if they are not somehow synthesized out of simple ones'. From this viewpoint one might well expect VFAs at an early processing stage, but this does not tell us how they cause VFAs for categorical tasks. Resorting to correlations between tasks does not help either.

The RH is implicated in studies with normals by the establishment of an LVFA or LEA. Correlations between the extent of VFAs will not produce an answer to the question of relationships between tasks. Correlations between VFAs are often spurious for statistical reasons (Stone, 1980) and may be so for the following reasons. Let us suppose that the VFA arises because of degradation of the message across the *corpus callosum* after the input arrives via the VF directed to the non-specialized hemisphere. Two connected RH categorical tasks (say identification of objects and faces) might, nevertheless, exhibit zero correlations for VFAs because of random variations in callosal transmission. On the other hand correlations found between these tasks for VFA may be just reflecting consistent individual differences in callosal transmission, rather than showing connected RH networks for the tasks. Relationships between levels of processing will always be difficult to disentangle as there is such a wealth of interconnections within and between modalities that there will not be a simple linear chain of processing.

For the present it might be more worthwhile to consider why higher-order visual processing is established in the RH rather than the LH? Better tuning in the RH may provide the answer to this. Crowell *et al.* (1973), in an EEG study, show that in the newborn it is the RH only which is 'driven' by light flashes whereas in the adult both hemispheres are 'driven'. In the child, formation of elementary higher-order visual units would be more likely set up in the nearby association areas of the active RH cortex. It is even quite possible to believe that once these units are established they become functionally independent of the lower-level systems which were essential for their formation. Clinical evidence (Newcombe and Russell, 1969) supports this view. They found that the RH was the locus for both a perceptual task (visual closure) and visual-maze learning. However, these tasks were affected by injury at different RH loci. Impairment on one of the tasks did not mean impairment on the other. Statements about the VFA for non-categoric perception will then tell us nothing about the VFA for categoric perception.

Processing modes

The hemispheres have without doubt different specializations. This is clearly shown by Levy (1974) in a study using split-brain patients. The patients were shown chimeric pictures formed from the left half of one object and the right half of another. The chimeric picture is presented at the midline so each half-object is projected to only one hemisphere. Completion of one of these objects takes place and the patient is unaware that the stimulus is really a composite of two pictures. After having been shown such pictures, the patients were given a choice of normal pictures and told to match what they had seen. A match based on visual similarity to the LVF was made with the left hand (RH) or based on the function of the object in the RVF if done with the right hand (LH). Specific instructions to match by appearance or function confirmed these findings. Analagously in normals, Niederbuhl and Springer (1979) found an RVFA if letter names were to be remembered, but an LVFA if asked to remember the letter shapes. But when we restate the RH advantage for non-verbal stimuli as an advantage for judgements based on appearance, we only prompt the question of what it is about the RH advantage that makes it better for dealing with appearance matches. Furthermore, sheer repetition of the findings of an RVFA or REA for verbal material does not help us understand the information processing required to obtain these results. We shall therefore consider attempts to define the processing modes which for normals are presumed present when a lateral advantage is found.

Gestalt/analytic processing

A simple division of the hemispheres into verbal and non-verbal is a somewhat imprecise account of findings from neuropsychology. Attempts have therefore been made, drawing upon our knowledge of the psychological processes involved in the analysis of stimuli, to give a greater understanding of why a lateral advantage is obtained. The first of these dichotomous distinctions to be considered suggests that the LH relies on sequential or analytic processing and the RH on holistic or gestalt analysis.

The view that the LH has a sequential mode of operation has held great currency and has been used, for example, by Gordon (1978) to sort out ear advantages for music. His research showed that rhythm aspects were processed better by the LH and tonal discrimination by the RH. The LH superiority for dealing with sequences of auditory material does not, therefore, apply just to speech. Nor is it said to apply just to the auditory modality, as more accurate LH judgements of sequences have been found for the tactile modality (Nachshon and Carmon, 1975). Clinical evidence also favours an LH superiority for dealing with sequences (Tallal and Newcombe, 1978; Archibald, 1978).

Kimura and Vanderwolf (1970) regard their finding of an LH superiority for motor sequencing as related to the anatomical proximity of the motor and speech areas in the LH. However, it is an oversimplification to regard language as just sequencing behaviour (Poeck and Huber, 1977) and, while the evidence for preferential LH involvement for sequencing is considerable, it is not sufficient for a task to have a sequential element to give LH superiority. The RH is preferred for velocity discrimination (Bertolini et al., 1978), Braille reading (Hermelin and O'Connor, 1971) and the Corsi span, which is the spatial equivalent of the digit span (Kim et al., 1980). The LH preference for sequencing is, however, built on firmer evidence than the supposed gestalt or holistic processing mode of the RH.

Recourse to the clinical literature shows that RH damage leaves the patient capable of a perceptual analysis only by detail (Hécaen and Angelergues, 1962), and that patients with LH or RH lesions carry out constructional tasks differently from each other (Piercy, Hécaen and Ajuriaguerra, 1960). Levy (1974) postulated an holistic strategy for the RH from such evidence. However, the LH and RH have different specializations, so unilateral brain lesions will force the patient to rely on only certain aspects of the input. Similarly, a superiority for normals in dealing with information presented to a hemisphere for which it is better suited does not need the explanation of a preferred processing mode. If attention is directed towards certain attributes of a stimulus, it should not surprise if lateral advantages are altered. Linguistic training, for example, reverses an existing LEA for identifying intonation contours of words (Blumstein and Cooper, 1974). This is not remarkable if the subject is trying to discriminate linguistic features. It is generally harder to force subjects to attend to non-verbal aspects of stimuli. The evidence offered by Webster and Thurber (1978) that a so-called gestalt training strategy improved RH performance was, to say the least, slight. It depended on a transformation of the raw scores for the dichaptic data and on ignoring the monohaptic results.

If we insist on calling the style of processing of the RH holistic or gestalt, then we must be clear what is meant by a gestalt. We must first distinguish a gestalt from the findings of Gestalt psychology, which give both RVFAs (Jasper and Raney, 1937 for the phi phenomenon) and others that give LVFAs (Nebes, 1973) for proximity. A gestalt has meant only too often what any particular author decided it meant. Gestalt processing is claimed by Bryden (1976) because more false alarms occurred in the LVF, by Clem and Pollack (1975) because the Müller-Lyer was stronger in the LVF only if parts of the figure appeared simultaneously, and by McKeever and Huling (1970) because an LVFA was obtained for dot figures, but not for outline figures. Gestalt processing is even claimed for the RH because the LVF is better at detecting mismatches of words and pictures (Tomlinson-Keasey et al., 1978). Most, if not all, of these results could be explained more parsimoniously by a RH which could extract visual information quicker than the LH.

Clinical studies have been even vaguer in their use of gestalt processing. A RH which operates on a gestalt basis is concluded because form is overweighted compared to area in the judgement of the similarity of rectangles (Bisiach and Capitani, 1976). Gardner et al. (1977) even claim disturbed RH function from patients unable to deal with the supposedly gestalt associations of high v. low musical notes corresponding to red v. blue, and loud v. soft notes corresponding to filled v. open circles.

A gestalt is talked of in some instances as being the formation of a unified percept and this may be the RH function that is lost when objects cannot be identified (De Renzi and Spinnler, 1966). Martin (1979) argued that if the RH was really specialized for dealing with the whole shape (global processing) rather than portions of the shape (local processing), then hemifield presentations of a letter constituted from smaller letters would exhibit an LVFA for the whole, but not the local shapes. There was little evidence for this global processing in the RH. Indeed, the shape of a word, which could be misconstrued as a gestalt, has been found to give an RVFA (Bradshaw et al., 1977). A gestalt in its more proper meaning of a whole processed more efficiently than its constituent parts, also applies to verbal as well as to non-verbal stimuli. Reicher (1969) showed that a word can take less time to process than its constituent letters. This word-superiority effect has been tested for hemifield differences and is accompanied like the majority of verbal stimuli by an RVFA (Krueger, 1975).

It is with a certain relief then, that we turn to the work of Cohen (1973), since here we at least have a testable statement of RH holistic processing. Gestalt processing (the mode of operation of the RH) is taken to mean parallel processing, i.e. it takes the same processing time to deal with many stimuli as it does for a single stimulus. The LH is taken to process stimuli sequentially and this view has a face validity, as parallel processing is confined to matching on the basis of physical identity (Neisser and Beller, 1965) and simple dimensions like size and brightness (Biederman and Checkosky, 1970).

Cohen (1973) obtained RTs for judgements of whether all the stimuli in a display were the same. The number of stimuli varied from two to five. The effect of set size for RVF displays was, unfortunately, not always the predicted increase in RT as set size increased. Also, parallel processing was not consistently shown for the LVF and even seen for the RVF. A replication of Cohen (1973) by White and White (1975) using a better design, found parallel processing for both hemispheres. The further replication by Polich (1980) tended to show serial processing for both visual fields. So while set-size effects appear variable, there is little supportive evidence for Cohen's hypothesis. The argument that the RH can act *only* as a parallel processor is certainly denied (Gross, 1972; Umilta *et al.*, 1979). Gross found an LVFA for judging the similarity of two arrays of black and white squares with RTs increasing along with the number of black squares (the critical features) and implying that the arrays were being processed in a serial fashion. Similarly Umilta *et al.* (1979) found an LVFA for dot detection with a serial search from fixation outwards.

It is a pity that the clearest definition of holistic processing made with respect to hemispheric involvement has been found lacking for empirical validation. The extension by neuropsychologists of serial v. parallel-processing differences to correspond to left v. right hemispheres seems ill-founded, but we have seen that less well-defined expressions of the gestalt fare no better.

Same/different

Nickerson (1967) reported the paradoxical finding that though search times for judgements of the difference between stimuli increased as the number of differing features decreased, judgements of sameness were performed relatively quickly. This is paradoxical, since the 'different' judgements show that the features of the stimuli are searched in a serial fashion. This should mean that 'same' judgements would be very long, as in order to be sure that the two stimuli are the same every feature must be searched. Therefore, there had to be a second mechanism involved in same v. different judgements which Bamber (1969) called an identity reporter. The neuropsychological extension of these findings is to place 'same' judgements in the RH and 'different judgements' in the LH (Patterson and Bradshaw, 1975; Bradshaw *et al.*, 1976). Non-verbal stimuli are not necessarily allocated to the RH, but to either hemisphere according to the judgement required. It might, however, be simpler to interpret their results with respect to the ease with which the stimuli might be labelled. Patterson and Bradshaw (1975) used schematic faces, and Bradshaw *et al.* (1976) simple geometric forms. With these types of stimuli it will be easy to assign labels, especially when looking for only one critical feature.

Hellige (1976) gives another compelling reason for different hemispheric advantages being associated with 'same' or 'different' responses. He considers 'different' responses more likely due to guesses based on insufficient information. As one might expect, the lateral advantages (which he finds only for 'same' responses) are, contra Patterson and Bradshaw (1975), not always for the LVF.

The bulk of pertinent studies (e.g. Gross, 1972; Simion et al., 1980) suggest that 'same v. different' is not a critical neuro-psychological variable in the judgement of stimuli. In any case, a complete hemispheric dominance for 'same' or 'different' judgements seems improbable. If this were so, 'same' information arriving at the LH would have to be recognized as the sort of information to be passed to the RH to make the judgement, and this is clearly an unnecessary, if not illogical state of affairs.

Easy v. difficult

This dichotomy has been suggested by Gates and Bradshaw (1977) to encapsulate the hemispheric advantages found for music perception with the RH dominant for easy judgements and the LH for difficult. This distinction certainly does not generalize to the visual modality where there is sufficient evidence that difficult discriminations make for an LVFA even for letters (Hellige, 1976; Jonides, 1979). If we are to consider seriously this dichotomy for hemisphere functioning, we must be told, a priori, how difficulty is to be measured in any study.

The role of task complexity does bear some relationship to hemispheric function, but it is not a simple one (Haun, 1981). Subjective ranking of the difficulty of block-design problems was found to relate to an increasing EEG activity in the LH (Galin et al., 1978). However, marked individual differences were seen and the increasing use of the LH for the harder tasks may be related in most subjects to an attempt to verbalize the problem.

Bever and Chiarello (1974) interpret LH involvement for complex tasks as showing the application of an analytical mode. In their experiment an REA for tone identification was found for musicians and an LEA for non-musicians. The mechanism for the switch-in-ear advantage with training is still unclear. Johnson et al. (1977) suggests that it relates to the ability to transcribe. Certainly, one wants to do more than postulate an analytical mode, as we have seen that this is no more than a label and not a constructive attempt to elucidate the mechanism involved.

Conclusions

The potential advantage of lateralized presentations for clarifying information processing rested on the hope that the two hemispheres would operate differently on stimulus input. Initial reception by one hemisphere, of course, does not mean sole processing by that hemisphere; nevertheless, it was hoped that this would at least cause some observable differences in processing. Certainly, it has been shown that verbal stimuli are favoured if presented to the LH, and likewise non-verbal to the RH, but this is hardly progress.

Perhaps the technique of lateralized presentations could never tell us a great deal about information processing. Moscovitch (1979) pointed out that hemispheric presentations cannot decide, for example, the issue of whether one or two codes are used for storage. What is being investigated with lateralized stimuli is the distribution of storage for different kinds of material, rather than the nature of storage itself. Moscovitch (1973) developed a scheme for deciding whether one or both hemispheres have control for a particular task based on the reaction time for each hand to the lateralized stimulus. This technique has been applied to face perception (Suberi and McKeever, 1977) and lexical storage (Barry, 1981). But the question of which hemisphere does what is an issue pertinent for neurology rather than for psychology.

If one wants to know how the LH or RH *per se* perform on any task the use of lateralized presentations are essential. However, if it is the understanding of information processing that is the aim, it seems cumbersome to adopt a methodology that will create variance as well as problems of interpretation. This is even more the case given the difficulties of conventional laboratory techniques to disentangle stages or categories of processing (Anderson, 1980). The use of the divided VF methodology and dichotic presentations would seem to have much greater application in the realm of applied psychology. There is, for example, the view that an unusual cerebral organization is related to dyslexia, a view supported from some VF studies (Witelson, 1977; Beaumont and Rugg, 1978). Indeed, there has been so much recent smoke from this old fire that it is certainly worth considering the technique of lateralized presentations for use as a diagnostic tool for cognitive assessment, both in educational and clinical psychology. (See Chapter 10 for the possible use of the technique for therapeutic purposes).

The impact of the work on hemispheric specialization on our knowledge of information processing must be said to have been limited. Moscovitch (1979) quite rightly stresses the importance of categorical perception for cognition, but it is not yet certain that the hemispheres are specialized only for categorical perception. The extension of the dual-coding theory to map onto the two hemispheres does gain some measure of support: the LH profits by verbal coding and the RH by non-verbal, and there is a certain amount of evidence for a RH site for imagery. While clinical research suggests that the two hemispheres have different processing modes, despite some considerable effort of research we have not been able to ascertain what these differences are. Both hemispheres would seem to deal with the material they are specialized for, in whatever way is appropriate to the demands of the task.

References

Anderson, J. R. (1980) *Cognitive Psychology and its Implications*. New York: W. H. Freeman.

Archibald, Y. M. (1978) Time as a variable in the performance of hemisphere-damaged patients on the Elithorn perceptual maze test. *Cortex 14*: 22-31.

Bamber, D. (1969) Reaction times and error rates for 'same – different' judgements of multidimensional stimuli. *Perception psychophysics 6*: 169-74.

Barry, C. (1981) Hemispheric asymmetry in lexical access and phonological coding. *Neuropsychologia 19*: 473-8.

Basso, A., Bisiach, E. and Luzzatti, C. (1980) Loss of mental imagery: a case study. *Neuropsychologia 18*: 435-42.

Beaumont, J. G. and Rugg, M. D. (1978) Neuropsychological laterality of function and dyslexia: a new hypothesis. *Dyslexia Review 1*: 18-21.

Bertolini, G., Anzola, G. P., Buchtel, H.A. and Rizzolatti, G. (1978) Hemispheric differences in the discrimination of the velocity and duration of a simple visual stimulus. *Neuropsychologia 16*: 213-20.

Bever, J. G. and Chiarello, R. (1974) Cerebral dominance in musicians and non-musicians. *Science 185*: 537-9.

Biederman, I. and Checkosky, S. F. (1970) Processing redundant information. *Journal of Experimental Psychology 83*: 486-90.

Bisiach, E. and Capitani, E. (1976) Cerebral dominance and visual similarity judgements. *Cortex 12*: 347-55.

Blumstein, S. and Cooper, W. E. (1974) Hemispheric processing of intonation contours. *Cortex 10*: 146-58.

Boller, F. and Spinnler, H. (1967) Visual memory for colors in patients with unilateral brain damage. *Cortex 3*: 395-405.

Bradshaw, J. L., Bradley, D., Gates, A. and Patterson, K. (1977) Serial, parallel or holistic identification of single words in the two visual fields. *Perception and Psychophysics 21*: 431-8.

42   The pathology and psychology of cognition

Bradshaw, J. L., Gates, A. and Patterson, K. (1976) Hemispheric differences in processing visual patterns. *Quarterly Journal of Experimental Psychology 28*: 667-81.

Bryden, M. P. (1976) Response bias and hemispheric differences in dot localization. *Perception and Psychophysics 19*: 23-8.

Bryden, M. P. and Allard, F. (1976) Visual hemifield differences depend on type faces. *Brain and Language 3*: 191-200.

Clem, R. K. and Pollack, R. H. (1975) Illusion magnitude as a function of visual field exposure. *Perception and Psychophysics 17*: 450-4.

Cohen, G. (1972) Hemispheric differences in a letter classification task. *Perception and Psychophysics 11*: 137-42.

Cohen, G. (1973) Hemispheric differences in serial versus parallel processing. *Journal of Experimental Psychology 97*: 349-56.

Cohen, G. (1975) Hemispheric differences in the utilization of advance information. In P. M. A. Rabbitt and S. Dornic (eds) *Attention and Performance* Vol. V. New York: Academic Press.

Cohen, G. (1976) Components of the laterality effect in letter recognition: asymmetries in iconic storage. *Quarterly Journal of Experimental Psychology 28*: 105-14.

Crowell, D. H., Jones, R. H., Kapunia, L. E. and Nakagawa, J. K. (1973) Unilateral cortical activity in newborn humans: an early index of cerebral dominance? *Science 180*: 205-8.

Davidoff, J. B. (1982) Studies with non-verbal stimuli. In J. G. Beaumont (ed.) *Divided Visual Field Studies of Cerebral Organization*. London: Academic Press.

Dee, H. L. and Fontenot, D. J. (1973) Cerebral dominance and lateral differences in perception and memory. *Neuropsychologia 11*: 167-73.

De Renzi, E. and Spinnler, H. (1966) Visual recognition in patients with unilateral cerebral disease. *Journal of Nervous and Mental Disease 142*: 515-25.

Faglioni, P., Scotti, G. and Spinnler, H. (1969) Impaired recognition of written letters following unilateral hemispheric damage. *Cortex 5*: 120-33.

Fontenot, D. J. (1973) Visual field differences in the recognition of verbal and non-verbal stimuli in man. *Journal of Comparative and Physiological Psychology 85*: 564-9.

Galin, D., Johnstone, J. and Herron, J. (1978) Effects of task difficulty on EEG measures of cerebral engagment. *Neuropsychologia 16*: 461-72.

Gardner, H., Silverman, J., Denes, G., Semenza, C. and Rosensteil, A. K. (1977) Sensitivity to musical denotation and connotation in organic patients. *Cortex 13*: 242-56.

Gates, A. and Bradshaw, J. L. (1977) The role of the cerebral hemispheres in music. *Brain and Language 4*: 403-31.

Gordon, H. W. (1978) Hemispheric asymmetry for dichotically presented chords in musicians and non-musicians, males and females. *Acta Psychologica 42*: 383-95.

Gross, M. M. (1972) Hemispheric specialization for processing of visually presented verbal and spatial stimuli. *Perception and Psychophysics 12*: 357-63.

Hardyck, C., Tzeng, O. J. L. and Wang, W. S-Y. (1978) Cerebral lateralization of function and bilingual decision processes. Is thinking lateralized? *Brain and Language 5*: 56-71.

Haun, F. (1981) Functionally lateralized information processing and its allocation to response inferences from those measures of letter identification performance following lateralised visual input. *Quarterly Journal of Experimental Psychology 33A*: 275-98.

Hécaen, H. and Angelergues, R. (1962) Agnosia for faces (prosopagnosia). *AMA Archives of Neurology 7*: 92-100.

Hellige, J. B. (1976) Changes in same - different laterality patterns as a function of practice and stimulus quality. *Perception Psychophysics 20*: 267-73.

Hellige, J. B. (1982) Visual laterality and cerebral hemisphere specialization: methodological and theoretical considerations. In J. B. Sidowski (ed.) *Conditioning, Cognition and Methodology: Contemporary Issues in Experimental Psychology*. Hillsdale, NJ: Lawrence Erlbaum Associates.

Hellige, J. B. and Webster, R. (1979) Right-hemisphere superiority for initial stages of letter processing. *Neuropsychologia 17*: 653-60.

Hermelin, B. and O'Connor, N. (1971) Functional asymmetry in the reading of Braille. *Neuropsychologia 9*: 431-5.

Jasper, H. H. and Raney, E. T. (1937) The phi test of lateral dominance. *American Journal of Psychology 49*: 450-7.

Johnson, R. C., Bowers, J. K., Gamble, M., Lyons, F. M., Presbrey, T. W. and Vetter, R. R. (1977) Ability to transcribe music and ear superiority for tone sequences. *Cortex 13*: 295-9.

Jones-Gotman, M. and Milner, B. (1978) Right temporal-lobe contribution to image-mediated verbal learning. *Neuropsychologia 16*: 61-71.

Jonides, J. (1979) Left and right-visual-field superiority for letter classification. *Quarterly Journal of Experimental Psychology 31*: 423-9.

Kim, Y., Royer, F., Bonstelle, C. and Boller, F. (1980) Temporal sequencing of verbal and non-verbal material: the effect of laterality of lesion. *Cortex 16*: 135-43.

Kimura, D. (1961) Some effects of temporal-lobe damage on auditory perception. *Canadian Journal of Psychology 15*: 156-66.

Kimura, D. (1967) Functional asymmetry of the brain in dichotic listening. *Cortex 3*: 162-78.

Kimura, D. and Vanderwolf, C. H. (1970) The relation between hand preference and the performance of individual finger movements by left and right hands. *Brain 93*: 769-74.

Kinsbourne, M. (1970) The cerebral basis of lateral asymmetries in attention. *Acta Psychologica 33*: 193-201.

Kinsbourne, M. and Warrington, E. K. (1962) The effect of an aftercoming random pattern on the perception of brief visual stimuli. *Quarterly Journal of Experimental Psychology 14*: 223-4.

44   The pathology and psychology of cognition

Klatzky, R. and Atkinson, R. C. (1971) Specialization of the cerebral hemispheres in scanning for information in short-term memory. *Perception and Psychophysics 10*: 335-8.

Kroll, N. E. A. and Madden, D. J. (1978) Verbal and pictorial processing by hemisphere as a function of the subject's verbal scholastic aptitude score. In J. Requin (ed.) *Attention and Performance*. Vol. VII. Hillsdale, NJ: Lawrence Erlbaum Associates.

Krueger, L. E. (1975) The word-superiority effect: is its locus visual – spatial or verbal? *Bulletin of the Psychonomic Society 6*: 465-8.

Lantz, D. and Stefflre, V. (1964) Language and cognition revisited. *Journal of Abnormal and Social Psychology 69*: 472-81.

Ledlow, A., Swanson, J. M. and Kinsbourne, M. (1978) Reaction times and evoked potential as indicators of hemispheric differences for laterally presented name and physical matches. *Journal of Experimental Psychology: Human Perception and Performance 4*: 440-54.

Levy, J. (1974) Psychobiological implications of bilateral asymmetry. In S. J. Dimond and G. Beaumont (eds) *Hemisphere Function in the Human Brain*. London: Elek.

McKeever, W. F. and Huling, M. D. (1970) Right-hemispheric superiority in graphic reproduction of briefly viewed dot figures. *Perceptual and Motor Skills 31*: 201-2.

McKeever, W. F. and Suberi, M. (1974) Parallel but temporarily displaced visual half-field metacontrast functions. *Quarterly Journal of Experimental Psychology 26*: 258-65.

Madden, D. J., Nebes, R. D. and Berg, W. D. (1982) Signal-detection analysis of hemispheric differences in visual-recognition memory. *Cortex* (in press).

Malone, D. R. and Hannay, H. J. (1978) Hemispheric dominance and normal color memory. *Neuropsychologia 16*: 51-9.

Martin, M. (1979) Hemispheric specialization for local and global processing. *Neuropsychologia 17*: 33-40.

Marzi, C. A. and Berlucchi, G. (1977) Right-field superiority for recognition of famous faces in normals. *Neuropsychologia 15*: 751-6.

Marzi, C. A., Di Stefano, M., Tassinari, G. and Crea, F. (1979) Iconic storage in the two hemispheres. *Journal of Experimental Psychology: Human Perception and Performance 5*: 31-41.

Metzger, R. L. and Antes, J. R. (1976) Sex and coding-strategy effects on reaction time to hemispheric probes. *Memory and Cognition 4*: 167-71.

Meyer, G. E. (1976) Right-hemispheric sensitivity for the McCollough effect. *Nature 204*: 751-3.

Miller, L. K. and Butler, D. (1980) The effect of set size on hemifield asymmetries in letter recognition. *Brain and Language 9*: 307-14.

Mishkin, M. (1979) Analogous neural models for tactual and visual learning. *Neuropsychologia 17*: 139-51.

Moscovitch, M. (1973) Language and the cerebral hemispheres: reaction time studies and their implications for models of cerebral dominance. In P. Pliner, T. Alloway and L. Krames (eds). *Communication and Affect: Language and Thought*. New York: Academic Press.

Moscovitch, M. (1979) Information processing and the cerebral hemispheres. In M. S. Gazzaniga (ed.) *Handbook of Behavioral Neurobiology*. Vol. 2: *Neuropsychology*. New York: Plenum Press.

Moscovitch, M., Scullion, D. and Christie, D. (1976) Early v. late stages of processing and their relation to functional hemispheric asymmetries in face recognition. *Journal of Experimental Psychology: Human Perception and Performance 2*: 401–16.

Nachshon, I. and Carmon, A. (1975) Hand preference in sequential and spatial discrimination tasks. *Cortex 11*: 121–31.

Nebes, R. D. (1973) Perception of spatial relationships by the right and left hemispheres in commissurotomized man. *Neuropsychologia 11*: 285–9.

Neisser, U. (1967) *Cognitive Psychology*. New York: Appleton-Century-Crofts.

Neisser, U. and Beller, H. K. (1965) Searching through word lists. *British Journal of Psychology 56*: 349–58.

Newcombe, F. and Russell, W. R. (1969) Dissociated visual perceptual and spatial deficits in focal lesions of the right hemisphere. *Journal of Neurology, Neurosurgery and Psychiatry 32*: 73–81.

Nickerson, R. A. (1967) Same-different reaction times with multiattribute stimulus differences. *Perceptual and Motor Skills 24*: 543–54.

Niederbuhl, J. and Springer, S. P. (1979) Task agreements and hemispheric asymmetry for the processing of single letters. *Neuropsychologia 17*: 689–92.

Paivio, A. (1971) *Imagery and Visual Processes*. New York: Holt, Rinehart & Winston.

Paivio, A. (1975) Perceptual comparisons through the mind's eye. *Memory and Cognition 3*: 635–47.

Paivio, A. and Ernest, C. H. (1971) Imagery ability and visual perception of verbal and non-verbal stimuli. *Perception and Psychophysics 10*: 429–32.

Patterson, K. and Bradshaw, J. L. (1975) Differential hemispheric mediation of non-verbal visual stimuli. *Journal of Experimental Psychology: Human Perception and Performance 1*: 246–52.

Piercy, M., Hécaen, H. and de Ajuriaguerra, J. (1980) Constructional apraxia associated with unilateral cerebral lesions. Left and right sided cases compared. *Brain 83*: 225–42.

Poeck, K. and Huber, W. (1977) To what extent is language a sequential activity? *Neuropsychologia 15*: 359–64.

Polich, J. M. (1980) Left hemisphere superiority for visual search. *Cortex 16*: 39–50.

Posner, M. I. (1969) Abstraction and the process of recognition. In G. H. Bower and J. T. Spence (eds) *The Psychology of Learning and Motivation*. Vol. 3. New York: Academic Press.

Pring, T. (1981) The effects of print-size and exposure duration in visual-field asymmetries. *Cortex 17*: 227–40.

Pylyshyn, Z. W. (1973) What the mind's eye tells the mind's brain: a critique of mental imagery. *Psychological Bulletin 80*: 1–24.

Reed, S. K. (1973) *Psychological Processes in Pattern Recognition*. New York: Academic Press.

Reicher, G. M. (1969) Perceptual recognition as a function of the meaning-fulness of the material. *Journal of Experimental Psychology 81*: 275-80.

Reitan, R. M. (1955) Certain differential effects of left and right cerebral lesions in human adults. *Journal of Comparative and Psychological Psychology 48*: 474-7.

Rizzolatti, G. and Buchtel, H. A. (1977) Hemispheric superiority in reaction time to faces: a sex difference. *Cortex 13*: 300-5.

Rothstein, L. D. and Atkinson, R. C. (1975) Memory scanning for words in visual images. *Memory and Cognition 3*: 541-4.

Schiller, P. H. and Wiener, M. (1963) Monoptic and dichotic visual masking. *Journal of Experimental Psychology 66*: 386-93.

Seamon, J. G. (1972) Imagery codes and human information retrieval. *Journal of Experimental Psychology 96*: 468-70.

Seamon, J. G. and Gazzaniga, M. S. (1973) Coding strategies and cerebral laterality effects. *Cognitive Psychology 5*: 249-56.

Semmes, J. (1968) Hemispheric specialization: a possible clue to mechanism. *Neuropsychologia 6*: 11-26.

Shepard, R. N. and Metzler, J. (1971) Mental rotation of three dimensional objects. *Science 171*: 701-3.

Sidtis, J. J. (1981) The complex tone test: implications for the assessment of auditory laterality effects. *Neuropsychologica 19*: 103-12.

Simion, F., Bagnara, S., Bisiacchi, P., Roncato, S. and Umilta, C. (1980) Laterality effects, levels of processing and stimulus properties. *Journal of Experimental Psychology: Human Perception and Performance 6*: 184-95.

Sperling, G. (1960) The information available in brief visual presentations. *Psychological Monographs 74* (II whole no. 498).

Stone, M. A. (1980) Measures of laterality and spurious correlation. *Neuropsychologia 18*: 339-45.

Strauss, E. and Moscovitch, M. (1981) Perception of facial expressions. *Brain and Language* (in press).

Suberi, M. and McKeever, W. F. (1977) Differential right-hemispheric memory storage of emotional and non-emotional faces. *Neuropsychologia 15*: 757-68.

Tallal, P. and Newcombe, F. (1978) Improvement of auditory perception and language comprehension in dysphasia. *Brain and Language 5*: 13-24.

Tei, E. B. and Owen, D. H. (1980) Lateral differences in sensitivity to line orientation as a function of adaptation duration. *Perception and Psychophysics 28*: 479-83.

Tomlinson-Keasey, C., Kelley, R. R. and Burton, J. (1978) Hemispheric changes in information processing during development. *Developmental Psychology 14*: 214-23.

Turvey, M. (1973) On peripheral and central processes in vision: inferences from an information-processing analysis of masking with patterned stimuli. *Psychological Review 80*: 1-52.

Umilta, C., Brizzolara, D., Tabossi, P. and Fairweather, H. (1978) Factors affecting face recognition in the cerebral hemisphere: familiarity and naming. In J. Requin (ed.) *Attention and Performance*. Vol. VII. Hillsdale, NJ: Lawrence Erlbaum Associates.

Umilta, C., Rizzolatti, G., Marzi, C. A., Zamboni, G., Franzini, C., Camarda, R. and Berlucchi, G. (1974) Hemispheric differences in the discrimination of line orientation. *Neuropsychologia 12*: 165–74.

Umilta, C., Salmaso, D., Bagnara, S. and Simion, F. (1979) Evidence for a right-hemisphere superiority and for a serial search in a dot-detection task. *Cortex 15*: 577–608.

Umilta, C., Sava, D. and Salmaso, D. (1980) Hemispheric asymmetries in a letter-classification task with different type faces. *Brain and Language 9*: 171–81.

Walker, P. (1978) Short-term visual memory: the importance of the spatial and temporal separation of successive stimuli. *Quarterly Journal of Experimental Psychology 30*: 665–79.

Ward, T. B. and Ross, L. E. (1977) Laterality differences under central backward masking conditions. *Memory and Cognition 5*: 221–6.

Warrington, E. K. and Taylor, A. M. (1978) Two categorical stages of object recognition. *Perception 7*: 695–705.

Webster, W. G. and Thurber, A. D. (1978) Problem-solving strategies and manifest brain asymmetry. *Cortex 14*: 474–84.

White, M. J. (1971) Visual hemifield differences in the perception of letters and contour orientation. *Canadian Journal of Psychology 25*: 207–12.

White, M. J. and White K. G. (1975) Parallel – serial processing and hemispheric function. *Neuropsychologia 13*: 377–81.

Witelson, S. F. (1977) Developmental dyslexia: two right hemispheres and none left. *Science 175*: 309–11.

3 Memory disorders

John T. E. Richardson

In clinical practice disorders of learning and memory are quite familiar; they are often a reliable sign of neurological damage or disease, and there are at least three main classes of patient in whom memory disorders are especially significant. First, they are often associated with endogenous neurological diseases, especially those of the arterial system such as cerebral thrombosis or haemorrhage, or those of a histopathological nature such as cerebral tumours. Under this heading one might also include the normal degenerative processes which are characteristic of old age, as well as more chronic conditions such as senile and presenile dementia. Secondly, memory disorders may arise not as a sign of the original neurological disease, but as a consequence of the surgical intervention necessary to alleviate its symptoms. These disorders tend to arise especially following surgical lesions of the cortical and subcortical structures of the temporal lobes, which may be undertaken in order to relieve chronic epileptic or depressive conditions that are not amenable to other forms of treatment. Finally, disordered learning and memory is typically apparent in cases of traumatic brain damage. In wartime such damage tends to be associated with open wounds produced by weapons or by shrapnel; in peacetime, accidents at home, at work or on the roads frequently give rise to closed head injuries in which the contents of the skull are not exposed.

As in the case of other types of cognitive disorder, there are two basic sorts of motivation for relating psychological theories of human memory to neurological practice. On the one hand the clinical description and analysis of memory disorders is severely hampered by an inadequate, pre-theoretical and largely intuitive understanding of the cognitive processes involved in normal learning and remembering. Contemporary experimental psychology offers the neurologist sophisticated and articulated models of human memory derived from the scientific study of intact subjects, and it follows that the use of these models should enable him to give a much more detailed and incisive account of the difficulties and problems encountered by his patients. Moreover, it might be possible to identify the hypothetical mechanisms and processes which are postulated by theories of normal memory function with specific physiological structures and systems. If this localization of cognitive function could be securely achieved, then in principle it would be possible to present recommendations for clinical treatment on psychological grounds, as well as on purely medical ones. In general, therefore, it is reasonable to expect that the application of psychological theories of normal memory function would enrich and inform the clinical understanding of cases of cognitive dysfunction.

On the other hand the neurological application of psychological theories might also be expected to generate an entirely new body of data with which to validate, refine and develop these theories, since neurological patients of the sort described above represent a radically different population of subjects. It is obvious that a theory which can describe the normal processes of learning and remembering in the general population is to be preferred to one based upon evidence derived solely from the study of college students. Nevertheless, a psychological theory which can in addition encompass and even predict the patterns of impairment to be found in a wide variety of neurological patients is to be preferred to either of these. Thus, the investigation of cases of impaired cognitive function can be regarded as an opportunity to submit to radical empirical testing those models of cognitive function which have been derived solely from the study of normal, intact subjects.

While the latter approach may well prove to be a heuristically powerful strategy in clinical neuropsychology, in practice it often tends to contain the hidden assumption that cases of cognitive disorder are essentially homogeneous with regard to the patterns of intellectual deficit which they manifest. This is a fairly natural assumption to make if one's knowledge and understanding of complex neurological function is somewhat limited, since such cases have in common that they have received damage to the same cerebral mechanisms. Nevertheless, it is characteristic of neurological patients that they demonstrate widespread heterogeneity in terms of their cognitive disorders, both qualitative and quantitative (cf. Kinsbourne, 1980). The precise nature of the impairment may vary considerably in terms of both the aetiology and the severity of the cerebral damage, and any account of the effects of brain damage upon cognitive function must specify both of these factors in establishing the domain of its applicability. For instance, it may be necessary to give quite different accounts of the effects of head injury from those of the effects of cerebrovascular disease, and quite different accounts of global amnesic disorders from those of the transient, and often trivial deficits which follow minor concussion.

In the case of human learning and memory the predominant theoretical perspective in experimental psychology has passed through several phases over the last twenty years or so. Before the development of the information-processing approach, human memory was typically conceptualized in terms of a unitary system in which representations or traces were rendered in some cerebral substance by a process of consolidation. Variations of this theory can be traced back over thousands of years of thought and discussion on the nature of remembering, but it was not capable of doing justice to the rich and complex phenomena generated in experimental investigations of human memory. With the rise of cognitive psychology, therefore, it became necessary to try to identify the component structures and processes which were responsible for those phenomena. The initial postulation of a two-component system consisting of a short-term store and a long-term store met with considerable success, but is now generally regarded as too restrictive a framework in which to develop interesting ideas and hypotheses. The last ten years or so have seen more attention paid to the various dimensions or levels in terms of which material may be actively processed by subjects during the course of learning, and the analysis of encoding processes is very much a primary focus for contemporary research in human memory. Finally, an appreciation of the dimensions in terms of which material may be encoded enables one to consider the strategies and cues employed when a subject attempts to retrieve information from memory. Accordingly, another important perspective to consider is that which emphasizes the role of retrieval processes. An excellent account of these theoretical developments is given by Baddeley (1976).

In this chapter, then, I shall consider in turn the extent to which empirical evidence on memory disorders tends to encourage the development of theories of normal memory function based upon consolidation, upon a two-component system, upon mnemonic encoding, or upon retrieval processes. Finally, I shall ask whether current research contains the most effective basis for relating the study of normal cognitive function to the understanding of dysfunction. This question has at least two important parts. First, is the study of neurological patients the most sensitive and methodologically sound means of evaluating whether psychological theories can give a satisfactory account of memory dysfunction? Secondly, are the methods and theories of experimental psychologists the ones which are most appropriate to neurological practice?

Consolidation theories of memory dysfunction

As was implied above, consolidation theories represent one of the oldest models of remembering in psychology. They admit of a fairly natural application to cases of disordered memory, according to which the patient is assumed to lack the ability to develop consolidated memory traces. It follows that experiences may be available in memory for a short period of time, but that they leave no durable or long-term record. This was originally proposed by Milner (1966) as an explanation of the amnesic disorder which follows bilateral temporal lobectomy. In this case it is supported by the fact that the patient may be quite unable to learn new information, yet his immediate memory span may be normal, and his memory for the distant past may appear to be unimpaired. It is also a fairly natural way of explaining retrograde amnesia following cerebral trauma: that is, the failure to recall events experienced just before the injury or accident.

Unfortunately, consolidation theory attempts to explain the amount of forgetting without really accounting for the nature of forgetting. Many of the more interesting phenomena surrounding cases of impaired memory relate to the conditions of testing, the characteristics of the material to be learned, the strategies being employed by the subjects, and the dimensions along which material is encoded and retrieved. In a balance sheet drawn up by Baddeley (1975) in order to compare different theoretical explanations of amnesia, consolidation theories came out worst simply because they failed to specify predicted outcomes when these additional phenomena were considered. Baddeley appeared to excuse consolidation theory on the grounds that 'so little appears to be known about consolidation', but this seems excessively generous. Consolidation is not a real entity waiting to be uncovered by empirical investigation; rather, it is a metaphor or analogy used to make sense of particular phenomena. Additional metaphors are required in order to make interesting predictions in the study of memory disorders, and the idea of trace consolidation appears to have outlived its usefulness in the development of psychological theories.

Nevertheless, the notion of a consolidation impairment would constitute an adequate explanation of memory dysfunction if the apparently qualitative aspects of the disorder could be attributed merely to the patient's memories being weaker. This was pointed out by Woods and Piercy (1974), who suggested that amnesic patients might simply be showing a pattern of results which would also obtain in normal subjects if their memories were relatively weak. Their idea was pursued in a series of experiments by Meudell *et al.* (1979), who equated the overall level of performance (and hence the assumed level of trace strength) by manipulating the retention intervals used for amnesic patients and controls. In each case there was no evidence for a different pattern of performance between the two types of subject across different experimental conditions, and it was concluded that 'much of the extant data on human amnesia is [sic] consistent with a consolidation deficit'. These studies constitute a major methodological objection to an uncritical acceptance of the idea that amnesic patients manifest a qualitatively distinct pattern of performance. Indeed, alternative accounts of memory dysfunction may be refutable just to the extent that they continue to predict a qualitatively different pattern of performance in amnesic patients when their overall level of performance is matched with that of the control subjects. However, it is obvious that the consolidation idea would normally not explain whatever pattern of performance had been manifested by both groups of subjects. That is, it would once again handle the *fact* of impaired memory without having anything interesting to say concerning the nature of the processes underlying either impaired or normal memory. In short, the consolidation metaphor must be regarded as being of little use for the purposes of understanding the nature of memory disorders.

Structural theories of memory dysfunction

The prevalent strategy in much of the contemporary research on human memory involves the specification of structural components and connections. Its origins lie in the two-component model of memory which was presented by Waugh and Norman (1965), and which was later developed by Atkinson and Shiffrin (1968). According to this theoretical framework, performance in immediate memory tasks reflects the contributions of two hypothetical stores: primary memory, which is considered to be a relatively transient, phonemic store of limited capacity; and secondary memory, which is considered to be a relatively permanent semantic store of indefinitely large capacity. Originally, the two stores were assumed to be connected in a serial fashion, so that the permanent storage of information in secondary memory was only brought about by the rehearsal of material held in primary memory. This model can be regarded as a central example of the information-processing approach in cognitive psychology, and it represents a clear conceptual advance upon earlier ideas concerning consolidation in human memory.

Although the two-store model was initially developed solely on the basis of experimental results obtained with normal subjects, it also appeared to be entirely consistent with neuropsychological evidence, and especially with the pattern of findings obtained in patients with global amnesic disorders. For instance, Drachman and Arbit (1966) found that patients with temporal-lobe amnesia had a normal memory span, but experienced great difficulty on material which exceeded the span of immediate memory. Similarly, Wickelgren (1968) used a mathematical analysis of short-term retention to argue that bilateral temporal lobectomy severely disrupted long-term storage without affecting short-term storage. The direct use of a neurological sample to attempt to validate the two-store model was undertaken by Baddeley and Warrington (1970). In a heterogeneous group of amnesic patients, the results of a variety of experiments tended to converge upon the idea that such patients demonstrated a severe and selective impairment of long-term storage. In particular, while the patients were impaired in both immediate and delayed free recall, they produced a normal recency effect with immediate testing, which was taken to reflect an intact primary or short-term memory.

More recently, a similar conclusion was reached by Brooks (1975) in studying patients with severe closed head injuries. He reported the following findings:

(1) Patients with severe closed head injury were impaired in free recall but not in their span of immediate memory.

(2) The impairment in free recall was more pronounced when recall was delayed by an irrelevant distractor task.

(3) In immediate free recall the impairment was mainly at the early and middle serial positions, leaving a normal recency effect.

(4) When long-term and short-term components of immediate free recall were quantified, the patients were impaired on the former, but not on the latter.

(5) The head-injured patients differed from control patients in terms of the frequency of semantic intrusion errors, but not in terms of the frequency of phonemic intrusion errors.

This evidence indicated that severe closed head injury produced a selective deficit in a patient's ability to store information in a long-term, semantic memory. Comparable findings have been obtained by Craik (1968) in studying the effects of normal ageing, and by Richardson (1978a) in the case of patients with spontaneously arrested congenital hydrocephalus.

The researches of Baddeley and Warrington (1970) and Brooks (1975) are consistent with the idea that profound memory dysfunction of the type engendered by severe temporal-lobe damage or severe closed head injury is the result of a selective impairment of secondary memory. Unfortunately, they do not critically support the two-store model of memory against reasonable alternatives. In particular, the rapid forgetting of supra-span material in the case of amnesic patients had been known for many years, and was regarded by Milner (1966) as entirely in accord with a consolidation interpretation of disordered memory. Moreover, other patients have produced evidence which is consistent with the idea of two memory stores, but which is inconsistent with the original formulation of the model. These are patients with damage to the parietal or parieto-occipital region of the dominant cerebral hemisphere, who demonstrate a severe impairment in the short-term retention of sequences of items, but no general disorder of long-term memory (Shallice and Warrington, 1970; Warrington *et al.*, 1971). The finding of a selective deficit of short-term storage is consistent with the distinction between primary and secondary memory, and is difficult to reconcile with a consolidation approach. Indeed, if we take this finding together with the analysis of disorders of long-term memory, we have what Teuber (1955) called a 'double dissociation' between the effects of damage to the parietal lobes and the effects of damage to the temporal lobes: that is, the two types of memory appear to be vulnerable to lesions at distinct and non-overlapping anatomical sites, and so it may be concluded that the short-term and long-term forms of memory storage are functionally independent. Equally, however, it is difficult to reconcile the findings of a selective deficit of short-term storage with the specific proposal of Waugh and Norman that long-term retention is dependent upon the rehearsal of information within a short-term store. On this view, any disruption of primary memory should have profound and direct effects upon the contribution of secondary memory as well. On the contrary, the pattern of a double dissociation implies that the two hypothesized memory stores must be organized in a parallel, rather than in a serial fashion in the total information-processing system (Shallice and Warrington, 1970). It should be pointed out, however, that the same conclusion had been reached independently and on the basis of purely experimental data by Kintsch and Buschke (1969), on the grounds that phonemic similarity among the stimulus material also had a selective effect upon the contribution of primary or short-term memory.

This research is a good illustration of the two major epistemological trends noted earlier. First, the application of the two-store model undoubtedly increased our knowledge and understanding of a variety of clinical conditions, and provided a clear conceptual framework within which to organize our thinking and speculations concerning the underlying neuropathology of those conditions. Secondly, these neuropsychological applications con-fronted the two-store model with a radically different form of empirical validation; it was obvious that the basic premise of the model was supported by the findings, but that a major assumption concerning the structural relationship between the two hypothesized memory stores had to be rejected. Consequently, the collection of relevant data from neurological patients constituted an important opportunity to evaluate and to develop the basic theoretical framework. Unfortunately, the framework itself has been subjected to radical criticism on empirical, methodological and heuristic grounds (Baddeley and Hitch, 1974; Craik and Lockhart, 1972; Watkins, 1974); in particular, its application to the paradigm of immediate free recall was almost certainly misguided (Baddeley and Hitch, 1977). Nevertheless, the two-store model is generally agreed to have been a useful first approximation in thinking about the structures and processes involved in human memory, and its applications to neurological conditions represent an important body of knowledge in the neuropsychology of memory.

Encoding theories of memory dysfunction

Although the two-store theory of human memory originally characterized primary and secondary memory in terms of their storage capacities and in terms of their rates of forgetting, evidence was soon forthcoming concerning the likely forms of coding to which the two hypothetical stores might have access. Of course, any theory concerning the cognitive processing of information must sooner or later specify not only the structures involved, but also the forms of encoding or representation which are employed. In this case the evidence tended to show that performance in short-term memory was influenced by phonemic properties of the stimulus material, whereas performance in long-term memory was influenced more by semantic properties of the stimulus material. Once the two-store theory was open to question as a coherent or appropriate model of human memory, however, there developed an alternate conception that the level of retention in any learning situation was directly dependent upon the level of coding or processing employed, with the basic general assumption that more abstract, semantic levels of representation would be associated with superior performance (Craik and Lockhart, 1972). In this sort of theoretical framework impaired retention is to be attributed to a failure or an inability to employ optimal levels of processing or encoding in learning and remembering.

Although it is possible to construct experimental tasks in which the optimal level of encoding is visual or phonemic, for most purposes this last assumption can be translated into the idea that memory disorders are the result of an impairment of semantic coding. This is mentioned by Baddeley (1975) as a potential explanation of the defective long-term memory performance of amnesic patients, but one which as it stands is refuted by the findings that amnesics are able to exploit taxonomic organization in order to improve their performance, and that they are assisted by being given an appropriate semantic cue at the time of recall (Baddeley and Warrington, 1973; Warrington and Weiskrantz, 1971). Butters and Cermak (1975) did find that the amount of proactive interference in short-term recall and the incidence of false–positive errors in a recognition task tended to be related to superficial, non-semantic properties rather than to taxonomic or semantic properties of the stimulus material with amnesic patients. However, Cermak and Reale (1978) found no evidence that instructions to process the material semantically helped amnesics any more than it helped controls. Thus, the hypothesis of a semantic coding deficit does not appear to be a useful account of amnesic disorders.

This hypothesis does appear to be more successful in explaining the effects of normal ageing upon human memory. The wealth of experimental evidence on age differences in learning and remembering has been conveniently summarized by Eysenck (1977, Chapter 11) and by Craik (1977), and this research has reliably shown that older subjects are inferior to younger subjects in their use of more complex and abstract forms of information processing and storage. Not only are older subjects likely to engage in less abstract and elaborative levels of processing in dealing with individual stimulus items (Erber et al., 1980; Kausler and Puckett, 1979; Puglisi, 1980); they also appear to be less able to integrate the semantic information contained in separate stimulus presentations (Pezdek, 1980). Moreover, since performance in short-term memory is considered to be less likely to involve these deeper levels of processing than is performance in long-term memory, these results also explain why short-term retention is affected much less by age differences (Eysenck, 1977, p.263).

To some extent, the value of any processing-deficit explanation depends upon whether the general notion of 'deeper levels of processing' can be specified in terms of particular encoding strategies. A form of mnemonic representation which has received considerable attention in the experimental literature is the construction of elaborative and integrative mental images, which is known to produce substantial and reliable improvements in memory performance (Richardson, 1980). The idea that impaired memory performance can be attributed to a selective deficit in the use of mental imagery has been investigated in the case of a variety of subject populations:

(1) When the use of different learning strategies is inferred from post-learning questionnaires, it appears that older subjects are less likely to use imaginal mediation in paired-associate learning than are young or middle-aged subjects (Hulicka and Grossman, 1967; Rowe and Schnore, 1971), even when they are explicitly instructed to employ such techniques (Hulicka *et al.*, 1967). However, this approach to the study of mental imagery is purely correlational, and assumes that older subjects are just as capable as younger subjects of remembering the mediators which they employed (Eysenck, 1977, p.258; cf. Richardson, 1978b).

(2) Baddeley and Warrington (1973) investigated the effectiveness of different mnemonic codes in a heterogeneous sample of amnesic patients. These patients were able to improve their recall performance when the stimulus material could be organized on either a phonemic or a semantic basis. However, unlike a group of control patients, they showed no sign of any improvement when sequences of unrelated words were connected by sentences which they were instructed to visualize.

(3) Jones (1974) considered the effects of stimulus concreteness and of imagery mnemonic instructions in patients following temporal lobectomy. Although patients with lesions of the left temporal lobe showed an overall deficit compared to normal performance, whereas those with lesions of the right temporal lobe did not, both groups showed a normal superiority on concrete material as opposed to abstract material and a normal benefit from imagery mnemonic instructions. These results imply that the neuroanatomical basis of mental imagery is probably not contained within the structures of the temporal lobes (Richardson, 1980, pp.139–40).

(4) Richardson (1978a) studied two cases of spontaneously arrested congenital hydrocephalus. They were found to be

impaired both in free recall and on the performance subtests of an intelligence scale, and it was concluded that their memory impairment resulted from a reduced ability to use mental imagery as an elaborative code.

(5) Richardson (1979a) examined a sample of patients admitted to hospital following minor head injuries. They were found to be impaired in the free recall of concrete material, but not in the recall of abstract material. In fact, although a sample of control subjects showed the normal pattern of superior recall on concrete material, the head-injured patients showed no significant difference between the recall of concrete and abstract material. It was concluded that closed head injury leads to an impairment of imaginal encoding, but does not affect verbal encoding.

The use of mental imagery in learning and remembering can be regarded either as a specific mnemonic device for improving retention, or as merely one example of non-verbal processing in human cognition. The latter interpretation suggests that memory disorders should be especially apparent in a wide variety of non-verbal tasks, including the retention of pictorial information and the storage and processing of spatial arrays. In the case of research on ageing, for instance, it would appear that older subjects are less able to recognize visual, auditory, or tactile stimuli which cannot be easily labelled or described (Riege and Inman, 1981). Similarly, Perlmutter et al. (1981) found that older subjects were impaired in remembering spatial arrays, but not in remembering verbal sequences; however, Schear and Nebes (1980) found no evidence for a greater decline with age in the case of memory for spatial locations than in the case of memory for individual verbal items. This sort of approach might then be developed by reference to the known functional asymmetry of the two cerebral hemispheres. Since linguistic skills appear to be localized within the left cerebral hemisphere in most subjects, a recurrent pattern of greater cognitive dysfunction on non-verbal tasks would entail that the physiological mechanisms of the right cerebral hemisphere were more vulnerable to widespread disruption as a result of brain damage than those of the left cerebral hemisphere. Once again, in the case of research on ageing, there is experimental evidence that the storage and processing efficiency of the right hemisphere declines with age more sharply than that of the left hemisphere (Johnson *et al.*, 1979). However, a recent study failed to find any clear relationship between the scores of neurological patients on verbal and non-verbal intelligence tests and the site of brain damage as diagnosed by means of computerized axial tomography (Wood, 1979).

Following on from this last point, it does appear to be true that performance in non-verbal cognitive tasks is especially vulnerable in patients with organic brain disorders, and shows a slower rate of recovery during the period of rehabilitation. This is certainly true in the case of closed head injury (Mandleberg, 1976; Mandleberg and Brooks, 1975), in the case of congenital hydrocephalus (Richardson, 1978a) and in the case of normal ageing (Botwinick, 1977). Nevertheless, these results must be treated with considerable care and scepticism, since verbal and non-verbal tasks differ not only in terms of the cognitive representations which they employ, but also in terms of the structures and processes involved. There may well be a quantitative difference, such that non-verbal tasks are inherently more complex and thus are open to disruption from a greater variety of sources (Mandleberg, 1975). There are certainly important qualitative differences, relating to the demands which the two sorts of task place upon various cognitive faculties. First, it may be the case that non-verbal tasks place greater emphasis upon attentional mechanisms, and that these are especially impaired with generalized organic disorders (cf. Kinsbourne, 1980). Secondly, non-verbal tasks often employ novel material which must be manipulated in an unfamiliar manner; it follows that they are more dependent upon the efficient use of memory, and will therefore show a greater deficit than verbal tasks in patients with neurological disorders which interfere with learning and remembering (Albert and Kaplan, 1980; Mandleberg, 1975). More precisely, non-verbal tasks appear to rely upon memory for particular episodes, whereas verbal tasks appear to rely upon general linguistic knowledge. In terms of the distinction proposed by Tulving (1972), one might thus conclude that episodic memory is more vulnerable to brain damage than is semantic memory. This has been proposed specifically as a characterization of the cognitive impairment associated with ageing (Eysenck, 1977, p.250), but here the distinction between episodic and semantic memory has been subsumed under the more general dichotomy between fluid and crystallized intelligence (Horn, 1975).

Insofar as it is possible to increase an individual's performance in learning and remembering by manipulating the encoding strategies which he employs, this sort of intervention might be expected to constitute a reasonable basis for developing programmes of therapy and rehabilitation in patients with memory disorders. Indeed, encoding theories of memory dysfunction appear to offer the most interesting and rewarding framework for anyone wishing to apply experimental research to clinical practice. Unfortunately, very little work has been carried out in this direction to date, and the clinical psychologist who is not content merely to monitor the changes in memory efficiency during degeneration or rehabilitation has to devise therapeutic strategies in the absence of any established principles. There has been considerable interest in the possibility of improving cognitive function in the elderly by means of training in particular techniques. While mnemonic aids based upon the use of mental imagery do seem to improve the performance of older subjects in formal experimental situations (Poon et al., 1980), these results cannot be accepted uncritically as defining the course which future training programmes should follow. First, it is exactly in the area of non-verbal encoding that elderly subjects appear to be deficient, and it might be more reasonable to train such individuals in the use of verbal mnemonic techniques (Winograd and Simon, 1980). Secondly, memory aids based upon the use of mental imagery seem to be of value only in remembering unrelated concrete items presented at a relatively slow rate; imagery mnemonics are much less useful under the conditions which normally arise in real life (Hunter, 1977; Morris, 1977). Nevertheless, it is also true that the efficacy of training programmes designed to improve the performance of neurological patients can only be formally and systematically evaluated under strict laboratory conditions with normal, intact subjects (cf. Chapter 10).

Retrieval theories of memory dysfunction

Memory impairment may transpire because of a failure to encode information in such a way that it can be held in storage throughout the retention interval. On the other hand, such an impairment may also arise because information which is adequately stored cannot be efficiently retrieved at the time of the retention test. At least three different sorts of retrieval-deficit account may be found in the literature on memory disorders:

(1) One idea is that retrieval failure is attributable to the absence of an effective retrieval strategy. Thus, the material represented in memory is not organized in such a way that items can be successfully retrieved using normal routes of memory search. This is often characterized by saying that these items are 'available' in memory, but not 'accessible' at the time of recall (Tulving, 1968). Evidence for this sort of retrieval failure may be obtained by showing that the magnitude of a memory impairment is reduced when specific retrieval paths are supplied by the experimenter: for instance, by cueing the subject with the relevant taxonomic category.

(2) A somewhat different approach involves an emphasis upon competition or interference from irrelevant material. Even if the material to be remembered has been adequately encoded and stored, a failure to inhibit these competing or irrelevant responses may produce a deficit at the time of recall. In this case subjects who demonstrate a memory impairment should be disproportionately aided by being given cues to recall which restrict the possible range of responses (Warrington and Weiskrantz, 1974).

(3) In attempting to retrieve material from memory, subjects may generate a variety of items as possible candidates for recall. It is sometimes assumed that these items are subjected to covert recognition judgements, so that only those responses which are judged to be likely to be correct are actually emitted. If the subjects fail to produce an adequate number of correct responses, or if they produce an inappropriate number of incorrect responses, this might be the result of inadequate decision processes in these covert recognition judgements. This can be tested by requiring the subjects to make overt judgements in a formal recognition task, and by measuring separately their memory sensitivity and their response biases.

It is often supposed that explanations of memory dysfunction in terms of a failure to retrieve the appropriate material are distinct from explanations in terms of an encoding deficit. However, any alteration in the manner in which a stimulus item is encoded is likely to entail a change in the circumstances which would constitute optimal conditions for its successful retrieval. Conversely, the effectiveness of a specific retrieval situation in determining recall performance will depend upon the extent to which that situation is appropriate to or compatible with the manner in which the stimulus material was encoded at the time of its original presentation (Tulving, 1974). Thus, the distinction between encoding-deficit and retrieval-deficit views of memory dysfunction is not a clear-cut one by any means. The relationship between the two approaches can be clarified by considering that the act of retrieval from memory storage depends upon the operation of certain retrieval processes upon a particular representation. Retrieval-deficit explanations of memory dysfunction may, therefore, be categorized according to whether they postulate a failure of the retrieval processes or a failure of the representation to be retrieved (cf. Davis and Mumford, 1981). The latter class of theory assumes that the cues established at the time when a stimulus was originally encoded were inadequate for its subsequent retrieval; consequently, these theories are indisting-uishable from encoding-deficit models of memory dysfunction. Only those theories which postulate a failure of the retrieval processes can be regarded as a logically distinct category of explanations.

Given this point, one may, nevertheless, ask to what extent the evidence on particular memory disorders is consistent with each of the retrieval-deficit accounts mentioned above. In the case of global amnesic disorders it is true that patients manifest improved performance as a result of taxonomic structure in the material to be remembered, or as a result of being given appropriate semantic cues to recall (Baddeley and Warrington, 1973; Warrington and Weiskrantz, 1971). However, there is no evidence that the performance of amnesics is improved more than that of controls by these manipulations, and so their impaired retention cannot be attributed to a spontaneous failure to use an effective semantic retrieval strategy. Rather more emphasis has been placed upon the effectiveness of retrieval cues which serve to limit the range of possible responses. Using a variety of experimental procedures, Warrington and Weiskrantz (1968, 1970, 1973, 1974; Weiskrantz and Warrington, 1975) found that amnesic patients could show substantial retention if they were prompted by a perceptual fragment of the stimulus to be remembered. They argued that this procedure constrained the subjects' responses, and thus minimized interference from competing responses. However, since their procedure employed cues at a relatively superficial level of mnemonic processing, the results were also consistent with the hypothesis that amnesic patients were selectively impaired in the ability to encode information at deeper or more abstract levels (Baddeley, 1975). Moreover, the original findings have not always been replicated (Mayes *et al.*, 1978).

Another area where the analysis of the effectiveness of retrieval cues has proved interesting is the study of normal ageing and of senile dementia, though once again the results have not always been consistent. Laurence (1967) found that older subjects benefited more than younger subjects from the provision of retrieval cues at recall, but Drachman and Leavitt (1972) and Hultsch (1975) did not find this interactive relationship between age and cue effectiveness. Miller (1975) found that providing the initial letters of the words to be recalled raised the performance of patients with presenile dementia to normal levels, though it did not improve the recall performance of normal controls. This could be interpreted as evidence that presenile dementia impairs the retrieval processes necessary for normal recall, or as evidence that it encourages the use of rather more superficial, visual or phonemic levels of encoding in tasks where normals process material semantically. The latter idea was supported as an explanation of the memory disorder characteristic of senile dementia in a study by Davis and Mumford (1981). In two different experiments, normal elderly patients showed improved recall when provided either with the initial letters or with the taxonomic categories of the words to be remembered. However, patients with senile dementia only benefited from the letter cues, not from the category cues; and the effect of letter cues was similar in magnitude in the two groups of patients. Thus, dementia appears to lead to inadequate semantic processing of stimulus material at the time of encoding, but there is no evidence to support a retrieval-failure hypothesis in this neurological condition. As an interesting ancillary finding, Davis and Mumford divided their normal patients into forgetful and nonforgetful controls on the basis of their uncued recall performance, ans showed that the forgetful controls benefited more from the provision of semantic cues. They suggested that these patients might be manifesting an early or mild form of dementia where the memory dysfunction was largely one of a retrieval failure at the time of recall.

Retrieval problems are normally considered to be minimized in recognition memory, though it is known that in certain conditions recognition performance may still involve a substantial retrieval component (Tulving and Thomson, 1973). The comparison of performance in recognition and recall tasks enables one to attribute an impairment of memory function to retrieval processes rather than to storage processes, to the extent that the impairment is evident in a recall task but not in a recognition task. This approach has been used extensively in the study of human ageing (Eysenck, 1977, pp.263–5). In general, older subjects demonstrate fairly good performance in recognition-memory tasks, which suggests that, in normal ageing, encoding and storage processes are rather less impaired than retrieval processes (Craik, 1977), but somewhat different results are obtained when patients with senile dementia are matched with normal controls of similar ages. In these studies the memory impairment obtained in recall tasks does not appear to be reduced or alleviated when recognition procedures are used (Caird, 1965; Inglis, 1957; Miller and Lewis, 1977; Whitehead, 1973, 1975), and this supports the conclusion of Davis and Mumford (1981) that impaired retrieval processes cannot explain the memory disorder in senile dementia.

Nevertheless, performance in a recognition task may be influenced both by the subject's memory sensitivity and by his response criterion or tendency to accept any item as 'old' or 'new'. When specific techniques are employed to separate these two factors, the impairment of recognition memory which is found with normal ageing or with senile dementia is usually found to be associated with a lax decision criterion, as evidenced by an increased false-alarm rate (Ferris *et al.*, 1980; Harkins *et al.*, 1979; Miller and Lewis, 1977; Rankin and Kausler, 1979). This suggests that the impaired performance in recall demonstrated by these subjects is probably not attributable to their use of too strict a decision criterion in rejecting possible candidates to be emitted as their responses. Although older subjects sometimes make fewer intrusion errors in recall than do young subjects (Taub, 1967), this may be because their failure to remember previous stimuli reduces the class of items from which reasonable guesses may be drawn, rather than because they are more cautious in their production of responses (cf. Eysenck, 1977, p.248).

Unfortunately, the inferences of most published research on memory dysfunction in recognition tasks are invalidated by an inappropriate use of the relevant analytic techniques. This criticism has been made in detail elsewhere with specific reference to the study of closed head injury (Richardson, 1979b), but it will be summarized here since the same errors are made in research on ageing (e.g. Ferris *et at.*, 1980; Riege and Inman, 1981) and in other areas of clinical neuropsychology. Briefly, then, the analysis of recognition performance normally appeals to signal-detection theory, which claims that the two classes of stimulus presentation to which the subject has to respond (that is, old and new items) define separate probability density functions on some decision axis of 'oldness' or familiarity. The subject is assumed to make his response by determining whether the psychological effect of a given stimulus presentation on this continuum exceeds some criterial value. The difference between the means of the two distributions is typically employed as an index of recognition sensitivity, and the likelihood ratio (the ratio between the two distributions) at the response criterion is sometimes employed as an index of response bias. However, the subject can only respond on the basis of a criterion expressed in terms of the likelihood ratio if he has access to at least a good estimate of the two probability distributions. Accordingly, the use of the inferred likelihood ratio as an index of response bias presupposes that the subject remembers the value produced by all or most stimulus presentations on the decision axis, and that he receives information on the correctness of his response on all or most trials. In most studies of recognition memory in clinical neuropsychology the first assumption is quite implausible, and the second assumption is not satisfied at all. Thus, most of the research to date will have to be reworked before any clear conclusion can be reached on the effects upon response bias in memory dysfunction.

The limitations of clinical neuropsychology

The most natural manner in which to investigate the effects of physiological dysfunction upon cognitive processing is to consider the consequences of actual physical damage to the brain, whether that damage be caused by disease, surgery or trauma. This is the approach adopted in all of the research discussed in this chapter so far, and it is clear that the study of damaged brains can generate much useful information concerning the normal functioning of the intact human brain, and that it can often lead to theoretical innovation and development in cognitive psychology. This research is also directly addressed to the practical problem of the diagnosis, treatment and rehabilitation of neurological patients, who constitute a major burden upon the health services of every developed society.

Nevertheless, the question arises whether the approach of clinical neuropsychology is actually the most appropriate or the most methodologically secure manner of understanding normal brain function.

It is inherent in this approach that the primary source of empirical data is the psychometric assessment of samples of patients with damaged or diseased brains. There are two major methodological reservations concerning such samples. First, it is invariably not the case that these samples are selected at random from the general population. Rather, there are always a great many constitutional and environmental factors which predispose particular individuals towards brain injury or disease, though typically most of these factors are only poorly recognized and understood. It follows that it is in principle never possible to generalize the results of research in clinical neuropsychology to the general population as a whole. Secondly, it is extremely rare to have available adequate control data from the same subjects in this sort of research. Although some of the relevant predisposing factors are known in principle, in practice it is normally not possible to predict the occurrence of brain injury and disease in specific individuals. Consequently, it is normal not to have any direct information as to a patient's premorbid cognitive abilities, though it may be possible to arrive at a very rough estimate of those abilities by considering his occupational status and his educational background. This means that control data concerning normal levels of performance in a psychometric test must be obtained from a distinct group of subjects, and thus that research in clinical neuropsychology is typically restricted to between-subjects designs. Students of psychology are normally warned of the reduced sensitivity of such designs in formal laboratory experiments, but a more serious problem arises in studies of neurological patients. Since it is neither ethically permissible nor practically possible to allocate subjects at random to control and experimental groups by systematically exposing them to or protecting them from disease or trauma, and since the predisposing factors mentioned above will normally not arise with the same incidence in the case of an appropriate control group, the researcher is invariably trying to attribute differences in performance between the two groups to some neurological indicator in the full knowledge that the groups may well differ also on many other relevant characteristics. A fundamental methodological task in any area of research in clinical neuropsychology is the choice of a control group which minimizes this sort of confounding. However, the basic point to be remembered is that this research is essentially correlational rather than experimental in nature.

One important exception to these criticisms is research on the effects of ageing. Obviously, all subjects manifest developmental changes in cognitive skills, and all subjects can in principle be retested at different ages. Of course, the availability of survivors will depend upon constitutional and environmental factors, and it is quite probable that samples of subjects of a considerable age are really quite unrepresentative of the general population. It is more important, however, that in practice most research on the effects of ageing upon memory function has tested different age groups at the same point in time. This cross-sectional approach clearly confounds the effects of age with those of generation or cohort differences, and limits the value of any results which may be found (Schaie and Strother, 1968). An additional problem is that chronological age is not an intrinsically psychological variable, and so any findings must be reinterpreted in terms of known or hypothesized chronological changes in cognitive structure and processes (Eysenck, 1977, p.245).

There do exist circumstances in which it is considered permissible to induce a permanent or temporary disruption of cerebral function, and such procedures might be regarded as experimental manipulations for the purposes of overcoming the second methodological problem mentioned above. Several of these procedures have an established role in clinical practice, and have generated useful research findings. They include the surgical removal of cerebral tissue in order to alleviate chronic, intractable epilepsy or depression, the electrical stimulation of local anatomical areas of the brain, and the global application of electroconvulsive shock in psychiatric treatment. None of these procedures handles the first methodological problem mentioned above, since each is employed exclusively in the case of patients whose brains are already believed to be diseased in some respect.

An ideal procedure for research on the effects of brain dysfunction would be one which could be applied to randomly selected groups of subjects and whose effects were entirely under experimental control. An approach which satisfies these requirements is that of psychopharmacology, which exploits the transient effects of specific chemical preparations to induce a temporary disruption of cerebral activity in normal, healthy volunteers. In this sort of research the induced impairment of cognitive function constitutes a reversible experimental manipulation, and so each subject can be employed as his own control. The effects of pharmacological preparations upon brain function are discussed in detail in Chapter 8, so it will be sufficient to mention here some of the more interesting findings in the study of human memory.

A considerable amount of research has investigated the cholinergic system of neurotransmission (Drachman and Sahakian, in press). Acetylcholine acts as a neurotransmitter at various sites in the central nervous system, and especially within the limbic system. Its importance in long-term memory was established by Deutsch (1971) on the basis of animal experiments. In humans the effects of acetylcholine are blocked by hyoscine (scopolamine), which is noted for its interference with memory function. Indeed, a variety of experimental studies have demonstrated that hyoscine has a fairly specific effect upon the encoding of new memories into long-term storage. Acetylcholine is hydrolysed by the enzyme acetylcholine-sterase, which is inhibited by the drug physostigmine (eserine); the latter reverses the amnesic action of hyoscine, and in isolation tends to enhance memory function. Finally, the role of the cholinergic system in long-term storage is supported by the fact that the memory impairment characteristic of presenile and senile dementia is associated with a deficit of the enzyme choline acetyltransferase in parts of the hippocampus.

Nevertheless, it is generally assumed that other systems of neurotransmission are implicated in learning and remembering. Another important system which has been extensively investigated is that involving the inhibitory neurotransmitter γ-Amino-n-butyric acid (GABA). There are high concentrations of GABA receptor sites within the hippocampus, and the availability of this neurotransmitter is facilitated by the class of chemical compound known as the benzodiazepines. The latter drugs produce relatively selective depression of limbic system activity, and experimental evidence has demonstrated that they also have a specific effect upon the encoding of new memories into long-term storage.

Psychopharmacological research is not without its problems, however. First, many of the procedures are rather dangerous and require careful clinical supervision, and secondly, it is often difficult to direct the preparation of interest to specific anatomical areas of the brain, so the research findings may well be relatively uninformative concerning the cerebral localization of cognitive function. Thirdly, our present understanding of the neurochemical basis of the effects of pharmacological preparations is often slight and itself dependent upon future research efforts. Consequently, it may be difficult to relate established effects at the level of cognitive function to specific processes at the level of neurochemical transmission.

Conclusions

It is clear, even from the relatively brief account given in this chapter, that neuropsychological research on disorders of learning and memory constitutes a major area of investigation which has the potential to bring about significant developments in theorizing concerning normal memory function and in understanding a wide variety of neurological conditions. Nevertheless, it is important not to accept this research uncritically, but to try to arrive at an overall assessment of its importance both for psychological theory and for clinical practice. It should be emphasized that the following remarks are intended to apply only to research and theorizing concerning human learning and memory.

One question to be asked is whether research in clinical neuropsychology is directed at the appropriate sorts of phenomena. The experimental manipulations and procedures which are employed tend to use one of two approaches. The first is that many of the studies which have been carried out have taken the well tried methods of the psychological laboratory and have applied them to samples of clinical patients. As was indicated in the introduction to this chapter, this has the advantage that procedures with a clear theoretical context are being submitted to testing on a radically different population of subjects. With the second approach the remaining studies have tended to take the somewhat arbitrary and theoretically naïve methods of the clinical psychologist, and to submit them to analysis by means of experimental investigation. This has the advantage that the results of research can be readily located within the sorts of psychometric assessment which are routinely administered to neurological patients. Unfortunately, both of these approaches have the important disadvantage that the methods and procedures employed are often not at all like the concrete tasks of learning and remembering which confront those patients in everyday life. In terms of the prevalent jargon of cognitive psychology one can certainly say that the research methods of clinical neuropsychology are typically low in 'ecological validity'.

Related to this issue is the question whether research in clinical neuropsychology is concerned with the appropriate sorts of empirical evidence. Both the approaches just described involve the collection of behavioural observations under standardized conditions. In particular, it is normally taken as a prerequisite of the scientific objectivity of cognitive psychology that the evidence which it employs should be public and behavioural in nature. A corollary of this is that a subject's own account of his thoughts, sensations and feelings is not considered appropriate as an item of data (Richardson, 1980, pp.7, 11-12). Nevertheless, clinicians typically do pay attention to a patient's introspective reports, and may well allow the symptoms which are presented to suggest a provisional diagnosis before more formal investigations are carried out. To some extent, therefore, there is a conceptual gap between psychological theory and clinical practice over the epistemological status of introspective reports. This hiatus is bound to limit the possibility of collaboration and communication between the two disciplines.

A rather different problem is whether research in clinical neuropsychology is actually directed towards the appropriate theoretical issues. Obviously, the models of human memory which have been discussed in this chapter have been at one time or another central topics of debate and research in cognitive psychology. Moreover, some of the most important research in this area has been carried out by investigators who are also at the forefront of work on normal learning and remembering. However, it has to be acknowledged that many other researchers in the field of clinical neuropsychology are not within the mainstream of this work, and as a consequence their theoretical context tends to be somewhat anachronistic. For instance, research on human ageing and memory appears to take the model of primary and secondary memory as a definitive account rather than as a rather outmoded first approximation, and has only recently discovered the use of signal-detection theory in analysing performance in recognition memory. Most other areas of clinical neuropsychology also seem to be susceptible to a time-lag of up to fifteen years in the appreciation of current theoretical sophistication, and this will obviously tend to counteract the process of creative theory development.

Similarly, another issue is whether research in clinical neuropsychology is directed towards the appropriate aspects of neurological practice. In principle, the work which has been described in this chapter should provide the clinician with a sounder basis for appreciating the various conditions presented by his patients. Unfortunately, there is little evidence that this research has had any appreciable effect upon the way in which professional medical staff actually think about their patients, in terms of their diagnosis, their treatment or their rehabilitation. To be fair, at the level of individual patients it is not clear that the procedures employed in this research have any greater reliability or prognostic value than the techniques which are already employed. Nevertheless, research workers in clinical neuropsychology must pay more attention to the needs and objectives of neurologists themselves if their findings are to be regarded as having clinical relevance.

If there is a general problem of the applicability of research in clinical neuropsychology, then a final point is whether such research is even necessary to ensure optimal conceptual and theoretical development in cognitive psychology. One would like to feel that clinical neuropsychology makes available to experimental psychologists a body of evidence relevant to their models and theories which could not be obtained in laboratory research with normal, intact subjects. Unfortunately, in the few major instances where neuropsychological findings have appeared to necessitate a revision of the prevalent cognitive theory of human memory, such changes have typically been dictated simultaneously and independently by normal experimental research. For instance, the assumption of serial sequential processing from primary to secondary memory had been questioned on experimental grounds before Shallice and Warrington (1970) reported their case study of a patient with a selective deficit of short-term storage. Nevertheless, even in these cases the neuropsychological research has provided additional, convergent evidence to motivate a significant revision to the accepted theory. Moreover, clinical neuropsychology is certainly the most direct means of providing an adequate material basis for the hypothetical entities of theoretical psychology in terms of the physiological structures of the human brain.

References

Albert, M. S. and Kaplan, E. (1980) Organic implications of neuro-psychological deficits in the elderly. In L. W. Poon, J. L. Fozard, L. S. Cermak, D. Arenberg and L. W. Thompson (eds) *New Directions in Memory and Aging*. Hillsdale, NJ: Lawrence Erlbaum Associates.

Atkinson, R. C. and Shiffrin, R. M. (1968) Human memory: a proposed system and its control processes. In K. W. Spence and J. T. Spence (eds) *The Psychology of Learning and Motivation: Advances in Research and Theory*. Vol. 2. New York: Academic Press.

Baddeley, A. D. (1975) Theories of amnesia. In A. Kennedy and A. Wilkes (eds) *Studies in Long Term Memory*. London: Wiley.

Baddeley, A. D. (1976) *The Psychology of Memory*. New York: Basic Books.

Baddeley, A. D. and Hitch, G. J. (1974) Working memory. In G. H. Bower (ed.) *The Psychology of Learning and Motivation: Advances in Research and Theory*. Vol. 8. New York: Academic Press.

Baddeley, A. D. and Hitch, G. J. (1977) Recency re-examined. In S. Dornic (ed.) *Attention and Performance*. Vol. VI. London: Academic Press.

Baddeley, A. D. and Warrington, E. K. (1970) Amnesia and the distinction between long- and short-term memory. *Journal of Verbal Learning and Verbal Behavior 9*: 176-89.

Baddeley, A. D. and Warrington, E. K. (1973) Memory coding and amnesia. *Neuropsychologia 11*: 159-65.

Botwinick, J. (1977) Intellectual abilities. In J. E. Birren and K. W. Schaie (eds) *Handbook of the Psychology of Aging*. New York: Van Nostrand Reinhold.

Brooks, D. N. (1975) Long and short term memory in head injured patients. *Cortex 11*: 329-40.

Butters, N. and Cermak, L. S. (1975) Some analyses of amnesic syndromes in brain-damaged patients. In R. Isaacson and K. Pribram (eds) *The Hippocampus*. Vol. 2. New York: Plenum Press.

Caird, W. K. (1965) Memory disorder and psychological test performance in aged psychiatric patients. *Diseases of the Nervous System 26*: 499-505.

Cermak, L. S. and Reale, L. (1978) Depth of processing and retention of words by alcoholic Korsakoff patients. *Journal of Experimental Psychology: Human Learning and Memory 4*: 165-74.

Craik, F. I. M. (1968) Two components in free recall. *Journal of Verbal Learning and Verbal Behavior 7*: 996-1004.

Craik, F. I. M. (1977) Age differences in human memory. In J. E. Birren and K. W. Schaie (eds) *Handbook of the Psychology of Aging*. New York: Van Nostrand Reinhold.

Craik, F. I. M. and Lockhart, R. S. (1972) Levels of processing: a framework for memory research. *Journal of Verbal Learning and Verbal Behavior 11*: 671-84.

Davis, P. E. and Mumford, S. J. (1981) The nature of the memory impairment in senile dementia: a brief review and an experiment. Paper presented to the Annual Conference of the British Psychological Society, University of Surrey.

Deutsch, J. A. (1971) The cholinergic synapse and the site of memory. *Science 174*: 788-94.

Drachman, D. A. and Arbit, J. (1966) Memory and the hippocampal complex: II. *Archives of Neurology 15*: 52-61.

Drachman, D. A. and Leavitt, J. (1972) Memory impairment in the aged: storage versus retrieval deficit. *Journal of Experimental Psychology 93*: 302-8.

Drachman, D. A. and Sahakian, B. J. (in press) The effects of cholinergic agents on human learning and memory. In R. J. Wurtman, J. H. Growdon and A. Barbeau (eds) *Uses of Choline and Lecithin in Neurologic and Psychiatric Diseases*. New York: Raven Press.

Erber, J., Herman, T. G. and Botwinick, J. (1980) Age differences in memory as a function of depth of processing. *Experimental Aging Research 6*: 341-8.

Eysenck, M. W. (1977) *Human Memory: Theory, Research, and Individual Differences*. Oxford: Pergamon Press.

Ferris, S. H., Crook, T., Clark, E., McCarthy, M. and Rae, D. (1980) Facial recognition memory deficits in normal aging and senile dementia. *Journal of Gerontology 35*: 707-14.

Harkins, S. W., Chapman, C. R. and Eisdorfer, C. (1979) Memory loss and response bias in senescence. *Journal of Gerontology 34*: 66-72.

Horn, J. L. (1975) Psychometric studies of aging and intelligence. In S. Gershon and A. Raskin (eds) *Aging*. Vol. 2: *Genesis and Treatment of Psychologic Disorders in the Elderly*. New York: Raven Press.

Hulicka, I. M. and Grossman, J. L. (1967) Age-group comparisons for the use of mediators in paired-associate learning. *Journal of Gerontology 22*: 46-51.

Hulicka, I. M., Sterns, H. and Grossman, J. L. (1967) Age-group comparisons of paired-associate learning as a function of paced and self-paced association and response times. *Journal of Gerontology 22*: 274-80.

Hultsch, D. F. (1975) Adult age differences in retrieval: trace-dependent and cue-dependent forgetting. *Developmental Psychology 11*: 197-201.

Hunter, I. M. L. (1977) Imagery, comprehension and mnemonics. *Journal of Mental Imagery 1*: 65-72.

Inglis, J. (1957) An experimental study of learning and memory function in elderly psychiatric patients. *Journal of Mental Science 103*: 796-803.

Johnson, R. C., Cole, R. E., Bowers, J. K., Foiles, S. V., Nikaido, A. M., Patrick, J. W. and Woliver, R. E. (1979) Hemispheric efficiency in middle and later adulthood. *Cortex 15*: 109-19.

Jones, M. K. (1974) Imagery as a mnemonic aid after left temporal lobectomy: contrast between material-specific and generalized memory disorders. *Neuropsychologia 12*: 21-30.

Kausler, D. H. and Puckett, J. M. (1979) Effects of word frequency on adult age differences in word memory span. *Experimental Aging Research* 5: 161-9.

Kinsbourne, M. (1980) Attentional dysfunctions and the elderly: theoretical models and research perspectives. In L. W. Poon, J. L. Fozard, L. S. Cermak, D. Arenberg and L. W. Thompson (eds) *New Directions in Memory and Aging*. Hillsdale, NJ: Lawrence Erlbaum Associates.

Kintsch, W. and Buschke, H. (1969) Homophones and synonyms in short-term memory. *Journal of Experimental Psychology 80*: 403-7.

Laurence, M. W. (1967) Memory loss with age: a test of two strategies for its retardation. *Psychonomic Science 9*: 209-10.

Mandleberg, I. A. (1975) Cognitive recovery after severe head injury: 2. Wechsler Adult Intelligence Scale during post-traumatic amnesia. *Journal of Neurology, Neurosurgery and Psychiatry 38*: 1127-32.

Mandleberg, I. A. (1976) Cognitive recovery after severe head injury: 3. WAIS Verbal and Performance IQs as a function of post-traumatic amnesia duration and time from injury. *Journal of Neurology, Neurosurgery and Psychiatry 39*: 1001-7.

Mandleberg, I. A. and Brooks, D. N. (1975) Cognitive recovery after severe head injury: 1. Serial testing on the Wechsler Adult Intelligence Scale. *Journal of Neurology, Neurosurgery and Psychiatry 38*: 1121-6.

Mayes, A. R., Meudell, P. R. and Neary, D. (1978) Must amnesia be caused by either encoding or retrieval disorders? In M. M. Gruneberg, P. E. Morris and R. N. Sykes (eds) *Practical Aspects of Memory*. London: Academic Press.

Meudell, P. R., Mayes, A. R. and Neary, D. (1979) Is amnesia caused by a consolidation impairment? In D. J. Oborne, M. M. Gruneberg and J. R. Eiser (eds) *Research in Psychology and Medicine*. Vol. 1. London: Academic Press.

Miller, E. (1975) Impaired recall and the memory disturbance in presenile dementia. *British Journal of Social and Clinical Psychology 14*: 73-9.

Miller, E. and Lewis, P. (1977) Recognition memory in elderly patients with depression and dementia: a signal detection analysis. *Journal of Abnormal Psychology 86*: 84-6.

Milner, B. (1966) Amnesia following operation on the temporal lobes. In C. W. M. Whitty and O. L. Zangwill (eds) *Amnesia*. London: Butterworth.

Morris, P. E. (1977) Practical strategies for human learning and remembering. In M. J. A. Howe (ed.) *Adult Learning: Psychological Research and Applications*. London: Wiley.

Perlmutter, M., Metzger, R., Nezworski, T. and Miller, K. (1981) Spatial and temporal memory in 20- and 60-year-olds. *Journal of Gerontology 36*: 59-65.

Pezdek, K. (1980) Life-span differences in semantic integration of pictures and sentences in memory. *Child Development 51*: 720-9.

Poon, L. W., Walsh-Sweeney, L. and Fozard, J. L. (1980) Memory skill training for the elderly: salient issues on the use of imagery mnemonics. In L. W. Poon, J. L. Fozard, L. S. Cermak, D. Arenberg and

L. W. Thompson (eds) *New Directions in Memory and Aging.* Hillsdale, NJ: Lawrence Erlbaum Associates.

Puglisi, J. T. (1980) Semantic encoding in older adults as evidenced by release from proactive inhibition. *Journal of Gerontology* 35: 743-5.

Rankin, J. L. and Kausler, D. H. (1979) Adult age differences in false recognitions. *Journal of Gerontology* 34: 58-65.

Richardson, J. T. E. (1978a) Memory and intelligence following spontaneously arrested congenital hydrocephalus. *British Journal of Social and Clinical Psychology* 17: 261-7.

Richardson, J. T. E. (1978b) Reported mediators and individual differences in mental imagery. *Memory and Cognition* 6: 376-8.

Richardson, J. T. E. (1979a) Mental imagery, human memory, and the effects of closed head injury. *British Journal of Social and Clinical Psychology* 18: 319-27.

Richardson, J. T. E. (1979b) Signal detection theory and the effects of severe head injury upon recognition memory. *Cortex* 15: 145-8.

Richardson, J. T. E. (1980) *Mental Imagery and Human Memory.* London: Macmillan.

Riege, W. H. and Inman, V. (1981) Age differences in non-verbal memory tasks. *Journal of Gerontology* 36: 51-8.

Rowe, E. J. and Schnore, M. M. (1971) Item concreteness and reported strategies in paired-associate learning as a function of age. *Journal of Gerontology* 26: 470-5.

Schaie, K. W. and Strother, C. R. (1968) A cross-sequential study of age changes in cognitive behavior. *Psychological Bulletin* 70: 671-80.

Schear, J. M. and Nebes, R. D. (1980) Memory for verbal and spatial information as a function of age. *Experimental Aging Research* 6: 271-81.

Shallice, T. and Warrington, E. K. (1970) Independent functioning of verbal memory stores: a neuropsychological study. *Quarterly Journal of Experimental Psychology* 22: 261-73.

Taub, H. A. (1967) Paired-associate learning as a function of age, rate of presentation and instructions. *Journal of Genetic Psychology* 107: 43-8.

Teuber, H. L. (1955) Physiological psychology. *Annual Review of Psychology* 6: 267-96.

Tulving, E. (1968) Theoretical issues in free recall. In T. R. Dixon and D. L. Horton (eds) *Verbal Behavior and General Behavior Theory.* Englewood Cliffs, NJ: Prentice-Hall.

Tulving, E. (1972) Episodic and semantic memory. In E. Tulving and W. Donaldson (eds) *Organization of Memory.* New York: Academic Press.

Tulving, E. (1974) Recall and recognition of semantically encoded words. *Journal of Experimental Psychology* 102: 778-87.

Tulving, E. and Thomson, D. M. (1973) Encoding specificity and retrieval processes in episodic memory. *Psychological Review* 80: 352-73.

Warrington, E. K., Logue, V. and Pratt, R. T. C. (1971) The anatomical localization of selective impairment of auditory verbal short-term memory. *Neuropsychologia* 9: 377-87.

Warrington, E. K. and Weiskrantz, L. (1968) A study of learning and retention in amnesic patients. *Neuropsychologia 6*: 283–91.

Warrington, E. K. and Weiskrantz, L. (1970) Amnesic syndrome: consolidation or retrieval? *Nature 228*: 628–30.

Warrington, E. K. and Weiskrantz, L. (1971) Organizational aspects of memory in amnesic patients. *Neuropsychologia 9*: 67–73.

Warrington, E. K. and Weiskrantz, L. (1973) An analysis of short-term and long-term memory defects in man. In J. A. Deutsch (ed.) *The Physiological Basis of Memory*. New York: Academic Press.

Warrington, E. K. and Weiskrantz, L. (1974) The effect of prior learning on subsequent retention in amnesic patients. *Neuropsychologia 12*: 419–28.

Watkins, M. J. (1974) Concept and measurement of primary memory. *Psychological Bulletin 81*: 695–711.

Waugh, N. C. and Norman, D. A. (1965) Primary memory. *Psychological Review 72*: 89–104.

Weiskrantz, L. and Warrington, E. K. (1975) The problem of the amnesic syndrome in man and animals. In R. Isaacson and K. Pribram (eds) *The Hippocampus*. Vol. 2. New York: Plenum Press.

Whitehead, A. (1973) Verbal learning and memory in elderly depressives. *British Journal of Psychiatry 123*: 203–8.

Whitehead, A. (1975) Recognition memory in dementia. *British Journal of Social and Clinical Psychology 14*: 191–4.

Wickelgren, W. A. (1968) Sparing of short-term memory in an amnesic patient: implications for strength theory of memory. *Neuropsychologia 6*: 235–44.

Winograd, E. and Simon, E. W. (1980) Visual memory and imagery in the aged. In L. W. Poon, J. L. Fozard, L. S. Cermak, D. Arenberg and L. W. Thompson (eds) *New Directions in Memory and Aging*. Hillsdale, NJ: Lawrence Erlbaum Associates.

Wood, R. L. (1979) The relationship of brain damage, measured by computerised axial tomography, to quantitative intellectual impairment. In D. J. Oborne, M. M. Gruneberg and J. R. Eiser (eds) *Research in Psychology and Medicine*. Vol. 1. London: Academic Press.

Woods, R. T. and Piercy, M. (1974) A similarity between amnesic memory and normal forgetting. *Neuropsychologia 12*: 437–45.

4 Disorders of visual perception

Jules Davidoff

Introduction

The study of disorders of visual perception had different origins from the study of visual perception in the laboratories of experimental psychology. Early research into perceptual disorders was medical, and there were never the systematic attempts to relate input to output as there were in classical psychophysics. However, nineteenth-century neurologists observed faults in perception which did seem to have a certain consistency with respect to site of injury. This led to the building of models of brain function and wiring diagrams not, in essence, dissimilar to our recent models of information processing. In the early twentieth century progress, at least from a medical viewpoint, was accelerated as a consequence of the accidents of war. Previously, the patients were tumour or stroke victims who had often suffered damage to large areas of the brain; these patients were not only hard to test but were likely to have damage to mechanisms subserving substantial amounts of information processing. War victims, however, often had more localized and clearly defined injuries.

During the early part of this century the perceptual disorders considered tended to be simple ones, e.g. reaching behaviour. It may well have been due to the influence of the behaviourist doctrines then current that most cognitive disorders were largely ignored. In fact, not until the victims of the 1939-45 war were looked at by neuropsychologists was a return made to investigating cognitive disorders of visual perception. Then, from individual cases and also from reasonably large samples, selective deficits in what we would now call information processing were found. In what must at best be an incomplete attempt, this chapter will try to describe disorders found from neuropsychological examination and link them to our present way of thinking about visual perception.

Disorders of reception

Visual perception may be considered cognitive in nature because the visual system operates on and controls the input. Perception is not a passive record of the output of the system's physiology, i.e. the data base, at the visual cortex. Nevertheless, the control processes by which the input is fitted to our perceptual aims are, nevertheless, useless without an adequate data base. Disruption of this data base may be considered to be a disorder of reception. Disease of the eye, connections from the eye to the visual cortex and damage to the early stages of visual processing in the cortex itself will all affect reception. This will lead to disturbances of stimulus detection, colour, line and depth perception, or what one might call early stages of information processing. To a limited extent, if control processes organizing the input are disordered, later processing stages may also have some effect on reception.

The simplest perceptual disorder in terms of information processing is one which alters our ability to detect stimulation. From a theoretical viewpoint, this can occur for quite trivial reasons. Cutting the fibres which transmit visual information received at the eye will result in a total loss of vision from that area of the visual field which the fibres serve. The blind spots (scotomata) so formed can be very well defined if the fibres are cut, or disease causes destruction of the entire visual cortex of one hemisphere. The whole right visual field (i.e. that part of the visual world which lies to the right of your midline in the vertical plane) will disappear if the left hemisphere striate cortex, or connections to it, are totally severed. In disease the scotomata may not be absolute or dense, and the patient may be able to detect a bright or large spot of light when a small one is invisible.

Indeed, precise testing of the area around a known scotoma will often show that there are raised thresholds for light detection. Raised sensory thresholds can accompany damage to many parts of the cortex so are not necessarily diagnostic of the locus of the lesion. In fact, a general neurological disorder such as multiple sclerosis may affect simple visual thresholds for flicker and contrast. Psychiatric groups, too, exhibit changed sensory thresholds, but here one must be aware of response biases and unwillingness to respond which could artificially raise thresholds.

One interesting aspect of visual perception and its organization shown by investigation of scotomata, is that these blind spots are seldom noticed. The eyes, being constantly in motion, sweep over the object allowing each part of the object to be represented at the intact cortex. Furthermore, gestalt organizational forces (e.g. closure) complete the input so that, even without eye movements, the missing part of the field is still unnoticed. However, patients with cerebral lesions can be made to detect their scotomata. Hécaen and Albert (1978) report an observation of MacKay who showed patients a display of lines radiating from a central point. Due to perceptual closure their individual scotomatous region in the display were not noticed. On top of the lines was then placed a random collection of small dots. In the intact visual field the dots appear to be arranged at right angles to the lines but this was not the case for the scotomatous region where the patient sees random dots perceptually 'closed' where the lines are only.

Visual information arrives at the visual cortex into a system which is designed for orientation detection, and while it is still not clear how the system extracts lines from the input (Frisby, 1980), it is not hard to imagine that this constitutes a mechanism for feature detection. These orientation-specific cells in the visual cortex are open to alteration from experience. Blakemore and Cooper (1970) found that kittens raised from birth in vertically striped surroundings did not have neurones which were responsive to horizontal lines. Exposure to input lacking a specific orientation can occur naturally in humans with astigmatic eyes, and this refractive error causes blurring along one meridian on the retina, which, if not optically corrected in early life, can cause patients to suffer permanent reduction of acuity along that meridian (Mitchell et al., 1973).

Depth perception seems to be mediated fairly early in the visual system. In the first area of visual cortex that receives input from the retina (called V1), the hypercolumns of the striate cortex (Hubel and Wiesel, 1968) are in pairs of monocular dominance columns. At least by the next stage of processing (V2) there is, in the monkey, the facility for binocular fusion which has been verified by ablation techniques (Cowey, 1979). V2 is known to exist in man, but we do not know whether it has a corresponding function (Cowey and Rolls, 1974). In man the different estimates for the anatomical locus of stereoscopic depth disorder seem to depend upon the different methods which have been used to assess stereopsis (Danta *et al.*, 1978). The formation of a stereoscopic shape from monocularly presented random dot patterns (Julesz figures) may be tapping impaired perceptual closure and shape perception as well as depth perception, which might explain why damage to the right hemisphere (Carmon and Bechtoldt, 1969) is more frequently involved. The responsible lesion is without doubt in the posterior part of the brain though its precise location seems to vary. Lesions of variable sites are also responsible for other distortions of the visual world. Distortions can occur of size and slope (stretching or flattening) and may be limited to only part of the visual field; these defects take many forms (Hécaen and Albert, 1978) including illusions of movement.

Complete colour-vision loss (achromatopsia) through an acquired cortical disorder is rare, but disturbances of colour vision (dyschromatopsia) without total loss are more common. Achromatopsia has been known to occur in patients who have normal visual acuity and in whom colour information is processed normally at the retinal level and probably reaches the cortex intact (Mollon *et al.*, 1980). The rarity of the disorder is probably due to the infrequent occurrence of lesions which are sufficiently selective to damage the relevant cortical area without causing cortical blindness or other perceptual disorders as a result of damage to neighbouring regions. Lesions to cause the problem would appear to have to be bilateral to the inferior occipital lobes (Meadows, 1974), and such lesions would be likely to damage life-support mechanisms, which would again account for the rarity of the phenomenon.

Perceptual disorders of colour vision are investigated clinically by tests normally given to isolate the genetic disorder commonly known as colour blindness. The Ishihara test of colour blindness asks the subject to name numbers formed from coloured dots displayed in an ensemble of dots of other equally bright colours. Chromatic vision is necessary to allocate the coloured dots to groups and thence form a shape. The test contains plates which can be used with illiterate subjects or with patients who, because of their aphasia, have lost the ability to name. Acquired cortical loss can in some cases be distinguished from the genetic loss if the test performance differs between the eyes since this would not arise from a genetic complaint. An alternative test procedure for determining colour loss asks the patient to sort a random arrangement of twenty different blue and green discs into a line progressing from most blue to most green. This Farnsworth-Munsell Hundred Hue Test also uses three other colour ranges, and is a rather exacting task which is failed by patients with damage to a variety of sites in the cortex. Scotti and Spinnler (1970) repeated the earlier finding of De Renzi and Spinnler (1967) who showed most deficit for patients with damage to the posterior part of the right hemisphere. Capitani *et al.* (1978), however, also found patients with right frontal lesions to be severely impaired. The Farnsworth-Munsell test requires attentional, spatial and sorting as well as perceptual abilities. Disorders of sorting and decision making are well known to occur from frontal lesions (Milner, 1963; Luria *et al.*, 1963) and could easily account for the poor performance shown by these patients on this particular test.

Zeki (1980) has discovered what could be called a colour centre in the monkey visual area V4. Particular cells have the property of responding only to a very small range of colour even if the hue of the input changes, so this cortical area could be seen as a colour-constancy centre. Such a centre makes it at least possible to consider the loss of notion of colour without the loss of earlier stages for colour reception. This type of impairment has been called colour agnosia, and it is to that we turn next.

Colour agnosia

Colour-vision disorders are of interest to psychological theory because the processing of colour information can be determined not only by the incoming stimulation, but also by our knowledge about colours. We can, for example, mistake the colour of an object because we know the usual colour of that object. Our stored colour memory then dominates the mechanism for colour constancy which would normally allow us to perceive hue independently of the hue of the light incident upon the object. Colour as a sensation consists of a hue of a particular brightness and saturation, but the sensation is also categorized and named, and error can also occur at these later semantic stages.

The difference between a perceptual (pictorial) and a categorical judgement can be seen from experiments with normal subjects. Egeth *et al.* (1969) investigated this difference by observing the effect of irrelevant colour-name interference. It was found that subjects could judge the colour of printed words and completely ignore the fact that the words were of colour names that conflicted with the colours that were being matched. However, when judgements were requested that concerned the names of the colours in which the words were printed, then the name of the word did interfere. Such interference, first investigated by Stroop (1935), is due to reading speed being faster than naming speed. This primes the semantic colour code erroneously for the judgement of the colour of the print of the word, and thus causes interference. Judgements made only at the pictorial level in the Egeth *et al.* experiment were not amenable to this Stroop interference.

The pictorial code can be affected by what is currently active in the storage system. Rosch (1975) found that the judgement of whether two colour patches were identical could be speeded up by being given in advance (priming) the name of the colour. This applied only to hues that were typical for that colour name, and priming hindered judgements for peripheral variations of the colour. This shows that colours are stored categorically and that when, say, the word 'red' is spoken, it does not activate all examples of red, but only what were called focal examples. If the judgement was changed so that the subject had to say whether the colours were from the same colour category or not, then the combination of the effect of priming and typicality altered. Priming now helped all colours within the named category. It would seem that both our memory for colour names (lexical memory) and memory for hues (pictorial memory) are connected, but in different ways, to our categorical or semantic memory. Disturbance to colour perception can be looked for at all of these stages in information processing.

Patients who can perform colour perceptual tests and yet are still unable to name the colours, must have damage after the pictorial representation stage of visual processing. There are two main theoretical approaches taken to describe this inability to name colours. One is to consider that it is essentially a language disorder in which colour names have been particularly affected; the other is to consider that a much more central disturbance, presumably connected to semantic coding, has caused the colour disorder. The semantic disorder implies that patients no longer understand the meaning of colours and what colours objects should be – this has been called colour agnosia. The dissociation of an object from its colour can be seen in patients who are unable to appropriately colour, with crayons, objects they can name (De Renzi *et al.*, 1972). In the main it is aphasic patients who show this inability to colour-in drawings. Some dysphasic patients have even been noted to have more difficulty in naming coloured objects than non-coloured ones (Wyke and Holgate, 1973). It would be simple to regard this aspect of colour agnosia as related to a language disorder. Incorrect colour naming can be very unhelpful in colour tasks as the patients may act upon their incorrect labels. However, this explanation seems not entirely satisfactory when one is confronted with a patient who has coloured-in a baby, say, green, and does not immediately recognize from an intact perceptual store that he is wrong.

An anatomical explanation of an inability to name colours comes from Geschwind and Fusillo (1966), who argue that the disability arises from a disconnection of the visual input to the left-hemisphere language area. The disconnection hypothesis was put forward by Geschwind (1965) to explain alexia without agraphia (inability to read without inability to write) and extended to colour agnosia. The patient of Geschwind and Fusillo could not name colours, but could name objects, and this raised a problem for the disconnection hypothesis. Geschwind resolved this apparent paradox by pointing out that objects gave rise to associations of a somaesthetic nature. The intact right-hemisphere visual system cannot pass its message across the damaged visual pathways in the *corpus callosum* to the left hemisphere, but it can do so via the intact pathways of another modality. Even if the disconnection explanation is accepted, it cannot provide a complete explanation for all colour agnosias. The patient of Geschwind and Fusillo could indeed answer perfectly questions which relied only upon verbal input. For example: What colour is a telephone box? But there are patients who have difficulty with this sort of question, and assuming that they understand what a telephone box is, then there must be a need for an explanation apart from a disconnection.

An alternative explanation to colour agnosia considers the

disorder to be an aphasic problem with the aphasia restricted to colour names. Inability to do tasks which would seem to require only perceptual analysis arises, according to Kinsbourne and Warrington (1964), because even when colour names are not demanded, they may still out of habit be used. Some sort of aphasic disturbance would seem to be necessary to explain those cases where patients cannot name from memory the colour of a lemon or telephone box. Beauvois (1981) has, however, pointed out that the distinction between verbal and visual components of a task is not clear-cut. In order to produce the colour of a telephone box in its absence it may be necessary to create a coloured image of the object. In this case a disorder involving a connection between the visual imagery and language could be the cause of the colour disorder, even though the task is apparently entirely verbal.

Object agnosia

Object agnosia is a complaint in which an understanding of the function of an object is lost without there being any identifiable responsible loss at reception. The diagnosis of a visual agnosia for objects, nevertheless, includes a large proportion of diagnosis by exclusion. One must, for example, distinguish visual agnosia from a verbal loss, and the patient must be able to identify the object from a verbal description. There are other disorders in which the purely visual aspects of the stimulus are important, and it must also be distinguished from them. Patients suffering from lesions to the limbic system may react as if visually agnosic, trying to mouth inedible objects in their apathetic state, but in fact they can name the object. Their loss of meaning is not related to the visual aspect *per se*. One also does not want to include under the heading of visual agnosia disorders of attention or faulty visual scanning which could clearly cause an inability to recognize an object and may even not allow the object to be copied. One such disorder of visual scanning has been called simultagnosia or Balint's syndrome. In this condition the part of the visual field which can be analysed is very small, and the failure to recognize an object is due to an inability to combine the elements of an object. Visual agnosia is also different from memory loss in that visual agnosics will have little difficulty in recall provided that they see an object in the same way as they saw it before. Meaning is lost in some sense in many disorders, such as those which cause an inability to name or use an object, but the dispute concerning visual agnosia is whether meaning can be lost selectively through the visual modality.

The inability to deal with colours can be clinically separated from disorders of object recognition; each ability in principle being retained in the absence of the other. However, many of the explanations put forward to account for colour agnosia have also been proposed for object agnosia. Just as for colour agnosia, object agnosia could result from an anatomical disconnection between the visual representation and its name. This would result from a large posterior left-hemisphere lesion which disconnects the left-hemsiphere visual system (usually by destruction) from the language centre in the left hemisphere. The lesion would also have to disconnect the language centre from the intact right-hemisphere visual apparatus by damaging the interhemisphere pathway (*corpus callosum*). A difficulty for this explanation is that not all visual – verbal connections are lost. The inability to read while being able to write, and colour agnosia, may often accompany object agnosia but need not always do so. Geschwind has proposed that objects can, by their tactile association, reach an intact naming centre via the connections from the tactile association area which cross at a different point along the callosum. The co-existence of both visual and tactile agnosia (Taylor and Warrington, 1971), however, puts the disconnection theory under some great strain. The disconnection argument could, however, be maintained if different fibres in the splenium (which transmit visual information between the hemispheres) carry different sorts of information and there were to be relative sparing of some of them.

Disconnection certainly can cause visual agnosia in the visual half-field as shown by the patient of Albert *et al.* (1975) who recognized objects much better if they were presented in the right visual field. The disconnection hypothesis would, however, seem to be disproved by the split-brain work. In these patients, the right hemisphere seems to understand what the object is even though it cannot be named. Therefore, the meaning of an object is conveyed without left-hemisphere participation. Unfortunately, the split-brain patients can never by themselves disprove any hypothesis concerning brain function, as one could always argue that the brain organization in these cases is abnormal because of the years of uncontrolled epilepsy.

An attempt to give a more psychological account of visual agnosia stems from Lissauer, who, in the late nineteenth century, divided visual agnosia into two forms: apperceptive and associative. In order to be judged apperceptively agnosic it was necessary to prove that one could see well, e.g. one had to content the examiner that visual acuity as measured by the familiar optician's chart was good, that one had not lost peripheral vision and that one could copy what one saw even though one did not know what the object was. Reports of apperceptive agnosia are rare. Benson and Greenberg (1969) report a case where even simple forms such as a cross or a circle could not be distinguished even though colour discrimination was good, and Levine (1982) an inveterate card player who, after brain damage, could not tell a diamond from a club. The limited discrimination which is possible for the apperceptive agnosic is easily disrupted by an irrelevant line drawn over the figure.

There are several aspects of apperceptive agnosia which are of interest to formulation of models of visual object recognition. If the syndrome is convincing, it implies the need for a stage of processing, after reception, at which impairment can occur. It is clearly at an early stage, but is it, for example, prior to the organization of a three-dimensional version of the two dimensional input? Ratcliff and Newcombe (1982), drawing on the work of Marr (1980), suggest that their visual agnosic patient could be described as apperceptive in that what he could not do was mentally construct a three-dimensional model. This meant that he could not distinguish one object from a rotated version of itself, although a certain amount of visual information must have been processed since some cross-modal matching to the tactile modality was possible. In terms of information processing an apperceptive agnosic had been seen as deficient at different stages by different authors, although all would agree that it must be prior to semantic processing.

A semantic disturbance (corresponding to Lissauer's associative agnosia) as a cause of visual agnosia has been just as controversial as apperceptive agnosia. Whether perception can be intact and have no meaning is a question which has aroused considerable and continuing interest. In the late nineteenth-century Munk, describing the behaviour of dogs after bilateral occipital lesions, noted what he referred to as a psychic blindness. The animals appeared to see in that they walked about without colliding into obstacles. However, they did not seem to recognize visually either their food or master, and did not recoil from fire. These experiments were repeated with monkeys with similar results, the monkeys orienting their bodies and limbs correctly to the object, but investigating it by use of their other sense modalities. The extension of this work to man was due to Lissauer and Freud, and it is to the latter that we owe the term agnosia.

There has been considerable dispute concerning the extent of the perceptual loss in visual agnosia of a semantic nature. Bender and Feldman (1972) following Bay in the 1950s are surely correct in affirming that in cases of visual agnosia there is always some sensory loss, but sensory loss does not always and, in fact, rarely does mean that the patient has visual agnosia. The addition of a general dementia on top of the sensory loss which Bay proposed would hardly explain a loss specific to the visual modality. One could no doubt define perception in such a way that associative visual agnosia came under the heading of a perceptual loss, but this disregards differences in terms of information processing. Differentiation of impairments because they are based more on memorial processes would also seem valid from research carried out with monkeys. More anterior lesions of the infra-temporal lobe cause associative losses compared to posterior lesions in that region for which the loss is more of a discriminative nature.

Other recent accounts of the rare cases of visual agnosia in terms of information processing consider the difference between a semantic and non-semantic pictorial representation of an object. This distinction seems reliably established from work with normals in laboratory experiments. Matches which rely only on physical identity are not influenced by the typicality of the subjects for class membership, i.e. the latency for matching chairs is identical for that of ottomans. Similarly, the frequency of occurrence of the name of the object is not important, which it is for object naming. Priming with superordinate names (unlike priming with object names) does not help matches of physical identity, presumably because the attributes evoked by the superordinate name are not specific enough, whereas those evoked by the object name itself are. The frequency of the name does help if the match is of two views of the same object (Bartram, 1976), though there have been reports in dissension with this finding (Klatzky and Stoy, 1974). Seymour (1979) concludes, however, that the non-semantic representation does include the three-dimensional representation. The clinical evidence of apperceptive agnosia supports this view. Indeed, the patient of Ratcliff and Newcombe (see p.87) shows the inability to achieve this stage of processing within the non-semantic representation.

The existence of a semantic representation of a visual stimulus (Tversky, 1969; Posner *et al.*, 1969) can be seen as the origin from cognitive psychology of the view held by Warrington (1975) of the disruption of the semantic system in visual agnosia. Rosch *et al.* (1976) showed that different levels of classification were possible within the semantic system. Extending this to clinical work, Warrington showed that patients could have the retention of knowledge of superordinate categories, e.g. animal, without the knowledge of the subordinate example, e.g. poodle. Disruption of the semantic system was further suggested by the inability to retrieve the picture of an object from its description.

Warrington found that the semantic system for visual meaning operated in a similar way to that for verbal meaning, but patients were disrupted in one system and not the other. She therefore proposed that there were two semantic systems: one visual and one verbal. This distinction is based on the work of Paivio (1975), who argued the case for two forms of information storage. He showed the need for a visual code from experiments in which subjects were asked to decide which of two animals was bigger. This was performed more quickly from pictures than names, and was found to relate to the animals' real size. This result must, however, be tempered by the finding that non-verbal judgements, for example of intelligence, are also performed more quickly from visual stimuli (Banks and Flora, 1977). Visual stimuli would seem to access both lexical and pictorial memory better, and indeed, Pylyshyn (1973) argues the case for there being only one sort of semantic storage. If one central semantic store does exist, Warrington's view would have to be modified to be one of damage to access to that store from some preliminary material specific processing rather than damage to the central store itself.

One further aspect of visual agnosia which needs to be considered is damage that may result in the loss of appreciation of a specific class of visual stimuli. Of such classes the most documented (though still rare) is a loss of face meaning, called prosopagnosia. The loss of ability to recognize face stimuli could arise from disruption from many stages of information processing. As in other agnosic cases one must always be certain that general amnesic and aphasic problems are ruled out. The distinction between loss of recognition for famous and for unknown people (Warrington and James, 1967) strongly suggests that face recognition is multi-determined. Both naming and perceptual organization will differentiate these two types of face. The internal features (e.g. eyes, mouth) of a face are particularly important when dealing with unknown faces, and prosopagnosics may have difficulty putting these features together. It could also be the transformation of one view of a face into another for which the patient has difficulty. Impairment will then be demonstrated when rotating a face to recognize a person's profile from a full view.

In line with Paivio's view of dual coding Ratcliff and Newcombe (1982) have suggested that the semantic store may contain specific information about physical attributes of objects. One could then imagine that those physical attributes pertinent to face recognition are gathered together in one place and this has been suggested to be in the right hemisphere. A special face centre has also been argued by Yin (1970) from patients' ability to deal with inversion of faces. Upright faces were not dealt with normally by right-hemisphere patients, whereas inverted faces were recognized at the same level as controls. However, inability to recognize objects when inverted and the surprise at the identity of the object when placed the correct way up is not specific to faces. Many objects are orientation specific for identification. An agnosia for faces is not the only specific category recorded, and experts in many areas have suffered, after brain damage, a loss of identification ability for their specialization. It is quite possible that rather than having an evolutionarily specified face centre, we have all become experts at face discrimination.

Disorders of spatial perception

Defects in spatial manipulation can occur for the whole visual field. For example, our mental map of the outside world may be disturbed, and this topographical loss is exemplified by the inability to indicate the location of cities on an outline map of one's own country or to trace a route round a map of streets near where one lives. Not only are patients impaired for topographical concepts which have been learned in the past, but also for new learning of visually guided mazes (Milner, 1965).

The analysis of the psychological components of topographical skills may be helped by findings showing groups of patients with differently localized injury who can do one task but not another. Ratcliff and Newcombe (1973) showed by this means that learning a maze pathway by visual cues is a different task from learning a route with a visual plan in front of you. Defective route following was only present with bilateral lesions, whereas right-hemisphere lesions were sufficient to impair learning the visual maze. Psychological function is most clearly differentiated in cases of double dissociation. When this occurs the two groups show reciprocal impairments, being good at one task and poor at the other. Newcombe and Russell (1969) showed a double dissociation for the tasks of perceptual closure and visual-maze learning. Right-parietal patients were impaired on the maze, but not closure, and vice versa for more posterior right-hemisphere damage. Whiteley and Warrington (1977) discovered a similar dissociation for the recognition of an incomplete version of a letter and the recognition of an object which has been rotated to present an unusual view.

In terms of clinical symptoms a topographical disorder can be dissociated from visual agnosia. Prosopagnosia does often seem to be accompanied by a visual spatial disorder of this sort, but this may be a result of the geographical proximity of the two sites in the brain. In any case, the reverse of a topographical disorder being associated with prosopagnosia does not seem to true. The clinical disorders which seem to accompany topographical disorder are the neglect of one side of space (see below) and a constructional apraxia, i.e. our inability to construct an object from a plan.

The severe memory impairment found with hippocampal lesions suggests that spatial organizational components *per se* can be differentiated from memory aspects. However, visual spatial disorders can be divided into those which rely on short-term memory and those which rely on long-term memory. De Renzi *et al.* (1977b) found that patients who had a topographical disorder nevertheless had a normal spatial span; thereby implying that their short-term memory system was intact. It would seem that it is long-term spatial memory for which right-hemisphere, rather than left-hemisphere damage is important (De Renzi *et al.* 1977a).

One point that should be considered with regard to localization studies is that they may be more concerned with verbal versus non-verbal processing. Many of these complicated spatial tasks can be tackled by verbal recoding, so that different strategies used by the patients during their lifetimes may mean impairment on the same task from different loci after brain damage. Topographical tasks, for example, may be performed in two ways, as Paterson and Zangwill (1944) found: their patient learned the route home after a right-hemisphere lesion by referring to tram numbers and street signs without any spatial appreciation of where he was going.

Disorders of attention

Models of information processing such as that of Seymour (1979) though complicated in terms of number of processes involved, do not emphasize 'top-down' processing. Top-down or 'concept driven' processing refers to the effect of existing structure for the organization of information from the incoming stimulation. Most models of word or object recognition, for example, do not consider the mechanisms whereby the stimuli are paid attention to. Such processes, though in many ways more simple than identification processes, are vital to perception.

The parietal lobes are also very much concerned with attention, and work with monkeys has shown that certain parietal cells fire if the visual stimuli in their respective field is to be a target for an eye movement. In humans neglect of stimuli in the contralateral half space is common result of a right-hemisphere parietal lobe lesion, and this asymmetry has led theorists to predict that the right hemisphere must have some special visual spatial function. It has been argued that the right hemisphere contains a representation of both visual fields, whereas the left hemisphere's corresponding site contains only a representation of the contralateral half of space.

Posner (1981) has shown that certain attentional deficits found in normals are accentuated after right parietal lobe damage. He found that normals detected stimuli much better if the stimulus arrived at a place where attention was directed. This was not necessarily the same place as one was looking, since attention could be directed to a point away from the direction of gaze. Poor performance at an unattended locus was exaggerated for patients with right parietal lobe lesions though such patients could detect a stimulus if directed towards it. However, they exhibited a complete inability to notice a stimulus in the left visual field if attention was directed to the right visual field. This phenomenon of extinction exhibited by these patients, therefore, requires an explanation based upon a limited capacity for attention.

Damage to the posterior parietal cortex disrupts the accuracy of visually guided reaching. Unilateral lesions cause misreaching predominantly in the contralateral half field, whereas bilateral lesions cause a generalized spatial disorientation (Holmes, 1918). These functions of noticing, reacting to and keeping stimuli in attention are also controlled by frontal-lobe function. Part of what could be regarded as a visual control system also involves that part of the frontal lobe called the frontal eye fields (Luria, 1973).

Disorders of planning

Neuropsychological research has recently paid some attention to the consideration of the control of information processing when solving visual problems. Luria (1973) showed that routine tasks are not affected by frontal-lobe lesions which impair the planning required to solve new problems. The difference between controlled and automatic human information processing has now been shown experimentally (Schneider and Shiffrin, 1977: Shiffrin and Schneider, 1977). Making use of this research and concepts from artificial intelligence, Shallice (1981) has tackled this somewhat neglected aspect of disorders of visual perception, and found that left frontal patients are impaired on a visual task requiring planning. This asymmetric impairment from frontal-lobe damage might suggest that the problem was solved through verbal mediation but Shallice denies this. Nor was the task related to constructional ability, rather it was suggested that some control process was lost by these patients. In complex problems there comes a point where one has to stop analysing the problem and decide the best course of action. It was this supervisory role that was lost in the patients with left frontal lesions.

Models of information processing tell us very little about the creative aspects of spatial performance. Though the clinical work provides only a limited account of the production of new material, the research is by no means uninteresting. In a study of frontal lobe patients it was found by Jones-Gotman and Milner (1977) that the fluency with which new visual patterns could be created was severely impaired by lesions to the right frontal lobe.

Conclusions

The major advances in our understanding of the visual system that have been made possible from physiological investigation should not deceive us that these have explained visual perception *in toto*. Visual perception requires not only a mechanism for reception and recoding, but means by which the visual world can be searched, the input selected and then interpreted. Not only do we need to have recognition devices, we need ways in which the storage system can interact with the input, and ways in which the input may be manipulated. Physiological advances, just like model building, tend to see the perceptual process as a one-way hierarchical system, and while many boxes (stages of processing) seem to be necessary for recognition to take place, little mention is made of any feedback loops (top-down processing) to earlier stages. Nevertheless, models of object recognition and pictorial memory should not be discarded as irrelevant to the study of their impairment. However incomplete they may be as a means of explaining these skills, they still represent an important first step towards an explanation of these disorders of visual perception.

Cognitive psychology does pay some account to the organizational or concept-driven aspects of perception. For example, Garner (1966) says 'to perceive is to know', but generally there tends to be more a lip service paid to the need for concept-driven processes and control processes, rather than an integration of them into theory. Such control processes would very likely be needed for even a simple task such as drawing a picture from memory. Indeed, for the perceptual demands of search, selection, drawing, map reading and topographical orientation, the existing information-processing models do not offer more than a bare description of the operations involved. However the processes which control the stages of information processing and direct our attention are now receiving consideration in neuropsychological research.

References

Albert, M. L., Reches, A. and Silverberg, R. (1975) Associative visual agnosia without alexia. *Neurology 25*: 322–6.
Banks, W. P. and Flora, J. (1977) Semantic and perceptual processes in symbolic comparisons. *Journal of Experimental Psychology: Human Perception and Performance 3*: 278–90.
Bartram, D. J. (1976) The effects of familiarity and practice on naming pictures of objects. *Memory and Cognition 4*: 593–602.
Beauvois, M-F. (1981) Optic aphasia: a process of interference

between vision and language. Talk given at the meeting on 'The Neuropsychology of Cognitive Function' at the Royal Society, London.

Bender, M. B. and Feldman, M. (1972) The so-called 'visual agnosias'. *Brain 95*: 173-86.

Benson, D. F. and Greenberg, J. (1969) Visual form agnosia. *Archives of Neurology 20*: 82-9.

Blakemore, C. and Cooper, G. F. (1970) Development of the brain depends on the visual environment. *Nature 228*: 477-8.

Capitani, E., Scotti, G. and Spinnler, H. (1978) Colour imperception in patients with focal excisions of the cerebral hemispheres. *Neuropsychologia 16*: 491-6.

Carmon, A. and Bechtoldt, H. P. (1969) Dominance of the right cerebral hemisphere for stereopsis. *Neuropsychologia 7*: 29-31.

Cowey, A. (1979) Cortical maps and visual perception. *Quarterly Journal of Experimental Psychology 31*: 1-17.

Cowey, A. and Rolls, E. T. (1974) Human cortical magnification factor and its relation to visual acuity. *Experimental Brain Research 21*: 447-54.

Danta, G., Hilton, R. C. and O'Boyle, D. J. (1978) Hemisphere function and binocular depth perception. *Brain 101*: 569-90.

De Renzi, E., Faglioni, P. and Previdi, P. (1977a) Spatial memory and hemispheric locus of lesion. *Cortex 13*: 429-33.

De Renzi, E., Faglioni, P., Scotti, G. and Spinnler, H. (1972) Impairment in associating colour to form concomitant with aphasia. *Brain 95*: 293-304.

De Renzi, E., Faglioni, P. and Villa, P. (1977b) Topographical amnesia. *Journal of Neurology, Neurosurgery and Psychiatry 40*: 498-505.

De Renzi, E. and Spinnler, H. (1967) Impaired performance on color tasks in patients with hemispheric damage. *Cortex 3*: 194-217.

Egeth, H. E., Blecker, D. and Kamlet, A. S. (1969) Verbal interference in a perceptual comparison task. *Perception and Psychophysics 6*: 355-6.

Frisby, J. P. (1980) *Seeing*. Oxford: Oxford University Press.

Garner, W. R. (1966) To perceive is to know. *American Psychologist 21*: 11-19.

Geschwind, N. (1965) Disconnexion syndromes in animals and man. *Brain 88*: 237-94 and 585-644.

Geschwind, N. and Fusillo, M. (1966) Color-naming defect in association with alexia. *Archives of Neurology 15*: 137-46.

Hécaen, H. and Albert, M. L. (1978) *Human Neuropsychology*. New York: Wiley.

Holmes, G. (1918) Disturbances of visual orientation. *British Journal of Ophthalmology 2*: 449-68 and 506-16.

Hubel, D. H. and Wiesel, T. N. (1968) Receptive fields and functional architecture of monkey striate cortex. *Journal of Physiology 195*: 215-43.

Jones-Gotman, M. and Milner, B. (1977) Design fluency: the invention of nonsense drawings after focal cortical lesions. *Neuropsychologia 15*: 653-74.

Kinsbourne, M. and Warrington, E. K. (1964) Observation on colour agnosia. *Journal of Neurology, Neurosurgery and Psychiatry* 27: 296–9.

Klatzky, R. L. and Stoy, A. M. (1974) Using visual codes for comparisons of pictures. *Memory and Cognition 2*: 727–36.

Levine, D. N. (1982) Visual agnosia in monkey and in man. In D. Ingle, M. Goodall and R. Mansfield (eds) *Advances in the Analysis of Visual Behavior*. Cambridge, Mass.: MIT Press.

Luria, A. R. (1973) *The Working Brain*. Harmondsworth: Penguin.

Luria, A. R., Pravdena-Vinarskaya, E. N. and Yarbus, A. L. (1963) Disorders of the ocular movements in a case of simultagnosia. *Brain 86*: 219–28.

Marr, D. (1980) Visual information processing: the structure and creation of visual representations. *Philosophical Transactions of the Royal Society of London, Series B, 290*: 199–218.

Meadows, J. C. (1974) Disturbed perception of colours associated with cerebral lesions. *Brain 97*: 615–32.

Milner, B. (1963) Effects of brain lesions on card sorting. *Archives of Neurology (Chicago) 9*: 90–100.

Milner, B. (1965) Visually guided maze learning in man: effects of bilateral hippocampal, bilateral frontal and unilateral cerebral lesions. *Neuropsychologia 3*: 316–38.

Mitchell, D. E., Freeman, R. D., Millodot, M. and Haegerstrom, G. (1973) Meridional amblyopia: evidence for modification of the human visual system by early experience. *Vision Research 13*: 535–58.

Mollon, J. D. Newcombe, F., Polden, P. G. and Ratcliff, G. (1980) On the presence of three-cone mechanisms in a case of total achromatopsia. In G. Verriest (ed.) *Colour Vision Deficiencies*. Bristol: V. Hilger.

Newcombe, F. and Russell, W. R. (1969) Dissociated visual, perceptual and spatial deficits in focal lesions of the right hemisphere. *Journal of Neurology, Neurosurgery and Psychiatry 32*: 73–81.

Paivio, A. (1975) Perceptual comparisons through the mind's eye. *Memory and Cognition 3*: 635–47.

Paterson, A. and Zangwill, O. L. (1944) Disorders of visual space perception associated with lesions of the right cerebral hemisphere. *Brain 67*: 331–58.

Posner, M. I. (1981) Components of spatial orienting. Talk given at the meeting on 'The Neuropsychology of Cognitive Function' at the Royal Society, London.

Posner, M. I., Boies, S. J., Eichelman, W. H. and Taylor, R. L. (1969) Retention of visual and name codes of single letters. *Journal of Experimental Psychology Monograph 79*: 1–16.

Pylyshyn, Z. W. (1973) What the mind's eye tells the mind's brain: a critique of mental imagery. *Psychological Bulletin 80*: 1–24.

Ratcliff, G. and Newcombe, F. (1973) Spatial orientation in man: effects of left, right and bilateral posterior cerebral lesions. *Journal of Neurology, Neurosurgery and Psychiatry 36*: 448–54.

Ratcliff, G. and Newcombe, F. (1982) Object recognition: some deductions from the clinical evidence. In A. Ellis (ed.) *Normality and Pathology in Cognitive Functions.* London: Academic Press.

Rosch, E. (1975) The nature of mental codes for color categories. *Journal of Experimental Psychology: Human Perception and Performance 1*: 303-22.

Rosch, E., Mervis, C. B., Gray, W. D., Johnson, D. M. and Boyes-Braem, P. (1976) Basic objects in natural categories. *Cognitive Psychology 8*: 382-439.

Schneider, W. and Shiffrin, R. M. (1977) Controlled and automatic human information processing: I. Detection, search and attention. *Psychological Review 84*: 1-66.

Scotti, G. and Spinnler, W. H. (1970) Colour imperception in unilateral hemisphere damaged patients. *Journal of Neurology, Neurosurgery and Psychiatry 33*: 22-8.

Seymour, P. H. K. (1979) *Human Visual Cognition.* London: Collier-Macmillan.

Shallice, T. (1981) Strategy selection and frontal-lobe functions. Talk given at the meeting on 'The Neuropsychology of Cognitive Function' at the Royal Society, London.

Shiffrin, R. M. and Schneider, W. (1977) Controlled and automatic human information processing: II. Perceptual learning, automatic attending and a general theory. *Psychological Review 84*: 127-90.

Stroop, J. R. (1935) Studies of interference in serial verbal reactions. *Journal of Experimental Psychology 18*: 643-62.

Taylor, A. and Warrington, E. K. (1971) Visual agnosia: a single case report. *Cortex 7*: 152-61.

Tversky, B. (1969) Pictorial and verbal encoding in a short-term memory task. *Perception and Psychophysics 6*: 225-33.

Warrington, E. K. (1975) The selective impairment of semantic memory. *Quarterly Journal of Experimental Psychology 27*: 635-58.

Warrington, E. K. and James, M. (1967) An experimental investigation of facial recognition in patients with unilateral cerebral lesions. *Cortex 3*: 317-26.

Whiteley, A. M. and Warrington, E. K. (1977) Prosopagnosia: a clinical, psychological and anatomical study of three patients. *Journal of Neurology, Neurosurgery and Psychiatry 40*: 395-403.

Wyke, M, and Holgate, D. (1973) Colour-naming defects in dysphasic patients: a qualitative analysis. *Neuropsychologia 11*: 451-61.

Yin, R. K. (1970) Face recognition by brain-injured patients: a dissociable ability? *Neuropsychologia 8*: 395-402.

Zeki, S. M. (1980) The representation of colours in the cerebral cortex. *Nature 284*: 417-18.

5 Language disorders

Ruth Lesser and Shuli Reich

Information-processing analyses have been used extensively in the study of language over the last few years (e.g. Levelt, 1978; Cooper and Walker, 1979; Butterworth, 1980), but their employment to any degree in the study of language disorders is a much rarer event, and has been largely restricted to the acquired organic disorders in adults of aphasia and alexia. These are, respectively, disorders of the multi-modal use of language (in speaking, listening, reading and writing) and disorders which are primarily of reading.

Information-processing analyses of language are concerned with the mental processes involved in the comprehension and production of language. These include the reception of the acoustic waveforms of speech, the analysis of speech sounds (phonology), the interpretation of messages (semantics), the ability to read words aloud or silently, and the spontaneous production of spoken utterances and written texts.

There are three basic theoretical problems which differentiate research in this field. First, there is a division of opinion as to whether these processes are better conceived of as occurring in a series or in parallel, and each viewpoint has its adherents. Cooper (1979), for example, expounds a serial model of information flow during speech perception which begins with filters for frequency, time and amplitude, and leads to detectors, integrators and recognition devices; he holds that 'the speech-perception system does not process information instantaneously, but in stages whose operations are distributed over some short time interval' (p.15) probably of less than 15 ms. In contrast, other current psycholinguistic notions of language functions (Goldman-Eisler, 1968) are that speech analysis is performed in part simultaneously and interactively at various levels. It draws, at the same time, on different language mechanisms such as the phonological analysis of speech sounds, the grammatical analysis of sentences and the semantic analysis of word meanings. The differences in time required to process language are explained not primarily in terms of temporal stages, but in terms of the cognitive load imposed by the task (for example, in using semantic rather than verbatim processing, or in speaking spontaneously rather than by repetition).

A second and associated distinction is between processing conceived of as directed in a 'bottom-up' or in a 'top-down' direction. Early models assumed that stages of processing began at the lowest stage of analysing the characteristics (acoustic, auditory and phonological), and then proceeded upwards to higher, meaning-related components of the information. More recently, models have acknowledged that this constitutes only one of several possible routes, and that at least one other strategy has been identified. This is top-down processing, whereby knowledge or expectations of the signal to be received or formulated precedes and influences the decisions about the lower-level sensory characteristics of the message.

In a third approach a distinction is made between studies of language processing which are 'off-line' and those which are 'on-line'. Off-line studies are primarily concerned with testing language as a composite of fixed systems independently of their immediate employment at a point in time. These systems consist of sets of knowledge sources of a wide variety, and include knowledge about the phonetic shape of speech sounds and their phonological structure in the speaker's language (for example that /b/ and /v/ are different phonemes in English though not in Spanish). They include knowledge about the syntactic and morphological structure of language (for example that there is a high probability that words ending in *ly* will function as adverbs). They include knowledge about the meanings of words in the lexicon or mental dictionary, and about speech act intentions, e.g. that an utterance such as 'Can you close the door?' in most contexts is intended to function as a request rather than a question. Whereas off-line studies are concerned with examining the nature of these sources of language knowledge as mental structures, on-line studies are concerned with their inter-activity and accessibility as a dynamic process. Typically, they have used fast reaction-time measures to examine the millisecond-by-millisecond mental processes occurring while a listener hears an utterance or reads a word (Marslen-Wilson, 1980). The study of language disorders, however, has made little use of these distinctions in experimental work and has relied primarily on models of serially organized stages using a bottom-up and off-line perspective.

Since the nineteenth century there have been two powerful traditions in the study of aphasia. From one several reductionist models have been derived in which components of language which could be isolated by brain damage have been identified, and locations critical to them have been mapped onto the brain. From the other a holistic approach has emphasized the integration of language with other facets of cognition. It argues that when a particular area of the brain becomes damaged it is not a specific ability such as speech which is impaired, but the integrative functioning of the brain as a whole. In the opinion of Hughlings Jackson, a major exponent of this view a century ago, the important distinctions were not between speech and non-speech activities in the brain, or between comprehension and production of speech, but between high and low (abstract and concrete) levels of cognitive activity. Thus, the processes involved in formulating and in understanding speech at different levels of abstraction did not need to be conceived of as using functionally and structurally distinct subsystems, as identified by localizationist thinking. The holist approach has much in common with the most recent psycholinguistic models of language as an interactive cognitive process, a topic which we shall discuss more fully at the end of this chapter. Since, however, a reductionist approach dominates current research into information processing in aphasia, we have used this as a framework for the substance of this chapter.

We begin with an account of a popular localizationist model, and shall then show how psycholinguistic models of language disorders, and in particular of reading disorders, have used linguistic notions in order to provide greater elaboration of subcomponents. In illustrating some of the issues which have arisen from this elaboration, we shall refer to disorders of phonological, semantic and syntactic processing in aphasic patients. In contrast to these off-line studies the penultimate section will consider some issues relevant to the on-line processing of information in aphasia.

Fractionation of language

As several recent accounts of aphasic disorders from an information theory perspective have pointed out (Moscovitch, 1979; Butterworth, 1980), much of the study of aphasia has been based on a simple stage model not dissimilar to that of Lichtheim and Wernicke a century ago. This model identified three discrete stages of language processing in which heard language activated word images in a centre in the left temporal lobe of the brain, whereby these images were transferred to a concept centre, from which the output passed to a motor articulation centre in the left frontal lobe. Although current versions of this model identify even further stages, these are characterized by distinctions of facets of behaviour (modalities) rather than of mental functions. The model holds that each of these behaviours such as listening, generating speech, etc. can be selectively impaired by damage to specific areas of the left cerebral hemisphere or by disconnection between adjacent areas. Since Geschwind's seminal paper propounding the disconnection theory (1965), the terminology derived from the Boston localizationist model, as defined by Goodglass and Kaplan (1972), has been widely used in research into aphasia. In particular, four main syndromes of aphasia are identified (Broca's aphasia, Wernicke's aphasia, conduction aphasia and anomia) with two subsidiary rarer ones (transcortical motor aphasia and transcortical sensory aphasia). In Broca's aphasia the predominant feature is non-fluent speech with inconsistent and effortful articulation, and short phrasing with restricted grammar superficially resembling the language of tele-grams. Broca's aphasia is attributed to damage to the frontal lobe portion of the central zone of the left hemisphere in which the language functions are considered to be located. Disturbances of auditory verbal comprehension are said to be consequent upon damage to the temporal lobe portion of this zone, resulting in Wernicke's aphasia. This syndrome is characterized by speech which is fluent and well-articulated, but which includes varying amounts of unintelligible words or 'jargon' or inconsequential responses and associations. Damage to the parietal lobe portion disturbs the ability to name objects, characterizing the syndrome of anomia. Damage to the tracts which link the frontal and temporal portions of the language zone disconnects the area concerned with listening to heard speech from the area concerned with speaking (conduction aphasia). However, since this damage does not necessarily extend to the zones themselves, the ability to repeat heard speech is impaired selectively. Other disconnections arise from damage around the language zone, in the frontal region leading to transcortical motor aphasia, or in the parietal region leading to transcortical sensory aphasia. In the former case the ability to initiate propositional speech is reduced, and in the latter, the ability to comprehend information is severely impaired. Since the language zone itself is not inherently disrupted, patients with either of these syndromes retain the ability to reproduce heard speech. The Boston model can also incorporate findings from specific disorders of reading; visual information from printed words is said to be transferred from the occipital lobe to the central language zone. If this route becomes non-functional, and if the damage also prevents the transfer of information from the occipital lobe of the other hemisphere via the *corpus callosum*, then alexia results.

Influential though this model is, it has a rather limited application since it rests on the assumption that chunks of behaviour can be mapped isomorphically onto mental structures. It also ignores many aspects of the actual behaviour of language-disordered individuals. It speaks for example of 'failures to repeat' but makes little attempt to differentiate amongst the types of errors made and the clues these might provide to the disturbed processes. Furthermore, since disturbances of different underlying processes can result in secondary behaviours and adaptive strategies which are similar, attempts at objective classification by test scores of surface behaviours do not necessarily result in more accurate categorization of patients according to the essential nature of their disorder. Neurologically the model depends for evidence of localization on the technique of mapping the overlap of the sites of brain damage in a number of patients, as established from brain scans. This technique ignores the extent of the damage and can, therefore, give the illusion of finer and finer localization with larger numbers of patients studied, since the overlap becomes progressively smaller.

An alternative approach has been to move away from modalities of behaviour and consider the fractionation of language from the point of view of linguistic levels. In particular, three main levels have been identified: phonological, syntactic and semantic. An early application of linguistics to aphasia proposed a functional dissociation between the use of syntax and the lexicon or word store (von Stockert, 1972). It moved away from the localizationist interpretation of Broca's and Wernicke's deficits as problems of speech or comprehension, and considered them as deficits in syntactic or lexical abilities respectively, regardless of whether these abilities were being revealed in speech or comprehension. However, since the lexicon is generally held to include syntactic components as well as semantic and other components (for example words may be stored according to their grammatical function or their sound shape as well as by their meaning), such an explanation needs to be further refined.

Another similar attempt to delineate the two disorders in linguistic terms as disturbances respectively of syntagmatic and paradigmatic operations (Luria, 1975) also founders on the difficulty of separating these two aspects of the lexicon; word choice in an utterance is guided by the syntagmatic implications of a word (such as the grammatical compulsion to complete 'put' as a verb - in its primary meaning - with an object and a location) as well as by paradigmatic preference (such as selecting 'cottage' rather than 'house').

It is a major conceptual leap to use the descriptive terms of linguistics (as a theoretical study) as if they refer to psychologically real mental systems, but it is one which has proved irresistible to many students of aphasia. Brown (1979), for example, uses linguistic terms in claiming that different types of aphasia reflect the disruption of language at different stages of the mental operations involved in its production. He suggests that there are two dissociable systems, a semantic - phonological one and a grammatical - articulatory one which is also concerned with the motor production of speech. The type of error made by a patient in using, for example, the word 'chair' as a referent reveals the stage to which he has progressed on this occasion on the semantic -phonological system: a semantic failure might result in 'wheelbase', an associative one in 'throne', a categorical one in 'table', an evocative one in 'you sit on it' and a phonological one in 'shair'. According to Brown, conduction aphasia may be equated with a disturbance at the last stage and varieties of Wernicke's aphasia and anomia with the earlier stages.

A further problem in the use of linguistic terms in neurolinguistic analysis is that their definitions are often controversial. For example, the distinction between function and content words has been hotly debated. Function (or closed-class) words include prepositions, articles and pronouns; content (or open-class) words include nouns, verbs and adjectives. Both groups are heterogeneous, and it is not clear whether the distinction between them is grammatical (as the labels suggest) or semantic (Klosek, 1979), or even phonological in that function words are usually unstressed (Kean, 1979). In general, the bulk of aphasia studies have preferred to use a psycholinguistic framework which makes convenient assumptions about such ill-defined linguistic terms. Indeed, some have argued that aphasia offers a means for testing the validity of such definitions and for determining the psychological reality of the linguistic distinctions (Schnitzer, 1978).

The most developed of the psycholinguistic fractionating models relates to disorders of reading, even though acquired language disorders which affect only the ability to read are relatively rare.

An information-processing model which has been partly influenced by evidence from the behaviour of alexic adults' reading of words is the 'logogen' model (Morton and Patterson, 1980), logogen being a term for the mental representation of a word. This model provides for modality-distinct systems for vision, for audition and for output in which words are activated. These systems do not in themselves contain semantic or syntactic information but provide access to these knowledge sources. It is, therefore, a model which elaborates on relatively peripheral and modality-bound aspects of language use rather than on interactive cognitive processes. The logogen model also provides for separate routes for grapheme – phoneme conversion in reading, i.e. for translating written letters or letter combinations into symbols for speech sounds, and for auditory – phonological conversion in listening, i.e. for translating heard sounds into symbols for speech sounds. Newcombe and Marshall (1980) have recently added a further refinement to their development of the logogen model. Since certain brain-damaged adults produce misnamings when they are writing (paragraphias), but not when they are speaking (paraphasias), it is argued that there must be separate output logogen systems (with their associated response buffers) for speaking and for writing.

Another recent fractionating model of reading based on inferences from pathology is that of Shallice (1981). He distinguishes seven stages beyond the stage of early visual processing: a filter control system, letter-form analysis, visual word-form analysis, letter identification, the phonological system, the semantic system and the articulatory control system used in reading aloud. Shallice justifies the isolation of one aspect of a language disorder, i.e. reading, by arguing for the existence of the reading domain as a discrete functional system. It is not clear, however, at what stage the processes used cease to be specific to this one domain, and at the least it must be assumed that the articulatory control processes used in reading aloud are also those used in spontaneous speech.

However, the studies used to examine reading performance in these patients are often so artificial (reading aloud single words or non-words) that it is doubtful what relevance they have for performance on more realistic tasks such as the comprehension of a connected passage of prose in a novel or newspaper.

Having outlined some notions of the fractionation of language function by brain damage, we shall now look more closely at studies which bear on specific aspects of these fractions.

Studies of phonology in aphasic comprehension

It has been suggested that impaired recognition of the sounds of speech is a major component in the deficit in comprehension of three main classes of aphasic adult: the word deaf, Wernicke's aphasics, and patients with global aphasia with very limited speech as well as limited comprehension. Johnston (1980) refers to this last group as 'patients who have language and auditory processing dysfunction as a result of a lesion which includes the temporal cortex of the left (dominant) hemisphere. Language and supplementary tests indicate the presence of defective recognition of the sounds of speech' (p.176). Globally aphasic people present particular difficulties of analysis in attempting a differentiation of dysfunctions of processing, however, and tests of their abilities in auditory comprehension have often been at the basic level of asking them to distinguish between words and non-words. For example, Wapner and Gardner (1979) showed that fourteen such patients were able to reject nonsense words as inappropriate names for items of room furniture or geographical locations, but were uncertain about accepting correct words. Boller and Green (1972) have also shown that global aphasics can distinguish between phonemic jargon or a foreign language and acceptable English speech, and conclude that

> even the most severe aphasics tend to maintain an ability to discriminate phonological patterns (Is it English or not?) and overall syntactic structures (Is it a question or a command?). Their inability to respond correctly, however, to the messages they perceived, suggests that detailed semantic analysis is a separate and later stage of comprehension (p.394).

Boller and Green maintain that 'the evidence from aphasia supports, not a separation of linguistic levels in the analysis of speech, but a sequence of processes that lead by stages to a finer more detailed analysis of a message' (p.393).

It is in the rare group of people who have acquired word-deafness that a specific deficit in phonemic perception has been proposed. This syndrome has been reviewed by Goldstein (1974), who also describes it as 'auditory agnosia for speech'. These patients have profound disturbances in understanding spoken language, whether in an appropriate functional context or in metalinguistic tasks such as dictation or repetition. Unlike Wernicke's aphasics, however, they retain comprehension through reading, and their spontaneous speech shows intact articulation and grammar without jargon. Such patients typically complain of fluctuations of attention and of problems in recalling words. Although according to current theories of lateralization, auditory agnosia for speech should be possible without an associated auditory agnosia for non-verbal environmental sounds, studies of people who have acquired word-deafness from cortical lesions have all indicated that at some time the patient had deficits in the conscious perception of auditory non-verbal material as well as the more profound disturbance in understanding speech (Miceli, 1982). Goldstein et al. (1975), however, report on a woman patient whom they studied over three years who showed improvement in the ability to match non-verbal sounds with pictures, but remained unable to understand speech unless by lip-reading. This supports the essential independence of processing for speech and for non-linguistic sounds, for which Albert et al. (1972) also report evidence. They describe a man who had suffered bilateral posterior cerebral damage resulting in auditory agnosia for non-verbal sounds, without word-deafness. Albert and his colleagues suggest that there may be a step-wise series of neuropsychological processes dealing differentially with the perception of meaningful non-verbal sounds and word-sounds. Their tentative explanation of the deficit in information processing in auditory (non-verbal) agnosia is in terms of on-line asynchrony. After initial processing of acoustic impulses separately in each hemisphere, impulses which have been partially processed in the right hemisphere are transferred to the left hemisphere, in which meaningful associations are stored. With Albert's patient, however, cortical-evoked potentials suggested that the right hemisphere was delayed in its auditory processing, and that the consequential asynchrony between the hemispheres interfered with the formation of meaningful associations.

In contrast, recent studies of phonemic perception in Wernicke's aphasia show the deficit in verbal comprehension in these patients is at least partly attributable to disturbance at a higher stage than phonemic analysis. The disturbance formerly attributed to phonemic hearing in Wernicke's aphasia (described by Luria as 'a disturbance of auditory analysis and synthesis' (1970, p.115)) appears to be not so much in the phonemic analysis of heard words, but in the association of words, whether heard or read, with their meaning. By analogy with the reading models discussed earlier, direct lexical access may be achieved in other modalities, i.e. through audition or visual sign or tactile Braille symbols. If this is so, Wernicke's aphasia (or at least some subdivision of the symptom complex of Wernicke's aphasia) may represent a disorder of the lexicon in which the connexions between semantic and phonological components of words in the lexicon have become loosened, and direct lexical access is impaired. Luria (1976) comments on

> the poor recognition of the meaning of individual words, the frequent occurrence of 'alienation of word meaning' and some degree of 'imprecision of meaning' as a result of which a well-marked 'lexical paragnosia' forms the centre of the speech disturbances in the patients of this group (p.186).

In a series of studies Blumstein and her colleagues (Blumstein *et al.*, 1977) have examined the role played by phonemic comprehension in Wernicke's aphasia by comparing the ability of Wernicke's aphasics to make phonemic discriminations with that of other groups of aphasic patients. The method used was to present to the subjects through earphones pairs of words or nonsense syllables which differed in one aspect or were the same. Although the Wernicke's aphasics had been classed as the most impaired of the groups in verbal comprehension on an aphasia test, they performed slightly better than one of the other aphasic groups (described as mixed anterior) who had fared better on the aphasia test. Blumstein *et al.* found a suggestive (but not statistically reliable) correspondence between number of errors on phonemic discrimination and general auditory comprehension only in the Wernicke group, which keeps open the possibility that their temporal-lobe damage may be associated with a specific effect on phonemic discrimination, as Luria's original formulation proposed.

If the nub of the Wernicke's aphasic's problem in comprehension is the association of sound and meaning, then error rate should increase as the task requires more semantic processing. This hypothesis has been tested by Baker, Blumstein and Goodglass (1981) when three degrees of semantic loading were used by them in discrimination tasks with Broca's and Wernicke's aphasics. Auditory – auditory discrimination was first used, e.g. discrimination of whether '*pear*' and '*bear*' were the same word, followed by the linking of a heard word with a line drawing in a second experiment. In a third experiment semantic demands were increased by presenting the subjects with four drawings after the word was heard, the three incorrect drawings showing respectively the phonemic contrast (e.g. if the correct word was '*bear*', the phonemic contrast could be '*pear*'), a semantically related contrast (e.g. '*wolf*') and a contrast semantically related to the phonemic contrast (e.g. '*grapes*'). As predicted, Wernicke's aphasics were more impaired than Broca's aphasics on all the experimental tasks, but their performance was disproportionately depressed by the increase in the semantic load. Moreover, they made more semantic errors on the final task. The authors conclude that 'While Wernicke's aphasics have a phoneme discrimination deficit which is intensified by semantic processing demands, there is separate and concurrent breakdown at the semantic level which is in turn influenced by phonological factors' (p.15).

Wernicke's aphasia, therefore, seems to point to three possible components in the processing of single words beyond the stage of auditory analysis, i.e. phonemic discrimination, the association of the sound shape of a word with its meaning (an interaction of phonological and semantic levels) and a level of semantic organization at a more abstract level than that of single words identifiable with their phonologically realizable forms. If Wernicke's aphasia, or any other aphasia, is indeed to provide evidence of the validity of this last level, it needs to be demonstrated that semantic disintegration can occur independently of any phonological disorder. Not surprisingly, much of the evidence related to this necessarily supra-modal level comes from the study of aphasic and alexic people's metalinguistic judgements about the meaning of written words, i.e. in formal tasks where they are required to make decisions about words rather than use the words spontaneously.

Access to the semantic lexicon through reading

The study of access to the lexicon in language-disordered people is one of the more fertile areas of study, and much of the psycholinguistic work on alexia has been related to this end. (Alexia is here used synonymously with dyslexia, by analogy with aphasia and dysphasia.) There are four main types of acquired reading disorders which have been proposed sufficiently explicitly to gain common currency in information-processing models, i.e. visual, surface, phonological and deep dyslexias, to use their most popular labels. In one form of visual dyslexia, 'pure alexia', the patient is able to write, but not to read back his own writing unless he traces it with his finger. The etiology is generally a stroke, and the reported cases have, therefore, usually been from an older age group. Memory problems, including those of lexical retrieval, are usually noted in this infrequent but well-documented syndrome. It is generally assumed, however, that any associated problems such as a mild visual agnosia (inability to attach meaning to a seen object), or naming difficulties in other modalities, or word-retrieval problems in spontaneous speech, reflect co-occurring disorders rather than being germane. Visual dyslexia as such has not, therefore, been considered as supplying information about the nature of the lexicon itself, since the damage appears to be at a peripheral and modality-specific stage of access to it.

Surface dyslexia has been described relatively recently and the syndrome has not yet been unambiguously characterized. Theoretically, the impairment is of the direct access route to the lexicon, so that reading is predominantly achieved through the grapheme – phoneme conversion route. The limitations of this route are revealed in particular when patients encounter words which do not conform to regular spelling (e.g *colonel*). Under these conditions their behaviour resembles that of children beginning to read or people with a low level of literacy. Grapheme – phoneme conversion is presumed to be a little-utilized route in skilled readers, except when they are asked to pronounce unfamiliar or non-words. Marcel (1980) has pointed out, however, that the few reports of surface dyslexia available describe errors which cannot be accounted for only in terms of misapplied grapheme – phoneme rules, but which also point towards some involvement of an impaired lexicon itself. For example, concrete nouns are more likely to be read correctly than abstract nouns, and nouns more likely to be read correctly than adjectives or verbs. Marcel suggests that the nature of this lexical impairment in surface dyslexia is a loss of orthographic specification (or mental images of their written shape) for some words in the input lexicon, so that these patients are functioning in the same way as beginning readers who have not yet acquired these specifications. They draw on grapheme – phoneme conversion rules only for words for which they no longer have instant recognition, and these are likely to be the less frequently used words and those more recently acquired. As with visual dyslexia the aphasic signs associated with surface dyslexia seem to be limited to a moderate anomia.

Phonological dyslexia and deep dyslexia are related in that both are presumed to reflect a primary impairment of the grapheme – phoneme route, though deep dyslexia is accompanied by other difficulties as well. Few examples of phonological dyslexia have been described, perhaps because the syndrome is identifiable mainly through the unusual task of attempting to pronounce nonsense words. Beauvois and Dérouesné (1979) have described four cases, and Shallice and Warrington (1980) two. Typically patients come to the attention of a neuropsychologist or speech therapist because they complain of difficulty in spelling. Aphasic symptoms again seem to be limited to moderate anomia, and since such patients can read content words and function words well, but make poor shift with nonsense words or read them by analogy with real words (e.g. '*vag*' as '*vague*'), it is assumed that the direct route to the lexicon, and the lexicon itself, are intact.

The most fruitful dyslexia syndrome through which to obtain evidence about the nature of the semantic lexicon is, therefore, deep dyslexia. It is generally agreed that this syndrome includes several underlying dysfunctions: i.e. of the grapheme – phoneme route, of syntactic and semantic components of the lexicon and of some preliminary stages of the production of word names. According to Shallice and Warrington (1980) this last disruption is 'a post-lexical phonological ("nominal") deficit' or a difficulty in selecting the sound shape for the name of a word, while Morton and Patterson (1980) categorize it as impairment in the output logogen system. Deep dyslexia therefore seems to be interpretable as a form of aphasia in that it involves word-retrieval, rather than processes specific to reading input. In its purest form it has been suggested (Hécaen and Kremin, 1976) that it may be a nominal aphasia specific to the written word; most of the examples in the literature describe symptoms which are also those of Broca's aphasia or of a more general anomia. Like most aphasic patients (see Gardner and Zurif, 1976; Farmer *et al.*, 1979), deep dyslexics make semantic errors. This is consistent with the notion that access at will can be obtained only to a diffuse sphere of meaning for a word, e.g. *'brother'* may be undifferentiated from *'sister'*, *'father'*, etc. Theoretically, if the patient is aphasic this applies regardless of modality of access, but in the case of deep dyslexia it is claimed to be specific to access through the visual language modality. Coltheart's (1980) review of twenty-two cases of deep dyslexia in the literature since 1931 notes that all except one had a selective difficulty in reading out function words, and that a number were clearly classifiable as Broca's aphasics. Coltheart notes that the one defining characteristic of all deep dyslexics is that they make semantic errors in reading (the corollary being that the number of aphasic patients who make semantic errors in reading must also be experiencing deep dyslexia). The inability to apply grapheme – phoneme correspondence rules does not allow the deep dyslexic patient to correct his semantic misreadings by this means. If this dyslexia is considered to be an aspect of aphasia, such behaviour can be interpreted as one instance of a more general impairment in the ability to apply analytic rules.

On the other hand, if modality-specific lexicons derived from visual and auditory input are being proposed, as they seem to be in the distinction being made between inferences from dyslexia and those from aphasia, then studies of semantic organization in aphasia need to be re-examined carefully to see to what extent they have relied on material presented through reading.

Integrity of semantic organization in aphasia

To account for some data from aphasia it also seems necessary to postulate a prelexical stage of semantic organization for the concepts which eventually become realized as words. This stage may consist of organizations of experience into semantic fields whose elements are linked in an associative network of relationships. Before it can be realized as a word with a phonological form the semantic field has to become individualized. According to one notion, the 'lexicalist hypothesis', it also has to take on a specific syntactic form, so that, for example, '*destroy*' is differentiated from '*destruction*' at a prephonological level. Indeed, Bresnan (1978) has suggested that the lexicon may contain a good deal of syntactic information prior to lexical insertion in sentences. She proposes, for example, that the active - passive distinction, hitherto attributed to grammatical transformations in the formulation of the surface structure of sentences, may reflect functions of verbs as lexical elements.

Evidence as to whether lexical retrieval problems in different types of aphasia are caused by semantic problems as such or by difficulty in attaching label to concept can be provided by performance under conditions of phonemic priming. Goodglass and Stuss (1979, 1980) report that priming with a phonemic cue, i.e. helping the patient by giving him the initial sound of the word he is trying to retrieve, is considerably more facilitating for Broca's aphasics than it is with Wernicke's or anomic aphasics. In fact, the performance of anomic patients was even poorer than that of Wernicke's aphasics.

A variety of independent studies have revealed the presence of agnosic or visual-recognition/identification difficulties that accompany naming deficits in some patients, particularly in those with posterior lesions (Shanon, 1978; Tsvctkova, 1976; Whitehouse and Caramazza, 1978). These studies require the patient to draw or classify the pictorial version of the object. The results suggest that naming disorders are often accompanied by a failure to distinguish objects from other members of the same semantic category. An object may be classified as a table because it has four legs and a flat top, and a bird because it has two legs and wings, without the realization that these are the characteristic but not the defining features of objects. Similarly, when these patients classify objects or their names, they group them according to their visual similarities or local association rather than according to their inclusion within a given taxonomic category (Zurif and Caramazza, 1976; Grober *et al.*, 1980). These findings have serious implications for theories of word/object processing for three reasons. First, they indicate that anomia may not be purely a deficit in retrieval, but represents an aspect of a more extensive problem involving perception and storage of information. Secondly, they suggest that the concept of anomia as a unitary deficit may be misleading, and that it may be better considered as a set of deficits whereby different stages in the information-processing sequence of object identification and naming are impaired. Thirdly, they suggest that earlier assumptions that considered the deficit to be related to the expression of intentions rather than to the formulation of the intentions themselves, may be a simplistic and even misleading account of the facts. These findings have in turn cast doubt on the justification for using errors committed in a single task as evidence of deficits. Difficulties at the perceptual stages of processing information are not necessarily eliminated by having the stimulus object continually on view. It is also interesting to consider that had the investigations been confined to language functions, the possibility of a deficit at an earlier perceptual or later conceptual stage in the system might not have been established. At this point, the limitations of a strictly linguistic model of speech production become apparent. Since any high-level cognitive task involves the interaction between perceptual, conceptual, linguistic and other cognitive factors, the exmaination of the linguistic or memorial aspects of the process in isolation from the other factors provides a distorted view of and unlikely explanation for the cognitive deficit.

An apparent failure to find the intended words is frequently observed in the spontaneous utterances of patients with jargon-aphasia, a label which is often used as synonymous with Wernicke's aphasia, but which emphasizes speech characteristics rather than comprehension failures. The speech of jargonaphasics has been interpreted as the product of two complementary processes, word-finding difficulties and a failure to inhibit the phonological system. These processes have been investigated by Butterworth (1979) through an examination of pause time associated with neologisms (novel, and usually unmeaningful, 'words'). Butterworth reported that, in an interview with a patient which lasted 20 minutes, 51 per cent of the neologisms were preceded by a pause, in contrast to only 18 per cent of real words. This suggests that the failure to produce a real word represents a qualitatively different process from that involved in producing one. The fact that over half of neologisms are associated with a pause suggests that these are the product of an active though unsuccessful attempt to find a particular word. However, nearly half of the neologisms were not preceded by a pause, and these may have reflected a lack of inhibition. Fifteen per cent of the abnormal lexical content of the sample of jargonaphasia consisted of verbal paraphasias (real but inappropriate words), and only a third of these were preceded by pauses.

Butterworth's argument conforms closely to the model of lexical mediation in jargonaphasia proposed by Buckingham and Kertesz (1976). They put forward a two-stage model of neologistic speech production, whereby the neologism represents a verbal paraphasia which then itself becomes phonemically distorted into a non-word. It is unlikely that the failure is simply occurring late in the information-processing sequence at a stage where speech sounds are organized to express already selected words since this would not account for the failure of such patients to be aware of their own errors or of the inappropriateness of their long, rambling responses to simple questions. The result of such findings is to locate the site of the deficit in this type of anomia at the very early stage of pre-verbal cognitive representation of the intention. If the intention has failed to become adequately differentiated and the linguistic system is activated prematurely, it is not surprising that the jargonaphasic is unaware of his speech errors, since he has no model or target word with which to compare them. The alternative formulation of the disorder in jargonaphasia is that the speaker's output consists of meaningless clichés because of the cumulative failure to use pause time effectively. The striking aspect of jargon speech is not that 51 per cent of neologisms are preceded by pauses, but that 49 per cent are not. If the neologism were a substitute for an intended word the speaker's failure to realize a target would surely have been expected to occupy more time than the correct choice. The absence of a pause indicates the absence of high-level cognitive activity (since cognitive planning and speech cannot occur simultaneously in time, according to Goldman-Eisler, 1968). The mere presence of pauses cannot, however, be taken as a guarantee of cognitive activity.

The recovery from jargonaphasia to anomic aphasia is often marked by an increase in pause time (Buckingham, 1979), suggesting that silence can assume a more purposeful role in facilitating search activities. We are, therefore, speculating that silence participates in speech as a dependent as well as an independent variable.

A further consideration is whether the analysis of the speech production of jargonaphasics is justified at a purely linguistic level. On the basis of lexical and phonemic analysis several authors have drawn a comparison between the empty meaningless speech of jargonaphasics and that of patients with schizophrenia (Chaika, 1974; Lecours and Vanier-Clément, 1976). Superficially, the similarities between the two forms of speech are striking: relatively intact syntactic structures and fluent speech with full use of intonation in the face of meaningless and occasionally neologistic utterances. However, recent studies suggest that these seem to be the products of different dynamic strategies (Reich and Cutting, 1981). For instance, when groups of subjects were required to describe activities shown in a picture of a domestic scene, the schizophrenics, despite their jargon and occasional tangential thinking, attempted to provide a global interpretation of the scene as a whole followed by an occasional itemization of the objects in the scene. Posterior aphasics, however, invariably began their utterances by itemizing the objects, even though they were rarely able to access the correct names. Only rarely, and at the end of their responses, did they attempt to integrate the action in the scene as a whole. It is as if, being unable to construct a holistic schema, they devote themselves to an attempt to reconstruct it by stringing together a sequence of elements. Since sequencing and hierarchical ordering seem to be fairly well preserved in fluent aphasics (von Stockert, 1972), it may be that they use this device in an attempt to compensate for their conceptual deficits. Perhaps a similar failure of synthesis operates also at the lexical level, resulting in the serial selection of components of word-meaning rather than their integration into a semantic unit. Indeed, Deloche *et al.* (1981) have recently interpreted the retained ability of a globally aphasic man to categorize words he could not read, as evidence that lexical meaning has indeed to be reconstructed by an active synthesizing process rather than being stored in an all-or-none fashion.

Grammar

The syndrome which has been most closely examined for evidence of the fractionation of grammatical components of language is that of

Broca's aphasia. Pick (1931) considered that the agrammatism associated with this syndrome represented a regression from conventional syntax to 'thought syntax'; the thought content, in terms of the thought and language schemas, failed to be made explicit as a grammatical and ordered sequence of elements. He proposed that the content words were selected first, as they expressed the essentials of thought followed by a further linguistic differentiation of the psychological or cognitive/thought schema into function words. He argued that agrammatism (the failure of this last stage to be realized) did not imply a loss of memory for word forms but a reduction or elimination of all aspects of the expression redundant to the conveying of the message. He proposed that the organic impairment resulted in an economy of effort whereby only the essentials of the concept or intention were realized in words. Interestingly, while Pick identified agrammatism as a peculiarly linguistic and syntactic disorder, he still argued for the existence of a close relationship between conceptual and linguistic processes in the acts of speech production and perception, and emphasized that the intention or meaning of an utterance influences and was influenced by the choice of word order.

The subsequent advance in the understanding of the syndrome was associated with the first linguistic approach to the analysis of aphasic speech, which sought to differentiate between the parts of speech that caused difficulties. Patients with anterior lesions were found to experience greater difficulty in emitting function words than content words, and produced fewer syntactic constructions and grammatical inflections than those with posterior lesions.

Several recent studies have taken up this enquiry into the nature of the problems experienced by Broca's aphasics with function words. Bradley (cited by Zurif, 1980), using a task of deciding whether letter strings were real words or not, has shown that normal subjects responded more quickly to frequent words than infrequent in respect of content words, but that there was no effect of frequency in respect of function words. Moreover, non-words which incorporate a content word as their first syllable take longer to reject than do non-words which incorporate a function word. In contrast, Broca's aphasics are as sensitive to frequency with function words as they are with content words, but show no particular delay in reaction times to non-words which include function words. Their behaviour suggests that they recognize function words as belonging to their language, but they seem to have lost the specialized mechanism for using them. Zurif (1980) argues that this mechanism is not specific to speech but is drawn upon both for sentence construction in speech production and for sentence comprehension, and is located in the anterior portion of the brain. Recent investigations (Gordon and Caramazza, 1982) have, however, failed to replicate Bradley's findings with normal subjects of different effects of frequency for content and function words. Inferences about disturbance of mechanisms in Broca's aphasia may, therefore, be somewhat premature.

A substantial number of studies have examined the ability of small groups of patients clinically described as Broca's aphasics to monitor the significance of various kinds of function words and bound morphemes in sentences, as distinct from tasks which use only single words. For instance, Heilman and Scholes (1976) examined the ability of aphasic subjects to understand a change in the meaning of sentences signalled by the word '*the*'. Thus sentences like 'He showed her baby pictures' are ambiguous, when presented without prosodic cues; but the insertion of '*the*' disambiguates them into 'He showed her the baby pictures' or 'He showed her baby the pictures'. Heilman and Scholes proposed that patients who were not able to supply syntactic inference rules from monitoring the function word '*the*' should respond to either of these forms as if they were still ambiguous. This hypothesis was supported. Scholes (1978) concludes from such studies that

> normally full sentence comprehension, i.e. knowing what a sentence means – is accomplished by the application of both lexical and syntactic analysis and both are necessary. That the two types of analysis appear to be isolable through brain-damage, maturation or experimental manipulation suggests, however, that they operate in a parallel (rather than serial) fashion (p.173).

An alternative way of interpreting these data is that function words are selectively impaired relative to content words on the basis of their phonological rather than their syntactic roles (Kean, 1979). Since Broca's aphasics are generally described as having a phonological disorder in the articulation of speech , the inference has been made that they do not attend to function words because these are not phonologically marked by stress. This cannot be simply a matter of processing, however; for although Broca's aphasics, like normal subjects, respond faster to stressed rather than unstressed words in sentences, they still show an effect of vocabulary type by responding faster to content words than function words regardless of stress (Swinney *et al.*, 1980).

Amongst others who have challenged Kean's proposal are Schwartz *et al.* (1980), who suggest that agrammatic patients are impaired in a grammatical operation which does not depend on the processing of function words, i.e. word-order as used in the interpretation of semantically reversible sentences such as 'The man follows the dog'. Schwartz *et al.* propose a radical interpretation of their findings, i.e., that agrammatic patients lack the capacity to deal with language structures that encode relational meanings; in both comprehension and production they lack mediating linguistic structures such as the syntactic notions of 'subject' and 'predicate' or even the logical notions of 'agent' and 'patient'. Their lack of grammatical surface structure reflects in fact a lack of these deep syntactic structures; cognitive intent is mapped directly onto an utterance and vice versa.

A problem with this interpretation is that other kinds of aphasic patients (whose production is not agrammatic) can have difficulty with syntactic comprehension of word-order. Tests of word-order such as this commonly do show impairment in aphasics (Lesser, 1974) but they may reflect lexical confusion rather than specific difficulties in manipulating order. Heeschen (1980) reports that Wernicke's aphasics were significantly more impaired than Broca's aphasics on a thirty-two-item picture-choice test in which the sentences tested differed on two variables, reversibility and topicalization by word-order. For example, *Der Offizier schreit den Rekruten an* – 'The officer shouts at the recruit' (considered to be irreversible with any plausibility) could also be presented in a topicalized form as *Den Rekruten schreit der Offizier an* – 'It is the recruit the officer shouts at.' The group of Wernicke's aphasics made more errors on topicalized sentences than on normal sentences, and to a greater extent than did the Broca's aphasics, showing less responsiveness to the semantic plausibility of the sentences, but perhaps a greater reliance on the expected constituent order of subject prior to object.

Luria also reports (1975) that it is posterior aphasics ('semantic' aphasics) who have disturbances in logico-grammatical relationships which make difficult the integration into a meaningful whole of sentences such as 'The square is above the circle' (an example also used in Schwartz's study). In contrast to Schwartz, however, he suggests that the anterior patients' problem lies in the use of function words and inflections rather than in the use of grammatical relations as such.

Yet another proposal is that of Saffran *et al.* (1980), who suggest that there are two distinct varieties of agrammatism. In one type of disorder the problem is essentially in the ordering of the syntactic elements for sentence construction, while the use of grammatical inflections and function words is retained; in the other the problem is essentially the reverse. Futher support for such a subdivision is in the study by Caplan *et al.* (1981) of the comprehension of gerundive constructions by Broca's aphasics. These investigators found evidence for a subdivision of this category: some were sensitive to the significance of function words and some were not.

Whilst these investigations have sought to determine the level of processing within a linguistically based model of hierarchy of information processing, other non-linguistic studies have revealed comparable sequencing and ordering difficulties in the processing of acoustic and visual stimuli (De Renzi *et al.*, 1977; Carmon and Nachshon, 1971; Albert, 1976). Although these findings concern the decoding rather than the encoding behaviour of patients with anterior lesions, they have implications for the level in the processing of information that the deficit occurs. Either the deficit is peculiarly linguistic, in which case the missing structures are also normally used in the performance of non-linguistic tasks that involve the perception and memory of sequential non-meaningful information; or the deficient structures involve the non-lingusitic analytic strategies that permit the discrimination and reproduction of sequential item information in speech and non-speech stimuli.

One common approach to the question of the linguistic status of the impaired mechanism has been to invoke the relatively normal non-linguistic communicative ability of aphasic patients. Thus, Saffran and her colleagues (1980) argue that agrammatism is a linguistic rather than a cognitive deficit since otherwise 'agrammatics should be more impaired in their non-verbal interactions with the world than they are'. However, in view of the limited number of studies in this field and their lack of agreement (Goodglass and Kaplan, 1963; Gainotti and Lemmo, 1976; Cicone *et al.*, 1979), this statement seems anecdotal and rather premature.

Even if the deficit is considered within a purely linguistic framework, however, the experimental tasks which are used to elicit encoding difficulties are often unusual and artificial. Such sentences demand a high level of syntactic analysis in the face of minimal semantic and pragmatic cues to meaning. Early studies of normal subjects, concerned with the production of similar sentences with different syntactic constraints (for example, Mehler, 1963), were eagerly adopted in support of the psychological reality of transformational structures. These interpretations were subsequently discredited by the reports that first the tasks could be accomplished without any attention to meaning; and secondly, that the tasks imposed artificial and atypical requirements on subjects' processing capacities. Thus, an enquiry as to whether normal or aphasic subjects can perform certain operations, cannot be evaluated without reference to the significance of these operations within the normal range of behaviours. Several experiments using healthy subjects indicate that this strategy used by agrammatic aphasics may not be as pathological as it first appears (Herriot, 1969). Wason and Reich (1979), amongst others, have demonstrated the overriding influence of semantic and pragmatic factors relative to syntactic factors in determining sentence meaning. Thus, the agrammatic aphasic is striking because of his overreliance on one of the most popular normal strategies for dealing with meaningful information. As with normal subjects, the less meaningful the stimuli or task, the worse his performance (De Renzi et al., 1977; Gardner and Zurif, 1976).

A further aspect of the speech-production abilities of the anterior aphasic has been examined within the framework of reading tasks. Typically such patients are better at reading words than isolated letters (Saffran and Marin, 1977), and are more successful in reading aloud words embedded in restrictive phrases such as 'a *heart* attack' than in non-restrictive phrases such as 'a *heart* injury' or in isolation (Saffran et al., 1976).

These results have rarely been related to the strategies used by healthy skilled readers; they are even less frequently related to other aspects of the linguistic and cognitive performance of the aphasic patient. Thus the failure of the grapheme - phoneme conversion rules in the information-processing sequence of the reading behaviour is usually considered as independent from the failure to process word order in the speech of the same patients. The tasks of reading aloud, describing activities and ordering words into sentences probably involve different combinations of strategies, but nevertheless a single deficient cognitive or linguistic process may have implications (albeit different) for performance on all three tasks. Although lack of an overall theoretical model encourages a reductionist approach to investigations of language processing, this should not prevent an attempt to reconcile these apparently isolated findings in order to consider the functioning of the organism as a whole.

The dynamics of aphasia

Some attempts have been made at such a holistic approach. Kreindler and Fradis (1968) examined the ability to estimate time intervals in a test of imitating tapping. Most aphasics were found to shorten the long intervals, implying an excess of neurophysiolgical excitation over inhibition. The suggestion is that aphasic symptoms represent a translation into the language system of more general deficits in neurodynamic processing. Other researchers have considered that aphasia may be evidence of overloading of processors working with reduced efficiency rather than interruptions in the processes themselves. Aphasics were more disturbed by distractors than were normal subjects, and could not cope with intervening tasks between the stimulus and its response (De Renzi et al., 1978). This happened even if they were first allowed a 4-second silent interval to consolidate the message. The fact that the patients could perform the task after an unfilled delay showed that they could understand the information and retain it in verbal memory. The experiments suggest, however, that the information trace may have been in a weak, badly organized form, i.e. three-item information had not been recoded into a one-item chunk. Diggs and Basili (1978), also using instructions from De Renzi and Vignolo's Token Test (1962), compared presentations under conditions of quiet, white noise and speech babble. Both left and right-brain-damaged patients who were not significantly aphasic were more disturbed by speech babble than were non-brain-damaged subjects, who found equivalent disruptions from speech babble as from white noise. The inference is that brain damage on either side impairs total brain capacity and limits the ability to filter information from similar background competition.

Perseveration (the inappropriate repetition of an earlier response) is common phenomenon in aphasia, and Yamadori (1981) reported that over 86 per cent of his sample of non-global aphasics showed verbal perseveration on a repetition task. Perseveration in aphasia has been attributed partly to pro-active interference (Flowers, 1975); Yamadori considers the cause to be an instability of inhibition in excited neural systems resulting in confusion in the sequencing of elements in response to a new stimulus.

An overloaded system may be expected to cope better if it is given more time to organize its load without additional input being added. A number of studies have shown that slowing the rate of presentation of sentences or introducing pauses facilitates aphasic comprehension (Gardner et al., 1975; Weidner and Lasky, 1976; Salvatore and Davis, 1979). Baker and Goodglass (1979) addressed themselves to the question of whether a component of difficulty in auditory comprehension in aphasia was slowed processing of single lexical items; they found a marked slowness in Wernicke's aphasics though not in Broca's aphasics. Johnston (1980), following Schuell, describes several kinds of auditory processing disorders that occur in conjunction with aphasia. The patient may not retain input long enough to complete the processing of the signal, which has itself become a more extended procedure. Typically, the patient recalls the initial component of the message better than later ones, as if succeeding units jam the system. Slower presentation rates for normal subjects normally facilitate recall from long-term store but not from working memory, since they allow the acoustic image to fade. On the other hand, Porch (1981) has described patients who miss the incoming portion of the verbal message because of what is described as a slow rise time or time taken to shift from a passive state to an active processing state. This draws attention to the need for including orienting or attentional mechanisms in a model of the analysis of audiolinguistic process dysfunctions in language disorders.

Faulty auditory feedback has also been invoked as a source of processing problems in aphasia. Boller and Marcie (1978) have described a patient with conduction aphasia whose speech improved with delayed auditory feedback, and a number of investigators (reviewed by Boller, 1979) have reported that patients with phonemic jargon were not disturbed by delayed auditory feedback in the same way as were normal subjects. Boller (1979) and Chapin et al. (1981) also report that Broca's aphasics are, in contrast, more disturbed by delayed auditory feedback than are controls. Boller and Marcie suggest that there are two kinds of phonemic feedback for the speaker: internal feedback which is crucial in the selection of phonemic features, and external feedback through which sounds are monitored as they are uttered or have been uttered. They speculate that in conduction aphasia internal feedback is impaired so that the patient relies on external auditory feedback; the hesitations and self-corrections of such patients suggest that external auditory feedback is also abnormal and perhaps delayed. It is not clear, however, why a further delay in this external feedback should contribute to bringing language production closer to normality.

The deficit in comprehension in some examples of conduction aphasia has been explained as being one of auditory short-term memory (Warrington and Shallice, 1969; Saffran and Marin, 1977; Shallice and Butterworth, 1977). This can plausibly explain the failure of conduction aphasics to repeat what they have just heard, but it is uncertain how much of the 'on-line' comprehension of sentences depends on short-term memory; indeed, if processing proceeds in parallel as Marslen-Wilson (1980) suggests, auditory memory may play a minimal role in sentences in which homophones do not have to be disambiguated. Conduction aphasics usually can produce the gist of a heard sentence, but fail to reproduce the exact words and exact syntactic constructions. This suggests that, while a deficit in auditory memory precludes echoic repetition, it does not prevent semantic comprehension of the sentence.

As Saffran and Marin have remarked, it is as though conduction aphasics were operating as normal subjects after a given delay between input and output. Typically, normal subjects listening to a passage of prose remember the gist of individual sentences long after their memory for the order of the words (syntax) has decayed (Sachs, 1967), and these findings might tempt one into speculation that conduction aphasics decode information in the same manner as normal subjects, but suffer from faster decay rates. This view is similar to the argument proposed by Warrington and Shallice (1969) to account for the reduced recency effect in learning lists of letters or words. However, Albert (1976) and his colleagues and Tzortzis and Albert (1974) subsequently argued against the existence of a short-term memory deficit, since conduction aphasics in carrying out tasks of matching and reproducing lists of unrelated items performed no worse than patients with Broca's or Wernicke's aphasia. Instead, he used the large number of order errors as evidence in favour of a specific deficit in ordering information. Furthermore, the implication was that this deficit involved a cognitive and modality-free system, since it affected performance on non-linguistic (environmental noises, shapes) as well as on linguistic (numbers, letters and words) stimuli presented auditorily and visually. Given this approach, we are then faced with the problem of the apparent dissociation between the poor verbatim memory for sentences and the relatively good comprehension and memory for gist. Put another way: how can conduction aphasics understand the meaning of sentences when they are unable correctly to reproduce the order in which the words in the sentence occurred? There are two possible answers to this question. First, as we have discussed earlier, order information may have been decoded initially at the stage of semantic analysis and may decay at a faster rate than semantic information. Secondly, the analysis of order information may not be a necessary prerequisite for understanding sentences. The second point deserves particular consideration as it relates to a series of studies on information processing in normal subjects (Aaronson, 1976; Stanners and Headley, 1972). These studies indicate that tasks that require the verbatim analysis of sentences rely on different temporal processing strategies from tasks that require comprehension. Whereas the former usually elicits an immediate word-by-word continuous monitoring of the stimulus information, the latter is usually associated with a delay between the input and its decoding. Thus, although we are able to remember both meaning and order information in simple sentences under optimal viewing conditions, these analyses may be accomplished by different strategies, particularly under conditions of cognitive stress.

Conclusion

As can be seen from the preceding sections, our approach has been to examine the contribution of information theory to the analysis of several of the major aphasic syndromes. In this endeavour we have used a method of analysis that reflects a current trend in neurolinguistic research - that of fractionating each syndrome into a set of subcomponents according to the size of the unit of analysis (phoneme, word, sentence). The assumption underlying this has been that these logical units entail psychological units. However, this activity involves the confounding of level of description with level of psychological processing - a common difficulty in linguistic and in psycholinguistic research. A further difficulty arises when performance elicited by artificial stimuli such as phonemes, non-words or arbitrary sentences are used to explain the difficulties encountered in more realistic tasks (Blumstein *et al.*, 1977; Morton and Patterson, 1980; Schwartz *et al.*, 1980). Underlying these studies is the failure to recognize that different tasks and stimuli interact to elicit different psychological strategies. Aaronson (1976), Foss and Swinney (1973) and others have argued that the strategies used to decode information for verbatim recall or at a phonemic level, differ from and may even be antithetical to the strategies used to comprehend information at the sentence or clause level.

Similar arguments have been proposed to account for mechanisms underlying the production of speech (Hughlings Jackson, 1878; Goldman-Eisler, 1968). Hughlings Jackson differentiated between fluent automatic speech that required little thought or cognitive planning, and voluntary propositional speech in which new ideas were formulated and for which planning time was essential. Goldman-Eisler further differentiated between performance on different tasks in terms of the level of cognitive planning required to generate or comprehend the meaning of a response. Reproduction by means of repetition or reading aloud involves less cognitive planning than a completely novel utterance, and these are therefore executed with less effort and pause time than spontaneous speech. The relationship between different utterances in terms of the amount of cognitive effort required to generate them may account for some of the apparent dissociations that occur between the abilities to reproduce and to produce or comprehend information in aphasia (Blumstein *et al.*, 1977; Gainotti and Lemmo, 1976). Thus, there exists a substantial body of evidence to indicate that the dynamics of behaviour (strategies) are sensitive to the demands on performance that are imposed by the stimuli and responses.

These findings have profound implications for the study of linguistic behaviour since they indicate that performance at each of the different levels of analysis may be specific to that level. In other words, performance elicited in tasks that specify the phoneme or word as the target, or that use artificial stimuli in arbitrary combinations, may not be generalizable to performance under other stimulus and task conditions.

If this is the case, what then is the logic that could have prompted this type of reasoning in the first place? The answer is an obvious one:

an adherence to a bottom-up view of processing whereby the processing of small units of information is seen as the basis of and prerequisite for the processing of larger units. Such a view inevitably
considers high-level meaning analysis as the composite of a series of
lower-level, less complex analyses of the elements of behaviour. This
view is epitomized in the reasoning of Marr's principle of modularity,
adopted by Shallice in his recent review of Neurological Impairment
of Cognitive Processes (1981):

> Any large computation should be split up and implemented as a
> collection of small subparts that are as nearly independent of one
> another as the overall task allows. If a process is not designed in
> this way a small change in one place will have consequences in
> many other places. This means that the process as a whole be-
> comes extremely difficult to debug or to improve, whether by a
> human designer or in the course of natural evolution, because a
> small change to improve one part has to be accompanied by many
> simultaneous compensatory changes elsewhere. (p.187).

This view is also consistent with the former tradition in linguistics
that the meaning of a sentence can be 'constructed by combining the
meanings of single lexical items' plus syntactic structure (Caramazza
and Berndt, 1978). Thus, investigations of the lexicon and the
features of individual word meanings have been conducted with the
belief that they provide information as to higher-order semantic
structures or the comprehension of sentences (Saffran et al., 1976).
For example, experiments are reported in which phoneme analysis is
seen as the basis of word perception (Cooper, 1979), and featural
analysis as the basis of conceptual structures and lexical meaning
(Rips et al., 1973). The contrasting top-down view of behaviour is
suggested by the experiments that indicate the significance of pragmatic, contextual and meaning-related factors in the perception
and analysis of lower-order sensory information. The arguments are
neatly summarized by Cooper (1980) in her recent review of visual
information processing:

> For many purposes, specification of visual input as sets of features
> extracted independently works quite well. However, when we con-
> sider the processing of displays that are structurally rich, the case

for local features as the proper specification of the input or the unit of visual analysis becomes less compelling. In the area of word processing, the superior perceptibility of words – as compared with unrelated letter strings, various sorts of regular non-word strings and perhaps single letters – has led some investigators to propose that units larger than individual features of letters are the important ones in perceiving printed words. (p.322).

Similarly, Wason and Reich (1979) have indicated the primacy of semantic and pragmatic factors over syntactic factors in assigning meaning to a sentence. Typically, the solution in neurolinguistic studies has been to isolate the 'independent' contribution of syntax by neutralizing the semantic content, and utilizing meaningless objects and shapes in situations without contextual information as in the Token Test (de Renzi and Vignolo, 1962). However, whilst this approach may be logically valid, it represents an unlikely psychological account of linguistic and non-linguistic processing mechanisms (Navon, 1977; Marslen-Wilson and Welsh, 1978). The effect of these procedures is to eliminate the influence of world knowledge on performance, and limit the strategies that may usefully operate on the stimuli.

What relevance do these findings have for aphasia research? The first and perhaps most obvious lesson is that the experiments and methodology in aphasia research are lagging behind, and still have much to learn from current information-processing arguments in psycholinguistic and scene-perception research. In particular, performance in tasks that involve the presentation of or responses to artificial or isolated (word/shape/object) stimuli should be recognized as being qualitatively different from performance on more realistic and knowledge-based tasks. Since 'words obtain their meanings from the sentences in which they are used' (Kintsch, 1980), the practice of looking for the source of speech encoding and decoding disorders at the object, word or phonemic level as in the aphasia studies of Kean (1979), Butterworth (1980), Grober et al. (1980) Semenza et al. (1980) and many others, ignores the most crucial level of analysis. At the very least, performance under these conditions needs to be related to performance under several other experimental paradigms.

Occasionally this is accomplished, and performance involved in classifying or reading aloud words and non-words is considered alongside a patient's ability to comprehend sentences (Patterson, 1979). Even then the tendency is often to enumerate performances on a series of unrelated tasks without much attempt to integrate them psychologically. Thus, reading deficits are examined at the level of individual words and not related psychologically to aphasic deficits at the level of sentences. It is not difficult to see how this practice then encourages the experimenter to consider aphasic disorders in terms of the differences between the pathological behaviours or syndromes rather than looking for common factors that may link them.

In the present chapter we have tried to summarize current thinking in aphasia research – thinking which has sought to identify the distinct contributions of the lexicon and of grammatical constructions in language processing. We have also outlined and advocated the use of at least one alternative approach, whereby pragmatic, semantic and syntactic factors are seen as interacting at each level of processing. This view is based on the notion that language as a communication system operates in a meaningful context and interacts with other cognitive activities in the transmission of purposeful and meaningful information. In its emphasis on the role of cognitive and thought processes in language function this view represents a return to the models of early aphasiologists such as Pick. This thinking may best be summarized in his two quotes of von Humboldt:

> Only the connected speech has to be considered as true and primary in all investigations which attempt to penetrate the phenomenon of language. The splitting up into words and rules is only the dead machination of scientific differentiation. (p.42)

> Man originally thinks the whole thought as one and speaks it in the same way. He does not believe [himself] to have put it together from individual words, and he would have trouble to sort it into words. (p.445)

References

Aaronson, D. (1976) Performance theories for sentence coding: some qualitative observations. *Journal of Experimental Psychology* 2: 42–55.
Albert, M. L. (1976) Short-term memory and aphasia. *Brain and Language* 3: 28–33.

Albert, M. L., Sparks, R., von Stockert, Th. and Sax, D. (1972) A case study of auditory agnosia: linguistic and non-linguistic processing. *Cortex 8*: 427-33.

Assal, G., Butter, J. and Jolivet, R. (1981) Dissociations in aphasia - a case report. *Brain and Language 13*: 223-40.

Baker, E., Blumstein, S. E. and Goodglass, H. (1981) Interaction between phonological and semantic factors in auditory comprehension. *Neuropsychologia 19*: 1-16.

Baker, E. and Goodglass, H. (1979) Time for auditory processing of object names by aphasics. *Brain and Language 8*: 355-66.

Beauvois, M-F. and Dérouesné, J. (1979) Phonological alexia: three dissociations. *Journal of Neurology, Neurosurgery and Psychiatry 42*: 1115-24.

Beauvois, M.-F. and Dérouesné, J. (1981) Lexical or orthographic agraphia. *Brain 104*: 21-49.

Blumstein, S. E., Baker, E. and Goodglass, H. (1977) Phonological factors in auditory comprehension in aphasia. *Neuropsychologia 15*: 19-30.

Boller, F. (1979) Delayed auditory feedback: a possible clue to the mechanism of some types of aphasia. In Y. Lebrun and R. Hoops (eds) *Problems of Aphasia*. Amsterdam: Swets & Zeitlinger.

Boller, F. and Green, E. (1972) Comprehension in severe aphasics. *Cortex 8*: 382-94.

Boller, F. and Marcie, P. (1978) Note: possible role of abnormal auditory feedback in conduction aphasia. *Neuropsychologia 16*: 521-4.

Bresnan, J. (1978) A realistic transformational grammar. In M. Halle, J. Bresnan and G. Miller (eds) *Linguistic Theory and Psychological Reality*. Cambridge, Mass.: MIT Press.

Brown, J. W. (1979) Language representation in the brain. In H. Steklis and M. Raleigh (eds) *Neurobiology of Social Communication in Primates*. New York: Academic Press.

Buckingham, H. W. (1979) Linguistic aspects of lexical retrieval disturbances in the posterior fluent aphasias. In H. Whitaker and H. Whitaker (eds) *Studies in Neurolinguistics*. Vol. 4. New York: Academic Press.

Buckingham, H. W. and Kertesz, A. (1976) *Neologistic Jargon Aphasia*. Amsterdam: Swets & Zeitlinger.

Butterworth, B. (1979) Hesitation and the production of verbal paraphasias and neologisms in jargon aphasia. *Brain and Language 8*: 133-61.

Butterworth, B. (ed.) (1980) *Language Production*. New York: Academic Press.

Caplan, D. (1981) On the cerebral localization of linguistic functions: logical and empirical issues surrounding deficit analysis and functional localization. *Brain and Language 14*: 120-37.

Caplan, D., Matthei, E. and Gigley, H. (1981) Comprehension of gerundive constructions by Broca's aphasics. *Brain and Language 13*: 145-60.

Caramazza, A. and Berndt, R. S. (1978) Semantic and syntactic processes in aphasia: a review of the literature. *Psychological Bulletin 85*: 898-918.

Carmon, A. and Nachshon, I. E. (1971) Effect of unilateral brain damage on perception of temporal order. *Cortex 7*: 410-18.

Cermak, L. S. and Moreines, J. (1976) Verbal retention deficits in aphasic and amnesic patients. *Brain and Language 3*: 16-27.

Chaika, E. (1974) A linguist looks at schizophrenic language. *Brain and Language 1*: 257-76.

Chapin, C., Blumstein, S. E. and Meissner, B. (1981) Speech-production mechanisms in aphasia: a delayed auditory feedback study. *Brain and Language 14*: 106-13.

Cicone, H., Wapner, W., Foldi, N., Zurif, E. and Gardner, H. (1979) The relation between gesture and language in aphasic communication.*Brain and Language 8*: 324-49.

Coltheart, M. (1980) Deep dyslexia: a review of the syndrome. In M. Coltheart, K. Patterson and J. C. Marshall (eds) *Deep Dyslexia*. London: Routledge & Kegan Paul.

Cooper, L. A. (1980) Recent themes in visual information processing. A selected overview. In R. S. Nickerson (ed.) *Attention and Performance*. Vol. VIII.Hillsdale, NJ: Lawrence Erlbaum Associates.

Cooper, W. E. (1979) *Speech Perception and Production - Studies in Selective Adaptation*. New Jersey: Ablex.

Cooper, W. E. and Walker, E. C. T. (1979) *Sentence Processing - Studies in Honour of Merrill Garrett*. Hillsdale, NJ: Lawrence Erlbaum Associates.

Deloche, G., Andreewsky, E. and Desi, M. (1981) Lexical meaning: a case report, some striking phenomena, theoretical implications. *Cortex 17*: 147-52.

De Renzi, E., Faglioni, P. and Villa, P. (1977) Sequential memory for figures in brain damaged patients. *Neuropsychologia 15*: 43-9.

De Renzi, E., Faglioni, P. and Previdi (1978) Increased susceptibility of aphasics to a distractor task in the recall of verbal commands. *Brain and Language 6*: 14-21.

De Renzi, E. and Vignolo, L. A. (1962) The Token Test: a sensitive test to detect receptive disturbances in aphasia. *Brain 85*: 665-78.

Diggs, C. C. and Basili, A. G. (1978) Auditory processing of brain-damaged adults under competitive listening conditions. Paper presented at ASHA convention, San Francisco.

Farmer, A., O'Connell, P. F. and Jesudowich, B. (1979) Naming and reading errors and response latency in Broca's aphasics. Paper presented at ASHA convention, Atlanta.

Flowers, C. R. (1975) Proactive interference in short-term recall by aphasic, brain-damaged non-aphasic and normal subjects. *Neuropsychologia 13*: 59-68.

Foss, D. J. and Swinney, D. A. (1973) On the psychological reality of the phoneme: perception, identification and consciousness. *Journal of Verbal Learning and Verbal Behaviour 12*: 246-57.

Gainotti, G. and Lemmo, M. A. (1976) Comprehension of symbolic gestures in aphasia. *Brain and Language 3*: 451-60.

Gardner, H., Albert, M. L. and Weintraub, S. (1975) Comprehending a word: the influence of speech and redundancy on auditory comprehension in aphasia. *Cortex 11*: 155-62.

Gardner, H. and Zurif, E. (1976) Critical reading of words and phrases in aphasia. *Brain and Language 3*: 173-90.

Geschwind, N. (1965) Disconnexion syndromes in animals and man. *Brain* 88: 237-94, 585-644.

Goldman-Eisler, F. (1968) *Psycholinguistics*. London: Academic Press.

Goldstein, M. V. (1974) Auditory agnosia for speech (pure word deafness): a historical review with current implications. *Brain and Language 1*: 195-204.

Goldstein, M. N., Brown, M. and Hollander, J. (1975) Auditory agnosia and cortical deafness: analysis of a case with three-year follow-up. *Brain and Language 2*: 324-32.

Goodglass, H. (1968) Studies on the grammar of aphasics. In S. Rosenberg and J. H. Koplin (eds) *Developments in Applied Psycholinguistic Research*. New York: Macmillan.

Goodglass, H. and Kaplan, E. (1963) Disturbance of gesture and pantomime in aphasia. *Brain 86*: 703-20.

Goodglass, H. and Kaplan, E. (1972) *The Assessment of Aphasia and Related Disorders*. Philadelphia: Lea & Febiger.

Goodglass, H. and Stuss, D. T. (1979) Naming to picture versus description in three aphasic subgroups. *Cortex 15*: 199-211 (with 1980 correction, *Cortex 16*: 341).

Gordon, B. and Caramazza, A. (1982) Lexical decision for open- and closed-class words: failure to replicate differential frequency sensitivity. *Brain and Language 15*: 143-60.

Grober, E., Perecman, E., Kellar, L. and Brown, J. (1980) Lexical knowledge in anterior and posterior aphasics. *Brain and Language 10*: 318-30.

Hécaen, H. and Kremin, H. (1976) Neurolinguistic rescarch on reading disorders resulting from left hemisphere lesions. In H. Whitaker and H. Whitaker (eds) *Studies in Neurolinguistics*. Vol. 2. New York: Academic Press.

Heeschen, C. (1980) Strategies of decoding actor – object relations by aphasic patients. *Cortex 16*: 5-19.

Heilman, K. M. and Scholes, R. J. (1976) The nature of comprehension errors in Broca's, conduction and Wernicke's aphasics. *Cortex 12*: 258-65.

Herriot, P. (1969) The comprehension of active and passive sentences as a function of pragmatic expectations. *Journal of Verbal Learning and Verbal Behaviour 8*: 166-9.

Jackson, J. Hughlings (1878) On affections of speech from disease of the brain. *Brain 1*: 304-30. Reprinted in J. Taylor (ed.) (1932) *Selected Writings of John Hughlings Jackson*. Vol. 2. London: Hodder and Stoughton.

Johnston, K. L. (1980) Auditory processing in aphasic adults: relationship between language disorders and auditory processing disorders. In P. Levinson and C. Sloan (eds) *Auditory Processing and Language*. New York: Grune & Stratton.

Kean, M. L. (1979) Agrammatism: a phonological deficit. *Cognition 7*: 69-83.

Kinsbourne, M. and Warrington, E. (1963) Jargon aphasia. *Neuropsychologia 1*: 127-37

Kintsch, W. (1980) Semantic memory: a tutorial. In R. S. Nickerson (ed.)

Attention and Performance. Vol. VIII. Hillsdale, NJ: Lawrence Erlbaum Associates.

Klosek, J. (1979) Two unargued assumptions in Kean's 'phonological' interpretation of agrammatism. *Cognition* 7: 61-8.

Kreindler, A. and Fradis, A. (1968) *Performances in Aphasia.* Paris: Gauthier-Villars.

Lecours, A. R. and Vanier-Clément, M. (1976) Schizophasia and jargonaphasia. *Brain and Language 3*: 516-65.

Lesser, R. (1974) Verbal comprehension in aphasia: an English version of three Italian tests. *Cortex 10*: 247-63.

Levelt, W. J. M. (1978) A survey of studies in sentence perception, 1970-1976. In W. J. M. Levelt and G. B. Flores d'Arcais (eds) *Studies in the Perception of Language.* Chichester: Wiley.

Luria, A. R. (1970) *Traumatic Aphasia.* The Hague: Mouton.

Luria, A. R. (1975) Two kinds of disorders in the comprehension of grammatical constructions. *Linguistics 154/5*: 47-56.

Luria, A. R. (1976) *Basic Problems of Neurolinguistics.* The Hague: Mouton.

Mandler, G. and Worden, P. (1973) Semantic processing without permanent storage. *Journal of Experimental Psychology 100*: 277-83.

Marcel, T. (1980) Surface dyslexia and beginning reading: a revised hypothesis of the pronunciation of print and its impairments. In M. Coltheart, K. Patterson and J. C. Marshall (eds) *Deep Dyslexia.* London: Routledge & Kegan Paul.

Marslen-Wilson, W. D. (1980) Speech understanding as a psychological process. In J. C. Simon (ed.) *Spoken Language Generation and Understanding.* Dordrecht: D. Reidel.

Marslen-Wilson, W. D. and Welsh, A. (1978) Processing interactions and lexical access during word recognition in continuous speech. *Cognitive Psychology 10*: 29-63.

Mehler, J. (1963) Some effects of grammatical transformations on the recall of English sentences. *Journal of Verbal Learning and Verbal Behaviour 2*: 346-51.

Miceli, G. (1982) The processing of speech sounds in a patient with cortical auditory disorder. *Neuropsychologia 20*, 5-20.

Morton, J. and Patterson, K. (1980) A new attempt at an interpretation, or an attempt at a new interpretation. In M. Coltheart, K. Patterson and J. C. Marshall (eds) *Deep Dyslexia.* London: Routledge & Kegan Paul.

Moscovitch, M. (1979) Information processing and the cerebral hemispheres. In M. S. Gazzaniga (ed.) *Handbook of Behavioural Neurobiology.* Vol. II. New York: Plenum Press.

Navon, D. (1977) Forest before trees: the precedence of global features in visual perception. *Cognitive Psychology 9*: 353-83.

Newcombe, F. and Marshall, J. C. (1980) Transcoding and lexical stabilization in deep dyslexia. In M. Coltheart, K. Patterson and J. C. Marshall (eds) *Deep Dyslexia.* London: Routledge & Kegan Paul.

Patterson, K. E. (1979) What is right with 'deep' dyslexic patients? *Brain and Language 8*: 111-29.

Pick, A. (1931) *Aphasia*. Translated by Jason W. Brown (1973) London: Charles Thomas.

Porch, B. (1981) Therapy subsequent to the PICA. In R. Chapey (ed.) *Language Intervention Strategies in Adult Aphasia*. Baltimore: Williams & Wilkins.

Reich, S. S. and Cutting, J. C. (1981). Picture perception and abstract thought in schizophrenia. *Psychological Medicine 11*: 1-6.

Rips, L. J., Shoben, E. J. and Smith, E. E. (1973) Semantic distance and the verification of semantic relations. *Journal of Verbal Learning and Verbal Behaviour 12*: 1-20.

Sachs, J. (1967) Recognition memory for syntactic and semantic aspects of connected discourse. *Perception and Psychophysics 2*: 437-42.

Saffran, E. M. and Marin, O. S. M. (1977) Reading without phonology: evidence from aphasia. *Quarterly Journal of Experimental Psychology 29*: 515-25.

Saffran, E. M., Schwartz, M. F. and Marin, O. S. M. (1976) Semantic mechanisms in paralexia. *Brain and Language 3*: 255-65.

Saffran, E. M., Schwartz, M. F. and Marin, O. S. M. (1980) The word order problem in agrammatism. II. Production. *Brain and Language 10*: 263-80.

Saffran, E. M., Schwartz, M. F. and Marin, O. S. M. (1980) Evidence from aphasia: isolating the components of a production model. In B. Butterworth (ed.) *Language Production*. Vol. 1. London: Acadmic Press.

Salvatore, A. P. and Davis, K. D. (1979) Clinical treatment of auditory comprehension deficits in acute and chronic aphasic adults: an experimental analysis of within-message pause duration. In R. Brookshire (ed.) *Clinical Aphasiology 1979*. Minneapolis: BRK.

Schnitzer, M. L. (1978) Toward a neurolinguistic theory of language. *Brain and Language 6*: 342-61.

Scholes, R. J. (1978) Syntactic and lexical components of sentence comprehension. In A. Caramazza and E. Zurif (eds) *Language Acquisition and Language Breakdown*. Baltimore: Johns Hopkins.

Schwartz, M. F., Saffran, E. M. and Marin, O. S. M. (1980) The word-order problem in agrammatism. I. Comprehension. *Brain and Language 10*: 249-62.

Semenza, C., Denes, G., Lucchese, D. and Bisiacchi, P. (1980) Selective deficit of conceptual structures in aphasia: class versus thematic relations. *Brain and Language 10*: 243-8.

Shallice, T. (1981) Neurological impairment of cognitive processes. *British Medical Bulletin 37*: 187-92.

Shallice, T. and Butterworth, B. (1977) Short-term memory impairment and spontaneous speech. *Neuropsychologia 15*: 729-35.

Shallice, T. and Warrington, E. K. (1980) Single and multiple component central dyslexic syndromes. In M. Coltheart, K. Patterson and J. C. Marshall (eds) *Deep Dyslexia*. London: Routledge & Kegan Paul.

Shanon, B. (1978) Classification and identification in an aphasic patient. *Brain and Language 5*: 188-94.

Stanners, R. F. and Headley, D. B. (1972) Pupil size and instructional set in recognition and recall. *Psychophysiologia 9*: 505-11.

Swinney, D. A., Zurif, E. B. and Cutler, A. (1980) Effects of sentential stress and word class upon comprehension in Broca's aphasics. *Brain and Language 10*: 132-44.

Tsvetkova, L. S. (1975) The naming process and its impairment. In E. H. Lenneberg and E. Lenneberg (eds) *Foundations of Language Development*. Vol. 2. New York: Academic Press.

Tzortzis, C. and Albert, M. L. (1974) Impairment of memory for sequences in conduction aphasia. *Neuropsychologia 12*: 355-66.

Von Stockert, T. (1972) Recognition of syntactic structure in aphasic patients. *Cortex 8*: 323-34.

Wapner, W. and Gardner, H. (1979) A note on patterns of comprehension and recovery in global aphasia. *Journal of Speech and Hearing Research 22*: 765-72.

Warrington, E. K. and Shallice, T. (1969) The selective impairment of auditory verbal short-term memory. *Brain 92*: 885-96.

Wason, P. C. and Reich, S. S. (1979) A verbal illusion. *Quarterly Journal of Experimental Psychology 31*: 591-7.

Weidner, W. E. and Lasky, E. Z. (1976) The interaction of rate and complexity of stimulus on the performance of adult aphasic subjects. *Brain and Language 3*: 34-40.

Whitehouse, P. and Caramazza, A. (1978) Naming in aphasia: interacting effects of form and function. *Brain and Language 6*: 63-74.

Yamadori, A. (1981) Note: verbal perseveration in aphasia. *Neuropsychologia 19*: 591-4.

Zurif, E. B. and Caramazza, A. (1976) Psycholinguistic structures in aphasia. In H. Whitaker and H. A. Whitaker (eds) *Studies in Neurolinguistics*. Vol. 1. New York: Academic Press.

Zurif, E. B. (1980) Language mechanisms: a neuropsychological perspective. *American Scientist 68*: 305-11.

6 Studies of the deaf and the blind

Susanna Millar

Introduction

'There is nothing wrong with the blind except that they cannot see, and nothing wrong with the deaf except that they cannot hear'. This dictum of a blind headmaster is noteworthy, not because it says all that needs to be said, but because it indicates firmly the point from which research ought to start. Far from stating the obvious, the remark was made in irritation against a good deal of research on the blind and the deaf which regards them as 'special' populations, and proceeds by comparing them with 'normals' on all possible counts in the hope that this will establish the areas in which the blind and the deaf are 'deviant'. It may be doubted that this approach is particularly fruitful for understanding any handicap; for blindness and deafness it is certainly inadequate. The blind may well be more dependent and the deaf more socially isolated, but these are clearly secondary concomitants of loss of vision or hearing. Similarly, both the blind and the deaf tend to be retarded in reading, but the reasons for this are not at all the same. Differences, as such, between the blind or deaf and normally seeing and hearing people can tell us very little. Research questions and designs need to be geared to the important fact that vision and hearing are the major (distal) information-gathering systems. In principle, performance in conditions where either one or the other is absent ought to afford a unique insight into the role of that sensory system within the whole informational or cognitive frame that is needed to perceive, remember, think and act. In practice our knowledge is limited by methodological problems and by the fact that relatively few studies have been designed to answer questions raised by this approach. It should be stressed that far from conflicting, the practical aim to find means of compensating for handicaps which must be the primary consideration of research with blind or deaf people, and the theoretical aim to gain a better understanding of the role of the sense modalities in thinking, necessarily complement each other. Theoretical formulations that have no implication for actual behaviour are self-defeating. Equally, for interventions to be beneficial in practice, the implicit theories and beliefs on which they are inevitably based need to be made explicit and testable. A case in point is the practice, until quite recently, of discouraging sign language in young deaf children in the belief that this would foster their oral language and thinking, when in fact, it merely prevents them from gaining knowledge easily. Another example is that simply to press on with additional practice in reading without understanding precisely which subsidiary skill is the main stumbling block, is more likely to discourage the blind or deaf retarded reader than to get him to catch up. It is as important for adequate practical intervention as for theoretical description to unpack initial global questions, and to analyse the manner in which processing is affected by the absence of an informational channel. This is the orientation from which studies and findings will be discussed.

Questions and theories

The approach taken here comes under the umbrella of theories of information processing in the broad sense of that term. This means that technical definitions of information, in terms of probabilities of reducing uncertainty and rates of information transmission, are regarded as useful measures (e.g. Fitts and Posner, 1973), but the hypothesis that all sense modalities convey the same type of information is left open. The question whether, and if so in what way, vision or hearing convey unique inputs into the system is, of course, of major interest in the study of sensory handicap.

The common factor for viewpoints that come under the general heading of information-processing approaches is that models, concepts and (in principle, precise) measures are taken from communication engineering. Although originally designed for problems in telecommunication, it was soon recognized that the concepts could be useful in the biological sciences, including psychology (e.g. Yockley *et al.*, 1956). Questions of memory, perception, problem solving and thinking generally gained from the analogy of man as a processor and transmitter of information, with limited channel capacity, translating inputs into a suitable code, storing the information in memory, and retrieving it to produce the required output. The systems analysis used most commonly until the seventies was in terms of sequential stages of processing from input to output (e.g. Atkinson and Shiffrin, 1968). Information comes in via the senses, is briefly stored in sensory buffers from which it is lost, unless it can be read or translated into a limited capacity short-term store from which items are displaced by new items if they are not maintained by active attentional control processes (e.g. rehearsal), which also transfer the item to long-term memory. The important short-term control processes were tacitly or explicitly conceived as verbal in nature. The major difficulty for the deaf would thus be not merely an absence of verbal information through not hearing, but also difficulties with working memory. For the blind, the situation would be less drastic, so long as information about the world was given by verbal description.

Modifications in the 'bottom-up' models of information processing became necessary when it became clear that serial stage models did not adequately describe the interactive nature of processing within the system. Thus, so-called 'higher'-order information about what to expect, for instance, can influence early or peripheral processes of detection: the short-term store could no longer be regarded as entirely acoustic in nature, or as differing from the long-term store in not accepting semantic attributes; experimental estimates of sensory and short-term store durations differed in different paradigms; studies with choice reaction times to validate distinct information processing stages began to show that amount of practice, item repetition and the type of item being processed had to be taken into account; and the limits of attention as processing capacity could no longer be adequately described as pertaining to a single channel, or the system as passive (for review see Lachman *et al.*, 1979). Most of these issues had been controversial for some time.· But advances in computer technology have provided models for theories that can incorporate most of the apparently contradictory findings, as well as evidence from psycholinguistics and from other fields about cognitive aspects, such as knowledge of rules and knowledge of the world, without abandoning the view of man as a (this time active) processor of information, or the goal of precision in specifying models and measures. However, that goal is fairly distant as yet. The very flexibility of these models, in principle, makes it all the more important to find constraints within which they have to operate for particular issues. One way of doing this is to examine how far the evidence allows us to reject particular assumptions about the effects of the absence of vision and hearing. Most of these stem from hypotheses that have been held at various times. The questions arising from these assumptions will be discussed briefly below.

A theory which predicts the most pervasive cognitive deficit for the deaf is undoubtedly the somewhat simple-minded identification of oral language with thinking sometimes attributed to the early behaviourists. However, the view that internal (covert) speech is the vehicle of thinking in humans is implied in the views of Vygotzky (1962), Luria, (Luria and Yudovich, 1959) who considered speech as the 'second signal' system which regulates behaviour in the absence of external reinforcement, and Kendler (1959) who assumes that covert verbal responses mediate concept attainment and behaviour. Given that spoken language is severely impaired with hearing loss, and on the assumption that inner speech depends on internalizing overt speech (e.g. Vygotzky, 1962), concept attainment, problem solving and thinking should be severely impaired in the profoundly deaf. An opposing viewpoint (e.g. Piaget, 1960, 1962) is that thinking and language are distinct functions, and that thinking depends on the internalization of actions with regard to objects and events and the progressive abstraction of the internalized action schemata into logical operations. The question is thus apparently whether or not the deaf and dumb in not speaking are impaired cognitively. However, as will appear, answers to this question depend crucially on the distinction between language and oral speech.

The second question of importance for the deaf is, as suggested above, whether loss of hearing, and therefore loss of the acoustic and phonological features of speech, impairs 'working memory'. There is evidence against a sharp division into processing stages and totally separate memory stores definable by absolute time limits to describe the actual human cognitive system. But such categorization is useful for certain types of questions. It is important in psychology particularly to make a distinction between a 'metalanguage' which is useful for talking about or analysing certain types of behaviour, and models that are assumed to be isomorphic with structural elements of the system. The concept of a short-term or working memory as a shorthand for 'keeping in mind' or remembering in the short term a telephone number that we have just looked up, or some items of information that we need to solve a current problem, is extremely useful. Since there is ample evidence that acoustic and phonological features are used in this type of behaviour, it is perfectly legitimate, and even necessary, to ask whether the deaf perform less well, or remember less, or whether the same amount can be remembered by using visual, spatial or articulatory features of the input, and if so, what kinds of features these may be.

Questions of modality are given short shrift in many theories, particularly those intended to be implemented in computer programs (e.g. Anderson and Bower, 1973; Kintsch, 1974; Schank and Abelson, 1977). The assumption is that knowledge is represented by abstract 'propositions' and procedural rules for accessing them. Sensory modalities are totally irrelevant. The only possible prediction for sensory deprivation is that performance will be worse because less information is coming in. There has been considerable controversy as to whether 'representation' is in terms of propositions or images or both. But in fact, all such controversies are mis-conceived. The term 'proposition' refers to a *formal* description, not to an empirical fact (Millar, in press). It is part of the metalan-guage in which the total system is formally described. The term 'image', by contrast, refers to a reported experience, or to empirical findings of certain kinds, which means that the terms 'proposition' and 'image' do not belong to the same 'universe of discourse'. They are not at the same logical level of description, and thus cannot be alternatives. There is no *a priori* reason why different forms of peripheral information should not receive more or fewer transformations, or be organized or accessed by different routes. In principle, it should be possible to simulate effects of sense modalities on time, type of accessing routes, or even loci of information storage. If necessary, rules for such procedures could be built in as structural features or written into computer programs. Such simulation would not change the type of metalanguage in which the system is formally described. The modality question is whether people rely on acoustic, phonological, visual or tactual features in memory, and if so, whether and how this affects performance efficiency. This is an empirical question and an important one for the deaf.

Questions of modality are perhaps even more important for understanding blind performance. None of the theories mentioned so far predicts any deficit for the blind, except possibly the absence of a concept of colour, and a reduction in spatial information that the sighted have to guide their movements. Similar predictions follow from theories based on the 'unity' of the senses. Gibson (1969), for instance, assumes that there are 'amodal' features such as invariant intensity relations that have, according to the theory, no modality component, and are progressively detected with age and experience. Apart from a few, and by implication quite un-important, aspects of perception, like colour, the particular sense modality picking up the information is quite irrelevant, although there may be slight differences in the accuracy of discrimination. However, a number of researchers, particularly those concerned with studies for the blind (e.g. Hatwell, 1978; McKinney, 1964; Révész, 1950; Schlaegel, 1953; von Senden, 1960; Warren, 1977; Worchel, 1951) have suggested that without vision, spatial organization is not only poor, but different, and there is an added difficulty in integrating information from different sense modalities. The question thus seems to be first whether the blind are deficient or retarded in spatial notions, or organize space differently; and secondly whether they are less capable than the sighted of substituting information from one sense modality for the other.

A further question of importance for the blind is the use of information from modalities other than vision and hearing. Clearly, verbal instruction about spatial rules, even where this is given in sufficient detail, would be meaningless without concrete instances of what is meant by extent, direction, distance and angular turns. The question is whether touch and movement provide precisely the same inputs as does vision. The answer by theories assuming the unity of the senses would be decidedly in the affirmative. The answer by theories assuming separate sensory systems would also be positive, although they would posit the need for some translation mechanism into a common code. This code need not be verbal (e.g. a binary code would do), and contrary to common assumption, it is not necessary either to assume that such a common code needs to be learned, as it could be 'wired in' at almost any stage or locus in the system. In fact neither the notion of separateness nor of unity fit with what we know of the relation between sensory systems. At the physiological level there is an amazing amount of specialization both for receptors and in the cortical and subcortical systems, but there is also convergence at several levels. From the point of evolution it would make no sense to have elaborate specialized modality systems if they all provide exactly the same information except for some unimportant qualitative differences; nor would it be conceivable that animals would survive long if separate sense modalities all provided different information about an object. Even the same enemy might be conceived as many!

The view taken here is that the sense modalities should be regarded as providing complementary and converging information (Millar, 1981), and this means that no modality is crucial. The absence of information from one sensory system does not merely reduce the amount of imformation about a given topic, but also eliminates a specific form of selection and coding of the information. Hence, information converging on the same topic from another source has to be supplemented (usually deliberately) from yet another source. The notion of sensory systems as complementary and converging means of coding environmental information makes good sense of the evidence we have at present, to answer the questions considered above.

Methodological considerations

There are considerable difficulties in research with blind or deaf people, some of which are common to investigations of both types of handicap, and others that are specific. The most general of these is the need to find adequate control groups with which to compare performance. Measures of IQ depend on tests that have been standardized on different populations for the deaf or blind and for hearing and seeing people. Standardization populations for deaf or blind tests are likely, for instance, to include a larger proportion of people with brain damage (e.g. those whose handicap stems from brain injury). Thus, norms of tests for the 'special' populations may well be lower, and this could mean that a performance deficit on a critical task by a deaf or blind person who has the same IQ score as his control, may not actually be due to the task, but could stem from generally lower performance because the IQ score was an overestimate relative to the control. The opposite difficulty arises if the deaf or blind are matched with controls on norms that have been standardized on the general population. Thus, non-verbal scales standardized on general norms will be harder for the deaf than for the hearing, if only because task instruction is more difficult. Similarly, for blind children to achieve equal scores with controls on a verbal task may actually indicate higher potential, if only because they may have had less experience of the instance or context used to present a problem. In such cases, equal performance as the controls on the critical task would indicate that the handicapped had a higher potential than their controls.

Both age of onset and degree of residual sensory functioning are crucially important for interpreting findings on the blind or deaf. The percentages of deaf or blind who are congenitally totally handicapped are relatively very small (see Rapin, 1979), Nevertheless, in the last resort it is this population only which can give us answers to questions about the effects of total absence of a sense modality. For instance, even minimal light perception or early vision has some effects on responses to external stimuli (see below). A great many studies both on the deaf and the blind have been a little cavalier in reporting degrees of handicap or time of onset in the populations they have used, so that it is not always clear when discrepancies in findings are simply due to differences in the degree of handicap.

The fact that there are many sources which may confound results from studies on sensory handicap does not, of course, mean that there are no means of overcoming them. Probably the use of convergent methods, that is using several different paradigms to test the same hypothesis, is one of the best means of ensuring the outcomes can be replicated and interpreted unambiguously. If findings differ, on the other hand, this strategy has the advantage of drawing attention to confounding factors. It is also useful for many studies to concentrate on subjects who have no additional handicaps (e.g. severe mental retardation or known brain damage), and to compare performance on the criterion task with performance on other tasks that are formally similar to the criterion task except on the critical variable. Comparison on such tasks of the handicapped with non-handicapped subjects thus allows the controls not merely to be matched on IQ scores (see above), but also to be matched to the handicapped on current tasks, so that the critical variable of the criterion task is isolated. It is clear, however, that in all such studies the degree of residual hearing or vision must be taken into account. The effect of the degree of loss need not be direct. Minimal visual experience need not be sufficient to supply actual information about external spatial relations, but it may affect performance, nevertheless, by drawing the subject's attention to the use of external cues (Millar, 1979). Similarly for the deaf, degree of hearing loss is directly associated with clarity of speech. But this in turn affects the extent to which inner speech is used (Conrad, 1979). Degree of hearing loss is thus an important factor to control when inner speech is a critical variable. Another important control is to compare patterns of performance of handicapped and control groups on the critical and matching tasks at different ages. This is essential particularly to provide evidence for statements that are quite commonly made without such evidence, as to whether the handicapped are retarded, or perform differently on the criterion tasks.

Studies on the deaf

There can be no doubt at all that the most important and far-reaching effects of profound deafness from an early age are on understanding and producing language. In the past those who were born profoundly deaf, automatically became 'dumb' also. Having no speech input and no means of hearing themselves utter, made it virtually impossible for them to produce the kind of speech that normally surrounds the hearing child. The vocalizations which are common to all human babies at birth decline sharply in the deaf around six months of age, when the babbling of hearing children begins to take on some of the characteristics of speech sounds in their society (e.g. Mavilya, 1971). The deaf child thus grows up without oral language unless this is deliberately taught.

Oral methods are, of course, important for the deaf in order to communicate with hearing peers, and the methods of teaching are often extremely ingenious. Nevertheless, the majority of deaf with very severe hearing loss do not achieve intelligible speech (Furth, 1966), and the extent to which successful speech is achieved depends crucially on the amount of residual hearing. Comprehension of speech through lip-reading is also severely affected by hearing loss. The deaf are worse at interpreting mouthed information, although it is presented visually, than hearing controls whose auditory input is scrambled or absent for the experimental period (Conrad, 1979). The explanation turns on the question whether the profoundly deaf are impaired cognitively, and if so, what precisely that may mean.

Language and thinking in the deaf

The very extensive studies by Furth (1966) were undertaken to provide evidence for his conviction that intellectual functioning did not depend on verbal mediation; a conviction that was based partly on prior observation and partly on Piagetian theory, although he did not confine himself to Piaget-type tasks. Furth argued cogently that tests not only had to be non-verbal, but the experimenter also had to ensure that deaf subjects understood the instructions; otherwise failure might merely mean that subjects had not understood the task, rather than that they were unable to do so. Obvious though this may seem, neglect of this simple methodolgical principle, which is crucial for the deaf, vitiates a great deal of research with young children. For instance, Oléron and Herren (1961) found a lag of 6 years between deaf and hearing children on a Piagetian 'conservation' task although they used a pictorial method. Furth (1964) found a difference of less than 2 years. He ensured by prior training that the task was understood as well as by using a non-verbal method. Furth (1966) also reported that young deaf children did not understand the sign for 'more', which was crucial for this type of test. By the age of 10 their success rate was 95 per cent. The Piagetian conservation task is intended to test logical reasoning. The child is presented with an instance of a given concept (e.g. number, represented by rows of beads). The experimenter then produces some irrelevant change in the display. If the child uses logical reasoning he will disregard the irrelevant change in his answer about the number of items. The point argued by Furth, and many others since, was that failure on logical tasks did not necessarily imply lack of logical competence. The distinction is that made by Chomsky between 'competence' and 'performance': the deaf child could be logically competent, but his performance might be inferior for all sorts of irrelevant reasons, such as not understanding instructions or a crucial term, or even being more prone to attend to misleading perceptual cues.

There are now a host of studies which show that the age at which success on 'conservation' tasks is achieved varies widely with testing procedures and experimental conditions (e.g. Donaldson, 1978). However, it is important to question also whether we can necessarily infer 'competence' from success. The whole point of the conservation task is to produce a conflict between attributes that are crucial to a concept, and attributes that are often correlated with these in the perceptual situation, but which are irrelevant to the concept. Thus, length of a line of objects is irrelevant to the concept of number, while addition and subtraction are crucial, but in the concrete situation adding and subtracting are correlated with lengthening and shortening the physical extent of the line of objects. For Piaget the methodological issue is clear: success on logical tasks is not enough. The task must be so structured that it is impossible to arrive at the correct solution by other than logical means. It is for this reason that the child is put into a 'perceptually deceptive' situation where the normally correlated but irrelevant cues are unrelated. The perceptual 'deception' is crucial to the test of logic; otherwise the correct answer could be given on the basis of other than logical grounds. On Piagetian criteria, therefore, experimental conditions which reduce the potentially confusing perceptual cues bypass the issue of logic. There can be no doubt that making an error on a logical task implies that the result was not obtained by logical means, although *general* lack of logical competence cannot be inferred. Similarly, however, logical competence cannot be inferred from success on logical tasks unless correct solutions by non-logical means can be ruled out. Conservation tasks are thus not particularly good tests of cognitive competence; but detailed analysis of these tasks does clarify some common confusions about the issues involved in thinking and language.

In order to understand thinking by the deaf it is essential also to be quite clear that deficiency in concepts is not the same as deficiency in logic. The difference can again be illustrated by conservation tasks. These confound knowledge of concepts like number, mass, weight or volume with the 'ability to conserve'. The ability to conserve means no more and no less than to see that two identical statements are identical; that what is irrelevant is irrelevant; and that if nothing relevant has changed, nothing relevant has changed. To violate this would indeed be a violation of logic; but it is inconceivable that seeing such identity *can* be a matter of learning. There clearly is no such necessity about knowledge of concepts such as number, weight, mass and the like. No violation of a logical principle is involved if a child does not as yet know that length is irrelevant to number or shape to volume. But in that case the child does lack 'competence' with number, or whatever the concept is, in a very real sense. Such errors differ in kind from the 'performance' errors discussed in the earlier sections where the child knows what is crucial but fails to apply his knowledge for some reason. Obviously, since the concepts can be acquired, we must assume that children have the capacity to acquire them. But that does not mean that the child has to be born with the concept. A potential for acquisition is not equivalent to competence (for further discussion of this distinction, see section on the blind). The important point here is that the profound retardation reported of the deaf can probably not be attributed to 'performance' errors alone. The deaf child is also likely to lack important information about what are essential and what inessential attributes of various useful concepts like number, mass, weight and volume, since a great deal of knowledge of this kind is conveyed by language. In other words, he is likely lack conceptual competence in quite important areas. But logical competence, that is recognition of strict identity, cannot depend on hearing; it is a prerequisite rather than a result of learning.

Evidence has been reported that adult deaf subjects, at least, can perform logical and classification tasks that had previously been thought to depend crucially on verbal mediation (Furth, 1966). Given that only a minute proportion of the profoundly deaf arrive at oral language (Furth, 1971), this seems clear support for the independence of thinking and oral speech. But oral speech is not identical with language; it is merely one instance of it. This is not just a terminological quibble; it turns on the question of how deaf children code information from their remaining sensory modalities, particularly vision, and is probably most usefully studied in the context of short-term memory paradigms.

Working memory, inner speech, sign language and coding by the deaf

An important argument by Conrad (1979) is that it cannot be

assumed that the deaf automatically lack what is known as 'inner speech'. Designated variously as speech for oneself, or covert speech, the fact that people can and do talk to themselves when thinking has been documented by various types of evidence. Some of the most convincing evidence comes from electromyographical studies (e.g. Garrity, 1977), recording incipient lip and vocal tract movements during problem solving and memory tasks, and from paradigms comparing serial recall of lists of items with similar versus dissimilar sounding names (Conrad, 1963, 1965, Conrad and Hull, 1964). The assumption that the profoundly deaf do not have such inner speech stems mainly from Vygotsky's theory (1962) that inner speech as the vehicle of thinking develops progressively from overt speech. Overt speech develops into fully grammatical and enunciated social speech for communication with others on the one hand, and into elliptical, covert and shorthand speech for oneself, on the other. There can be no doubt that there is a close association between speech intelligibility and the degree of hearing loss (e.g. Fry, 1977), and this is so despite the enormous effort expended in attempting to teach oral language to the profoundly deaf. In fact, the association between deafness and internal speech as assessed by memory for phonologically confusable and non-confusable serial lists, is strikingly high also. But internal speech is not necessarily completely absent even in the profoundly deaf (Conrad, 1979), and covert 'oral' speech is not the only vehicle for thinking and memory, although it is an extremely important one, as will become obvious from the following short-term memory studies.

When deaf children are assessed on memory-span tests, experimenters clearly have to ensure that the presentation itself does not dictate the results. The presentation, therefore, is visual. The question is precisely how the deaf code this information.

Consider the theory that incoming information is first held in modality-specific stores for a very brief (millisecond) period of time, and is then lost unless it can be read into a verbal, mainly phonologically based, store and maintained by verbal rehearsal. On this theory a shorter span for the deaf would certainly be expected. Span deficits for the deaf have indeed been reported (e.g. Blair, 1957; Conrad and Rush, 1965; Wallace and Corballis, 1973), although other studies have not found this (e.g. Conrad, 1972; Thomassen, 1970). Conrad (1979) showed that the apparent contradiction can be resolved: when intelligence and degrees of deafness are held constant, the presence or absence of internal speech (sensitivity to phonological similarity) determines the size of recall spans. In other words, deaf children who showed internal speech recalled nearly as much as the hearing. Although this must, in the nature of the case, represent rather a small fraction of the profoundly congenitally deaf, it is an important corrective to the usual assumption. By itself, however, it does not alter the general model of a verbally based short-term or 'working' memory. The important questions are first, whether non-verbal, short-term coding occurs also, and if so whether this leads to smaller immediate memory spans; secondly, whether if non-verbal coding does lead to equal memory spans, it follows that it is linguistically or symbolically based; and finally, how inner speech is acquired by the profoundly deaf in the first place. The three questions will be discussed in reversed order below.

Myklebust (1964) and Dodd (1977) have argued that lip-reading, or using the visual input from the facial gestures of the speaker, could provide the deaf with the necessary linguistic input from which inner speech could be developed. Unfortunately, this seems to be a 'Catch 22' situation. Lip-reading is actually very difficult even when trained speakers are used. One reason is that 'visual speech' has few distinctive features. More important, perhaps, is that lip-reading itself is poor unless children already use a phonetic code. The difficulties in lip-reading thus reflect the general lack of verbal knowledge by the deaf (Conrad, 1977). It seems clear, however, that a phonological code need not be auditory; McGurk and McDonald (1976) and Dodd (1977) have shown that visual as well as auditory features of speech are picked up and affect what is heard by the listener. Opposing the visual and auditory features of speech results in distortion, rather than simply in the addition or omission of one or other of the features. This suggests that the input from the two modalities are complementary rather than separate and additive. In principle, it should be possible, therefore, for the congenitally profoundly deaf to pick up some aspects of oral language from being taught lip-reading, possibly together with redundant information from kinaesthetic and tactual cues from touching their own vocal chords while attempting to produce speech, and from other parameters of speech made visible to them. But lip-reading must be rather easier for those who have had language, and can, therefore, supplement the impoverished signals from vision alone by a knowledge of the rules and constraints of the particular language they used to hear. In other words, the route for the deaf in acquiring language is not only more cumbersome than for the hearing, it is also more indirect, and probably requires far more complementary and supplementary information, including knowledge of the rules, redundancies and probabilities of the given language. It is possible that the great concern with speech production by the deaf has overshadowed the amount of 'higher-order' knowledge that may be required to make the cues that the deaf can use more intelligible and, therefore, easier to perceive. A phonetic code without hearing is possible, but difficult to acquire.

The superiority in linguistic skills of deaf children of deaf parents who have had the advantage of learning sign language early has been known for some time (Schlesinger and Meadow, 1972). The concern with oral speech for the business of communicating with the hearing, and the doubt that manual languages had grammars and were thus 'languages' at all, has helped to perpetuate the belief that sign language was at best inferior to oral language, and at worst a hindrance to acquiring oral language. It is now recognized that there are a number of quite different sign languages (e.g. American sign language, finger spelling, Paget – Gorman sign system, British sign language), and that they are capable of semantic and syntactic sophistication comparable to oral languages, although they differ from these as well as from each other. The benefit of providing information for the deaf in sign language has been argued convincingly by Conrad (1979).

Perhaps the most exciting finding has been that 'inner' language can be other than acoustic. In fact, of course, it should not be surprising that articulatory and visual information about oral speech can be used to code phonologically. Nevertheless, inner language can evidently also be in terms of sign languages. This was shown by Bellugi, Klima and Siple (1974) since they found the deaf worse at serial recall of finger signs that shared common features. Locke and Locke (1971) provided further evidence. They divided deaf adolescents into two matched (on IQ score and age) groups on the basis of their speech intelligibility, and also had a hearing control group, although these were slightly younger. Locke and Locke used written recall of visually presented letter pairs; the letters in a pair were either similar phonologically or similar on a visual basis, or they were similar in terms of the finger-spelling signs. The rationale was similar to that of Conrad (e.g. 1963, 1965), but they also used the fact that items in a pair are recalled better if they share a feature. The basis of a subject's coding strategy can thus be inferred from better recall of such item pairs as well as from confusion errors. The interesting result was that the deaf, particularly those with unintelligible oral speech, recalled more pairs in which the letters had similar signs; their errors showed dactylic (finger-sign) confusions, and at least some of them were observed to overtly engage in finger spelling, evidently as a form of rehearsal. The hearing children, by contrast, mainly used phonological coding as assessed by these criteria. The deaf also relied more on visual features of letter pairs than did the hearing; the fact that the deaf do use visual features in memory also has been shown by Conrad and Rush (1965) and Conrad (1972), using Conrad's paradigm of recall for phonologically and visually confusable letter lists, respectively. The deaf, and particularly those with poor speech intelligibility, tended to be worse on the visually rather than on the phonologically confusable lists, while for the hearing the reverse was the case. It is clear, therefore, that the deaf, although not entirely precluded from phonological coding, can and often do rely on dactylic and visual codes in memory tasks.

Clearly, dactylic codes, whether based on finger spelling or other sign languages, are linguistic codes also, albeit not phonological in character. Since finger signs can be repeated, they could in principle be rehearsed as easily as name sounds and there is, thus, no particular reason to assume that memory based on sign coding should be less efficient than memory based on phonological coding as 'working' memory for other tasks. Conrad (1979) showed that memory span for the deaf was not different from that of the hearing when the ratio of using 'inner speech' is taken into account. Unfortunately, we have no similar evidence for inner language based on signing. It seems likely that familiarity with the material, and ease and speed of signing will have to be controlled if future studies are to provide us with this evidence. More intriguing, perhaps, is the relation of visual to phonological coding. Yik (1978) showed that both occurred in sequential recall of Chinese words by hearing Chinese speakers; so even for verbal material visual coding was almost as effective as phonological coding. Although it is less easy to demonstrate 'rehearsal' of visual codes, Posner (1967) showed that hearing subjects could maintain visuo-spatial information across delay without loss, unless interfering tasks were interpolated. There is thus no reason why visuo - spatial coding should be less efficient as a short-term memory code.

Given the evidence that memory for unrelated items for short periods of time does not depend crucially on verbal coding, we are on much surer ground in assuming that thinking and oral speech at least are not identical. We need not assume, either, that the deaf are necessarily impaired cognitively. Nevertheless, the profoundly congenitally deaf are usually severely handicapped in practice, as will be obvious from the findings on reading attainment. Hearing is not a necessary condition for the acquisition of language or its use in thinking; but in its absence the path to language skills is more circuitous and cumbersome.

Reading in the deaf

Reading, of course, requires a host of subsidiary skills, and these are usually taken for granted if there is no retardation. Nevertheless, it is clear that linguistic skills must be essential. In the context of education this means oral language. For the deaf child to acquire this requires very special teaching methods. However, despite the emphasis on oral language learning, the fact is that the deaf tend to be grossly deficient in linguistic skills (Conrad, 1979; Furth, 1971; Rapin, 1979). It is not perhaps surprising, therefore, that they are also grossly retarded in reading and in scholastic attainments that depend on reading and reading comprehension (Rapin, 1979). Conrad (1979) showed that both intelligence and the ability to use internal speech predict reading scores better than the degree of deafness alone. The ability to code in sounds has been shown to be an important factor in the reading skills of hearing children also (e.g. Liberman *et al.*, 1977). Clearly, those who cannot distinguish sounds, but first have to be taught phonological distinctions via visual, tactual and kinaesthetic paths will have much greater difficulty in learning the grapheme - phoneme correspondences, and rules which need to be used in decoding unfamiliar words from visual letter strings on the page. The duller deaf child is likely to lose out on both counts. However, most current models of reading (e.g. Coltheart, *et al.*, 1980) also assume that reading comprehension need not proceed from the visual letter via phonological re-coding to the 'internal lexicon' which gives meaning to the sounds, but that the route from visual strings on the page to the internal lexicon can also be direct. The further problem with this is that the deaf child's vocabulary, and consequently his internal lexicon, is also extremely impoverished. If reading comprehension is to be established so that it can lead to further knowledge, it is probably necessary to develop the deaf child's sign language, and to provide him with an adequate internal lexicon through teaching in terms of sign language also, rather than to restrict him to learning oral language (Conrad, 1979).

Information from hearing is neither necessary nor sufficient for logical thinking, working memory or for the acquisition and use of language, and language-based skills like reading. But the process of effectively substituting this information through other channels requires far more knowledge than we have at present. What the evidence we have does suggest is that in re-routeing the necessary information we need to concentrate far more on so-called 'top-down' effects, by supplying information and knowledge that can aid the discrimination of features via the other modalities, rather than by pegging away solely at improving oral discrimination.

Studies on the blind

The handicap produced by lack of vision is at the same time more immediately obvious than that of the deaf, but also possibly even less well understood. It is obvious that young blind babies cannot orient properly to objects, and detailed observations on delay in crawling, walking and other (normally) visually guided behaviours have been reported (Fraiberg, 1977). Beyond this, however, educators and researchers seem to have been, if anything, more concerned with the emotional, social and language development of the blind, than with the development of spatial notions. Until very recently, at any rate, it has certainly not been part of the normal school curriculum to provide systematic instruction on spatial relations. Even special 'mobility' training is not generally geared to this, but turns on attention to possible guiding cues and kinaesthetic or sound 'landmarks'. The reason for this neglect is that people assume either that the blind are incapable of developing adequate spatial concepts, or that they develop the same spatial notions as the sighted automatically without any special tuition, provided they are given enough 'experience' in the form of encounters with the environment. This form of dichotomous thinking is quite useless both as far as practical help is concerned, and even more for an adequate formulation of what is involved in loss of vision. Intuitively, the link of vision with notions of space and imagery is as immediate as that of hearing with language. In order to analyse how this link works in fact, the evidence from the blind will be reviewed first in terms of the question of imagery, spatial competence and representation.

Spatial concepts and representation in the blind

There is a need for an explicit distinction between the notion of 'capacity' and the notion of 'competence', as well as 'performance' in studying handicaps. The idea that task failure or inefficiency may be due to irrelevant 'performance' factors rather than to a lack of 'competence' has been used a great deal since its introduction by Chomsky, and in all sorts of contexts. So much so, indeed, that the notion of 'competence' from being quite precise, has come to mean anything from complete knowledge of the information required for a task as well as complete skill to carry it out in favourable circumstances, to the most minimal form of a disposition to acquire the knowledge or skill in question. But clearly, it is quite a different matter when a person fails to recall, say, the name of one of the American States because he has some temporary blockage, or the name is inaccessible for some reason, from when he fails to recall the name because he had never learned it in the first place. The distinction urged here is between 'competence' in the sense of being fully qualified, and 'capacity' in the sense of having the potential for the skill in question. It applies to knowing how to do something (sometimes called 'procedural' knowledge) as well as to knowing that something is the case (knowledge of the world). It also cuts across the usual distinction between innate and acquired skills. The human infant is genetically programmed for knowing who won the Derby as well as for walking and talking, in a way in which even the best earthworm is not. Similarly, the human infant's capacity to acquire spatial notions is likely to differ from that of the earthworm; but this does not necessarily have to imply that spatial concepts are innate. It will be argued that the distinction between capacity and competence explains some apparently contradictory results on spatial skills in the blind.

Leonard and Newman (1967) used a spatial inference task in order to test whether spatial thinking in the blind is necessarily impaired. Such tasks consist in familiarizing subjects with paths between A and

B in either direction, and between B and C in either direction, and then requiring them to indicate the direct path from A to C. Leonard and Newman's subjects were six intelligent, adolescent grammar school boys, five of whom were blind from birth, although not all were totally blind. The task was to infer detours between points on a tactual map after being acquainted with other routes between these points. Most subjects solved the problem on the map, and were then able to walk the new path also. Leonard concluded that visual experience was not a necessary condition for spatial thinking. Perhaps even more impressive is the two-and-a-half-year-old congenitally totally blind child who apparently solved a spatial inference problem in large-scale space (Landau et al., 1981). However, exciting though this is, this evidence is somewhat marred by the strong probability that sound cues were not excluded. The authors report that 'Kelli did not move ballistically towards the target. Instead, she seemed to adjust her movements as she went'. This type of adjustment, evident also from the reported paths Kelli took, is very like the evidence for updating of information on the introduction of extraneous and irrelevant noise cues which the present author found in studies with young blind children. It is not the path predicted if Kelli had had innate knowledge of the geometric principles that underlie spatial knowledge as Landau et al. wish to argue. There can be no doubt from Leonard's (1967) study that vision is not necessary for solving spatial problems. Indeed, to establish this it would be sufficient to show that a single, congenitally totally blind person can perform adequately on spatial problems. However, to say that the blind have the capacity to detect spatial relations does not in the least mean that they necessarily have, or even acquire adequate spatial concepts, or are necessarily spatially 'competent' in the sense of the term used here. If anything more than 'capacity' (potential) is meant by the assumption that 'geometric principles are innate', this is sufficiently counter-indicated by the careful studies on blind adults conducted by Worchel (e.g. Rouse and Worchel, 1955). These studies showed that his subjects had great difficulty with spatial inference (re-location) tasks, but there was no suggestion that his blind adults were incapable of deductive inference on any other type of material. Similarly, the careful training programme devised by Cratty and Sams (1968) to teach blind children adequate notions of their bodily relations would hardly be required. A simple Socratic method eliciting from the blind child the knowledge of spatial relations or of geometric principles he has already, would be all that was needed if such principles were innate. But intensive spatial training is most certainly necessary for congenitally totally blind children (Cratty, 1971; Hatwell, 1978; Warren, 1977), while the sighted need no special training to arrive at adequate spatial concepts. Vision is not a necessary condition for these; but it provides important information which has to be supplied by a much more circuitous route in its absence.

The second question of interest in considering the spatial thinking of the blind is their means of 'representing' spatial knowledge. For some psychologists 'spatial' and 'visual' coding are synonymous, and the notion of imagery carries implicitly the connotation of visual imagery, homologous – if possibly less strong or distinctive – with eidetic imagery. Others have argued that representation of knowledge is always 'abstract', or 'amodal' in nature. A great deal of this type of controversy actually centres on quite different uses of the term 'representation', and it was argued (see above) that the interesting empirical question has to be analysed in terms of informational coding. A literal interpretation of the term, however, refers to actual maps, models or representations as drawings. Some years ago the present author conducted a study with blindfolded sighted children matched to blind children, none of whom had ever drawn pictures before, or even, in many cases, held a pencil or pen for drawing (Millar, 1975a). The blind, particularly the congenitally totally blind, mainly produced scribbles before the age of about 10, but after that the type of schema they drew to represent a figure did not differ essentially from the schemata produced by the blindfolded sighted. What differed most was the placement of the figure: the sighted aligned the figure with the side of the page as would be expected for the conventional 'upright' figure in drawing, while placement on the page by the blind was essentially random. The floor or ground was indicated as being 'underneath', thus suggesting that these children had not yet come across the convention in question. It is not possible to infer the manner of internal representation from drawings (Kosslyn et al., 1977), and the findings on the blind allow us to state only that the blind are perfectly capable of the kind of external representation demanded by drawing. What the first drawings by congenitally totally blind children do show is that they produced shapes on the page to symbolize, rather than to picture, a given three-dimensional object or body-part. Further-more, blind children do not really seem to differ in this from the sighted.

The coding of spatial information by blind children and sighted children

A paradigm which has been used a great deal to assess spatial coding is the mental rotation or 'perspective' task. In this the subject is presented with some sort of spatial array, and has to indicate what the array would look like from an orientation that differs from the subject's own current or previous position. Shepard and Metzler (1971) obtained a linear increase in reaction time with increased angular rotation of a form relative to another for judgements whether the forms were identical or not. The finding is consistent with the notion that subjects used visual imagery to unravel the differences in rotation; but it does not necessitate this assumption. The present author tested the role of visual experience in mental rotation tasks (Millar, 1976). Blind children and blindfolded sighted children judged the orientation of a straight line indented in a rectangular frame. Subjects first felt the line from a 'home' position, and the frame was then rotated so that subjects could follow the rotation of the frame to different test positions by touch. In a second task the frame remained stationary and subjects walked around it from the 'home' position to each test position. After rotation subjects drew the orientation of the line to the given test position. I argued that visual experience was more likely to lead to map-like strategies. This would mean that the line was imaged relative to the frame. The strategy was not necessarily accurate, but the degree of error in orienting the line should have been much the same from any of the test positions on the frame. The blind, on the other hand, would have had to rely on memory of the movement sequence during rotation. On this strategy, orientation errors would have been significantly worse for the test position requiring the longest sequence of rotation, and for test positions from which the line appeared in oblique orientations, since these required a dual reference. The results were consistent with the predicted difference in strategy between the blind and the sighted, suggesting that the sighted used map-like strategies more, while the blind tended to code in terms of movement sequences.

The assumption of differential coding between the blind and the sighted was borne out by another task. The present author tested blind children and blindfolded sighted children on forward and backward recall of spatial locations on a five-sided figure which subjects traced with a stylus (Millar, 1975b). The figure was presented in four (unpredictable) orientations so that the locations had to be remembered either in relation to the spatial (imaged) lay-out of the figure, or in relation to the movement sequence in acquisition. The blind were very poor at backward recall, parti-cularly of the first location, which was the longest distance (and took the longest time) from input to recall, as would be expected on the hypothesis that they coded locations relative to the movement sequence. The sighted were, if anything, actually better on backward than forward recall, consistent with the assumption that they constructed some form of mental 'map' of the figure when they had come to the stopping point after presentation. In other words, blind children and sighted children tend to differ in the way in which they code the information that is available to them. This can, and often does, have consequences on solving specific spatial tasks, but does not mean that blindness impairs the ability (capacity) to solve spatial problems, in principle.

Not all rotation tasks produce differences between the blind and the sighted, and there are two reasons for this. First, a number of tasks that formally involve rotation of a figure can, in fact, be solved by discriminating a prominent feature (e.g. smooth versus jagged sides) and actually rotating the pieces so that the prominent features tally. There is no reason why the blind should be worse at this sort of task, on any hypothesis. The task reported by Marmor and Zabeck (1976), for instance, falls into this category. Secondly, mental-rotation tasks do not necessarily depend on visual imagery, but can be solved by using knowledge of rules (e.g. Flavell *et al.*, 1978) and inferences that allow a subject to update information about his present position. For instance, information about items that are currently on the left and right, knowledge of the rule that 180° rotations reverse left – right relations, and that such a rotation is taking place, should be sufficient to solve that type of rotation problem without the need to 'image' anything. Such strategies should be quite as efficient as, or even more accurate than coding directions in terms of imaged spatial relations. At the same time they would require knowledge of the rules, and quite complex processing of all the relevant information. This could explain the fact that adequate solutions of spatial inference and mental rotation (including detour) tasks are more often reported for intelligent adolescent and adult blind subjects (e.g. Leonard and Newman, 1967); while at earlier ages such problems produce very large differences between the congenitally totally blind and blindfolded sighted children (Gomulicki, 1961; Millar, 1981b).

Another important means of coding the location of objects is to use one's own body for spatial reference. For instance, if the light switch on your desk is on your right when sitting at your desk, it is quite sufficient to remember the relation of your hand position to your body midline to reach it, even in the dark. However, such self-referent coding is not useful if you must turn around; what is on the right at entrance is on your left on the way out. Errors of reversal after 180° rotation without vision suggest coding by reference to bodily cues. This does not mean that self-referent strategies can be inferred from all errors in mental rotation. Mental-rotation tasks involve a greater memory load than non-rotation tasks, since the original position has to be remembered. Poor memory rather than self-referent coding could thus cause more errors. The important criterion is the proportion of reversals when there is no fixed external cue that could produce a similar result. By no means all studies showing worse rotation by the blind have reported this evidence. But there can be no doubt, even on this more stringent criterion, that blind children use their own bodies to provide spatial reference far more than do blindfolded sighted children (Millar, 1981b). On Piagetian theory (Piaget and Inhelder, 1948) this would be explained by a delay in spatial development. The assumption is that there is an invariant progression from the use of 'ego-centric' (body-centred) cues by young children, to coding locations by reference to objective external, vertical and horizontal axes (as in the Euclidean co-ordinate systems) by adolescents. However, the notion of 'ego-centrism' confounds self-referent coding with the coding of movements or movement sequences. In fact, using the body as a means of spatial reference can be distinguished experimentally from remembering the movement made in locating a given object (Millar, 1981b). Furthermore, Piaget's theory predicts a statistical interaction between sightedness and age. This interaction was not found either in studies with mental rotation (Miller, 1981b), or in the results for a much simpler 'shift' task that distinguished between the use of external cues and coding in terms of movement or self-reference (Millar, 1979). Young sighted children made a great many mistakes in shifting objects (blind) from specific locations on one background shape to the same locations on an identical shape next to it in either horizontal or vertical directions. But their mistakes related to the difficulty of the background locations, showing that they had used an external cue as reference, whereas errors by the congenitally totally blind varied with the type of movement shift that had to be executed, although the blind were considerably older. Moreover, the shift task did not use rotation, or impose a memory load. This means that the difference in coding between the blind and sighted is not confined to difficult mental tasks.

Révész (1950) seems to have been quite correct in suggesting that the blind code information relative to their own bodies because they derive their spatial notions from haptic (touch and movement) information. However, his suggestion that they do not understand external spatial co-ordinates needs qualification. First, visual experience is not a necessary prerequisite for solving Euclidean problems (see above). Moreover, using a body-part or one's body midline as an anchor or reference in relation to which locations can be coded, is a strategy needed by all moving animals, including man, in order to relate the location of body-parts to each other. Nevertheless, for the sighted external spatial frames are important in orienting themselves from an early age (e.g. Lee and Aronson, 1974). For the blind, by contrast, there is little consistent or reliable feedback from external sources, and consequently little reason for them to believe that external references would be particularly useful. The manner in which information is coded thus depends not only on the current mode of input, but also on longer-term experience. In both cases subjects need to have knowledge of external spatial relations, and must be able to retrieve this knowledge for current use. But the choice of strategies also depends on knowledge of procedures that have paid off in the past.

From the evidence reviewed above it is clear that information for spatial tasks that is presented through movements (kinaesthetically) can be coded in a variety of ways. The choice of code depends on, among other things, its ease or difficulty in a given situation. For instance, blindfolded sighted, as well as blind children, code information from the movement made in locating an object (Millar, 1981b). It is only when it is obvious from the task that such easy strategies are inappropriate that the sighted use map-like coding in blindfold conditions. Cognitive maps do, after all, require retrieval of past information as well as the recoding of kinaesthetic information. It is not surprising, therefore, that such strategies by the sighted are found mainly when neither self-referent nor movement coding are very useful (e.g. Millar, 1975b). When the tasks involve judgements of movement extent rather than direction, so that spatial coding is neither disrupted nor essential (e.g. rhythmic counting can be used), the blind and sighted do not differ. But processing characteristics do change, with repetition of the input and responses (Millar, 1977a).

Vision seems to have three major advantages over movements for spatial coding. First, it elicits attention to external (beyond reach) cues. Thus, blind children who have had even minimal visual experience either in infancy or through light perception, tend to use background shape (external) cues for reference when the congenitally totally blind code in terms of movements, although the blindfolded sighted achieve accuracy with such reference much earlier (Millar, 1979). Secondly, vision provides experience of the manner in which external locations and directions relate to each other, and such knowledge is difficult to derive from blind kinaesthetic experience without special teaching. Thirdly, it provides reliable information and feedback about the use of external references. For the blind, kinaesthetic and movement information is reliable about directions only within personal space. It is, therefore, quite reasonable that self-referent and movement coding should become preferred strategies for the blind. In principle, the missing information can be supplied by other routes; but in practice, we are still far from knowing precisely what information needs to be supplied or how preferred strategies can be changed, so that many totally congenitally blind children still fall considerably short of attaining adequate spatial notions.

Tactual coding, spatial reference and reading by the blind

The difference between information in visual and in blind conditions is least obvious, but perhaps most instructive, for shape recognition. Given that mental reference to external co-ordinates is hardly required for this, differences between the blind and the blindfolded sighted should not be expected, and are not found (for brief review see Millar, 1981a). Nevertheless, shape recognition presents a serious problem in the early stages of blind reading. It is, of course, well known that tactual shape recognition is inferior to visual recognition (e.g. Goodnow, 1971; Millar, 1971), but the reasons for this have not always been very clear.

Two main explanations have been favoured for poor tactual shape recognition. One is that the tactual short-term store has poor retention characteristics, fading quickly with delay and having little access to attentional capacity (e.g. Goodnow, 1971; Gilson and Baddeley, 1969). The other is that tactual discrimination is poor, so that it operates like 'blurred' vision (e.g. Apkarian-Stielau and Loomis, 1975). Recent evidence suggests that neither of these accounts is adequate, at any rate for Braille shapes and other raised-dot patterns (Millar, 1981a). First, interference paradigms which compare retention after unfilled delay with delays filled with tasks that demand processing capacity, have shown that tactual information is sensitive to interference provided there is sufficient repetition and practice of the forms (Millar, 1974). Poor retention, shown by small recall spans and deterioration with delay (Millar, 1975c, 1978a), is indeed characteristic of memory for tactual inputs, unless they are quickly recoded into verbal form. But the reason for poor retention is not that the inputs are tactual, nor that they are poorly discriminated, but that tactual inputs are not spatially organized as easily as the same inputs in vision. Thus, specific tactual coding can be demonstrated by paradigms using tactually similar versus dissimilar and phonologically similar lists of items (Millar, 1975c), and by 'same' – 'different' judgements of letter pairs that are either identical on all counts, or differ solely in physical tactual features (Millar, 1977b), not in name or shape. The following findings show that despite quite accurate discrimination, these features are not necessarily organized spatially, let alone in global form:

(1) generalization to enlarged shapes is often difficult (Millar, 1977b); (2) the density of dots rather than their spatial relations or symmetry in a pattern determines recognition accuracy (Millar, 1978b); (3) blindfolded sighted children who have learned to name some Braille letters cannot draw their shapes (Millar, 1977c); (4) the usual advantage of matching identical versus different shapes is not found for tactual dot patterns; (5) the left hand (right

'spatial' hemisphere) is not necessarily better in the early stages of actual recognition (Millar, 1977c, 1981a).

Indeed which is the 'better' hand seems to be determined by the number of years subjects have spent on Braille reading (Fertsch, 1947). Early in learning there seems to be no hand advantage, suggesting tactual coding which is not yet spatially organized; later in learning left-hand (right-hemisphere) superiority is likely to be found, suggesting spatial coding; while really fast and proficient Braille readers seem to use the right hand more effectively (Fertsch, 1947), suggesting that they rely on fast verbal (left-hemisphere) codes.

In vision the Braille characters that are derived from two by three raised-dot matrices make very simple global shapes. The fact that they are not coded as such by touch very easily is actually perfectly intelligible. In blind conditions there are no spatial references which could determine the dot position; unless the pattern has already been recognized, the small, unsystematic exploratory movements cannot provide this either, in the absence of prominent features. The position is further complicated by the fact that although Braille letters are 'upright' in orientation, the Perkins Brailler which is now mainly used for writing has a horizontally arranged keyboard for the relevant dot combinations. Braille is difficult for many reasons, including lack of redundancy in the system, multiple meanings for the same characters, and so on (see Foulke, 1979). But many people never actually get beyond the initial difficulty of recognizing the shapes tactually, and it represents a considerable hurdle for the young, blind beginning reader. Retardation is thus quite common, but for quite different reasons from those retarding the deaf.

The evidence from touch again shows that information presented via tactual channels may be coded in a number of quite different forms: by physical tactual features that may not be organized spatially, as well as in spatially organized or shape form, or by verbal features (name). Which form of coding is chosen seems to depend on how quickly and easily it is available to a subject. Thus, fast naming is associated with phonological coding (Millar, 1975c; 1978a), while spatial coding is less easy by touch than vision, where reference information is more easily available.

Conclusion

Hearing is not necessary for the acquisition of language, and vision is not necessary for the acquisition of spatial competence. Nevertheless, absence from birth of information from either of these channels has profound and quite specific effects. Most obvious of these is the absence or severe reduction of knowledge that is normally acquired via the channel in question. Lack of hearing affects linguistic and semantic knowledge. In the case of vision the main effect is on knowledge of relations between external locations and directions. Given the distinction between capacity and competence, it is clear that such knowledge can be absorbed and used, provided we can find adequate means of imparting it.

However, there are also more subtle effects from the absence of sound and sight on the means of coding information. The auditory system is not unique in providing phonological features; phonological coding can also be derived from visual and kinaesthetic information. But the auditory system makes a large contribution. Similarly, spatial configurations are more easily, although not uniquely, derived from visual inputs than from touch and movement. Children, at least, prefer codes that they can access easily. Signing by the deaf, and movement and self-referent coding by the blind are obviously useful for mediating performance in many tasks. It is tasks for which such codes are not appropriate that differentiate performance by the deaf or blind from their hearing or seeing peers.

For models of how information is processed, there are several implications from studies of the deaf and the blind. First, sequential stage theories are obviously inadequate. The findings show that knowledge acquired from a variety of sources is particularly important for interpreting inputs from systems that are not the normal channel for given information. It is not possible simply to substitute one sensory channel for another; vision does not improve with loss of hearing or vice versa. 'Higher-order' knowledge is necessary for adequate 'lower-order' perception in these cases. For instance, the deaf must already have a good knowledge of spoken language in order to benefit from, or even to learn lip-reading. Another example is the fact that quite simple dot patterns are not recognized as shapes by touch early in learning. Similarly, the blind need prior knowledge of external spatial relations, or at least knowledge of reversal rules in order to perceive kinaesthetic inputs as information about external space rather than in terms of personal space or movement sequences. Processing is, therefore, not an invariant sequence of stages from 'lower-order' or peripheral sensory input to 'higher-order' or central organization. Theories have to incorporate the integration of information from all parts of the system in their descriptions. Secondly, the modality of input is not irrelevant to processing; although the modality of input does not uniquely determine the form of coding. In principle, coding derived from different modalities can be used interchangeably and flexibly, but this does not make coding 'amodal'. A figure can be felt and danced as well as viewed, but the form of coding can be remembered as well as its content, and can have effects on the ease of acquistion and use. There is no reason why the same level of efficiency should not be attained by alternative routes and modes of coding. Nevertheless, these do take longer in acquisition. Modes of coding and representation thus need to be included also in models of information processing if these are to describe processing adequately when a major input channel is missing.

Note

The work on the blind discussed in this chapter was supported by a grant to the author from the Social Science Research Council.

References

Anderson, J. R. and Bower, G. H. (1973) *Human Associative Memory*. Washington, DC: Winston.
Apkarian-Stielau, P. and Loomis, T. H. (1975) A comparison of tactile and blurred visual form perception. *Perception and Psychophysics 18*: 362–8.
Atkinson, R. C. and Shiffrin, R. M. (1968) Human memory: a propsed system and its control processes. In K. W. Spence and J. T. Spence (eds) *The Psychology of Learning and Motivation* Vol. 2.
Bellugi, U., Klima, E. S. and Siple, P. (1974) Remembering in signs. *Cognition 3*: 93–125.
Blair, F. X. (1957) A study of the visual memory of deaf and hearing children. *American Annals of the Deaf 102*: 254–63.
Coltheart, M., Patterson, K. and Marshall, J. C. (eds) (1980) *Deep Dyslexia*. London: Routledge & Kegan Paul.
Conrad R. (1963) Acoustic confusions and memory span for words. *Nature 197*: 1029–30.

Conrad, R. (1965) The role of the nature of the material in verbal learning. *Acta Psychologica* 24: 244-52.

Conrad, R. (1972) Short-term memory in the deaf: a test for speech coding. *British Journal of Psychology* 63: 173-80.

Conrad, R. (1977) Lip-reading by the deaf and hearing children. *British Journal of Educational Psychology* 47: 60-5.

Conrad, R. (1979) *The Deaf Schoolchild*. London: Harper & Row.

Conrad, R. and Hull, A. J. (1964) Information, acoustic confusions and memory span. *British Journal of Psychology* 55: 429-32.

Conrad, R. and Rush, M. L. (1965) On the nature of short-term memory encoding by the deaf. *Journal of Speech and Hearing Disorders* 30: 336-43.

Cratty, B. J. (1971) *Movement and Spatial Awareness in Blind Children and Youth*. Springfield, Ill.: Charles Thomas.

Cratty, B. J. and Sams, T. A. (1968) *The Body-image of Blind Children*. New York: American Foundation for the Blind.

Dodd, B. (1977) The role of vision in the perception of speech. *Perception* 6: 31-40.

Donaldson, M. (1978) *Children's Minds*. London: Fontana.

Fertsch, P. (1947) Hand dominance in reading Braille. *American Journal of Psychology* 60: 355-49.

Fitts, P. M. and Posner, M. (1973) *Human Performance* London: Prentice Hall International Inc.

Flavell, T., O'Manson, R. C. and Latham, C. (1978) Solving perspective-taking problems by rule versus computation. *Developmental Psychology* 14: 462-73.

Foulke, E. (1979) Investigative approaches in the study of Braille reading. *Journal of Visual Impairment and Blindness*, October.

Fraiberg, S. (1977) *Insights from the Blind: Comparative Studies of Blind and Sighted Infants*. New York: Basic Books.

Fry, D. (1977) *Homo Loquens*. Cambridge: Cambridge University Press.

Furth, F. G. (1964) Conservation of weight in deaf and hearing children. *Child Development* 35: 143-50.

Furth, H. G. (1966) *Thinking without Language* New York: Free Press.

Furth, H. G. (1971) Linguistic deficiency and thinking: research with deaf subjects. *Psychological Bulletin* 76: 58-72.

Garrity, L. I. (1977) Electromyography: a review of the current status of subvocal speech research. *Memory and Cognition* 5: 615-22.

Gibson, E. J. (1969) *Principles of Perceptual Learning and Development*. New York: Appleton-Century-Crofts.

Gilson, E. Q. and Baddeley, A. D. (1969) Tactile short-term memory. *Quarterly Journal of Experimental Psychology* 21: 180-9.

Gomulicki, B. R. (1961) *The Development of Perception and Learning in Blind Children*. Private Publication from the Psychological Laboratory, Cambridge University.

Goodnow, J. J. (1971) Eye and hand. Differential memory and its effect on matching. *Neuropsychologica* 42: 1187-201.

Hatwell, Y. (1978) Form perception and related issues in blind humans. In

R. Held, H. W. Leibowitz and H. L. Teuber (eds) *Handbook of Sensory Physiology* Vol. 8. Berlin: Springer Verlag.

Kendler, T. S. and Kendler, H. H. (1959) Reversal and non-reversal shifts in kindergarten children. *Journal of Experimental Psychology 58*: 56-60.

Kintsch, W. (1974) *The Representation of Meaning in Memory*. Hillsdale, NJ: Lawrence Erlbaum Associates.

Kosslyn, S. M., Heldmeyer, K. H. and Locklear, E. P. (1977) Children's drawings as data about internal representations. *Journal of Experimental Child Psychology 23*: 191-211.

Lachman, R. R., Lachman, J. L. and Butterfield, E. C. (1979) *Cognitive Psychology and Information Processing: An Introduction*. London: Wiley.

Landau, B. Gleitman, H. and Spelke, E. (1981) Spatial knowledge and geometric representation in a child blind from birth. *Science 213*: 1275-7.

Lee, D. N. and Aronson, E. (1974) Visual proprioceptive control of standing in human infants. *Perception and Psychophysics 15*: 529-32.

Leonard, J. A. and Newman, R. C. (1967) Spatial O orientation in the blind. *Nature 215*: 1413-14.

Liberman, I. Y., Shankweiler, D., Liberman, A. M., Fowler, C. and Fischer, F. W. (1977) Phonetic segmentation and recoding in the beginning reader. In A. S. Reber and D. Scarborough (eds) *Towards a Psychology of Reading*. Hillsdale, NJ: Lawrence Erlbaum Associates.

Locke, J. L. and Locke, V. L. (1971) Deaf children's phonetic, visual and dactylic coding in a graphemic recall task. *Journal of Experimental Psychology 89*: 142-6.

Luria, A. R. and Yudovich, F. I. (1959) *Speech and the Development of Mental Processes in the Child*. London: Staples Press.

McGurk, H. and McDonald, J. (1976) Hearing lips and seeing voices. *Nature 264*: 746-8.

McKinney, J. R. (1964) Handschema in children. *Psychonomic Science 1*: 99-100.

Marmor G. S. and Zaback, L. A. (1976) Mental rotation by the blind: does mental rotation depend on visual imagery? *Journal of Experimental Psychology: Human Perception and Performance 2*: 515-21.

Mavilya, M. (1971) Spontaneous vocalization in hearing impaired infants. *Proceedings of the International Congress on Education of the Deaf*, Stockholm.

Millar, S. (1971) Visual and haptic cue utilization by preschool children: the recognition of visual and haptic stimuli presented separately and together. *Journal of Experimental Child Psychology 12*: 88-94.

Millar, S. (1974) Tactile short-term memory by blind and sighted children. *British Journal of Psychology 65*: 253-63.

Millar, S. (1975a) Visual experience or translation rules? Drawing the human figure by blind and sighted children. *Perception 4*: 363-71.

Millar, S. (1975b) Spatial memory by blind and sighted children. *British Journal of Psychology 66*: 449-59.

Millar, S (1975c) Effects of tactual and phonological similarity on the recall of Braille letters by blind children. *British Journal of Psychology 66*: 193-201.

Studies of the deaf and the blind 167

Millar, S. (1976) Spatial representation in blind and sighted children. *Journal of Experimental Child Psychology 21*: 460-79.

Millar, S. (1977a) Spatial representation in blind and sighted children. In G. Butterworth (ed.) *The Child's Representation of the World*. London: Plenum Press.

Millar, S. (1977b) Tactual and name matching by blind children. *British Journal of Psychology 68*: 377-83.

Millar, S. (1977c) Early stages of tactual matching. *Perception 6*: 333-43.

Millar, S. (1978a) Short-term serial tactual recall: effects of grouping on tactually probed recall of Braille letters and nonsense shapes by blind children. *British Journal of Psychology 69*: 17-24.

Millar, S. (1978b) Aspects of information from touch and movement. In G. Gordon (ed.) *Active Touch*. New York: Pergamon Press.

Millar, S. (1979) The utilization of external and movement cues in simple spatial tasks by blind and sighted children. *Perception 8*: 11-20.

Millar, S. (1981) Crossmodal and intersensory perception and the blind. In R. D. Walk and H. L. Pick, Jr (eds) *Intersensory Perception and Sensory Integration*. New York: Plenum Press.

Millar, S. (1981) Self-referent and movement cues in coding spatial location by blind and sighted children. *Perception 10*: 255-64.

Millar, S. (in press) The problem of imagery and the blind. In B. de Gelder (ed.) *Knowledge and Representation*. London: Routledge & Kegan Paul.

Myklebust, H. R. (1964) *The Psychology of Deafness*. New York: Grune & Stratton.

Oléron, P. and Herren, H. (1961) L'acquisition des conversations et le language: étude comparative sur des enfants sourds et entendant. *Enfance 14*: 203-19.

Piaget, J. (1960) *The Psychology of Intelligence*. Paterson, NJ: Littlefield, Adams.

Piaget, J. (1962) *Play, Dreams and Imitation in Childhood*. New York: Norton.

Piaget, J. and Inhelder, B. (1948) *La Représentation de l'espace chez l'enfant*. Paris: Presses Universitaires de France.

Posner, M. (1967) Characteristics of visual and kinaesthetic memory codes. *Journal of Experimental Psychology 75*: 103-7.

Rapin, I. (1979) Effects of early blindness and deafness on cognition. In R. Katzman (ed.) *Congenital and Acquired Cognitive Disorders*. New York: Raven Press.

Révész, G. (1950) *Psychology and Art of the Blind*. London: Longmans, Green.

Rouse, D. L. and Worchel, P. (1955) Veering tendency in the blind. *New Outlook for the Blind 49*: 115-19.

Schank, R, and Abelson, R. (1977) *Scripts, Plans, Goals, and Understanding*. Hillsdale, NJ: Lawrence Erlbaum Associates.

Schlaegel, F. F. (1953) The dominant method of imagery in the blind as compared to sighted adolescents. *Journal of Genetic Psychology 83*: 265-77.

Schlesinger, H. S. and Meadow, K. P. (1972) *Sound and Sign*. London: University of California Press.

Shepard, R. N. and Metzler, J. (1971) Mental rotation of three-dimensional objects. *Science 171*: 701-3.

Thomassen, A. J. W. M. (1970) On *The Representation of Verbal Items in Short-term Memory*. Nijmegen: Drukkerij Schippers.

von Senden, M. (1960) *Space and Sight: the Perception of Space and Shape in the Congenitally Blind before and after Operation*. London: Methuen.

Vygotsky, L. S. (1962) *Thought and Language*. Cambridge, Mass.: MIT Press.

Wallace, G. and Corballis, M. C. (1973) Short-term memory and coding strategies in the deaf. *Journal of Experimental Psychology 99*: 334-48.

Warren, D. H. (1977) *Blindness and Early Childhood Development*. New York: American Foundation for the Blind.

Worchel, P. (1951) Space perception and orientation in the blind. *Psychological Monographs 65*: whole no. 332.

Yik, W. F. (1978) The effect of visual and acoustic similarity on short-term memory for Chinese words. *Quarterly Journal of Experimental Psychology 30*: 487-94.

Yockley, H. P., Platzman, R. L. and Quastler, H. (eds) (1956) *Symposium on Information Theory in Biology*. London: Penguin.

7 Cognitive impairment in schizophrenia

David R. Hemsley

Introduction

Disordered thought has long been viewed as one of the most distinguishing features of schizophrenia. Kraepelin (1919) provided numerous descriptive principles for schizophrenic thinking, but with little attempt to interrelate these principles. Thus, on attention he wrote:

> It is quite common for them to lose both inclination and ability on their own initiative to keep their attention fixed for any length of time . . . there is occasionally noticed a kind of irresistible attraction of the attention to casual external impressions. (pp.6-7)

Of schizophrenic thinking he observed: 'the patients lose in a most striking way the faculty of logical ordering of their trains of thought' (p.19). More generally he noted: 'Mental efficiency is always diminished to a considerable extent' (p.23).

Such descriptions are a necessary beginning to the understanding of schizophrenics' cognitive impairment. Bleuler (1911) was the first to attempt to specify a single underlying psychological defect that would account for all the symptoms of the disorder; in his view, these resulted from a disruption of the associative processes. The latter are the connections between ideas which enable normals to organize and interrelate many single thoughts and exclude irrelevant thoughts. Although this construct lacks explicit definition, Bleuler also made the important distinction between primary and secondary symptoms. Primary symptoms are those resulting directly from the organic disease that he presumed to underlie schizophrenia; the disturbance of association was considered a primary symptom. On the other hand, secondary symptoms reflect the normal psychic processes or attempts at adaptation to the primary disturbance. More recent investigators (e.g. McGhie and Chapman, 1961; Hemsley, 1977) have also viewed aspects of schizophrenic symptomatology as resulting from the interaction of the cognitively impaired individual with his environment.

Following Bleuler other clinicians proposed alternative constructs as the central disturbance in schizophrenia. One of the most prominent constructs was that of 'overinclusion', used by Cameron (1939) to describe certain types of schizophrenic behaviour in problem-solving situations. He noted that patients were frequently unable to limit their attention to the relevant stimuli of the task, often reacting to irrelevant stimuli and tending to 'overinclude' them in, for example, object-sorting tasks. Later the term 'overinclusive' was extended to cover any response made to any inappropriate stimulus.

Such formulations resulted in attempts to demonstrate specific performance deficits in schizophrenics which are not present in other subject populations. Psychological deficit was defined by Hunt and Cofer (1944) as the loss of efficiency or decrement in performance exhibited by psychiatric patients relative to normals on intellectual and laboratory tasks. However, as Oltmanns and Neale (1978) note, the results of such research with schizophrenics are often theoretically elaborated in two ways.

> First, the single empirical measure which has been assessed is assumed to index a more general construct .... Second, it is then postulated that the construct which is implicated in the deficit is causally related to schizophrenia and can account for a variety of schizophrenic behaviours. In other words it is held to be a primary symptom of schizophrenia (p.198)

The early research on cognitive deficits lacked the adequate model of normal cognitive functioning which might justify such elaboration.

The tasks employed, although ostensibly tapping one cognitive function, were invariably open to alternative interpretations.

Among the most influential data in suggesting hypotheses about the nature of schizophrenic disorganization were the subjective reports of the patients themselves. An extended interview study by McGhie and Chapman (1961) of newly admitted schizophrenics concentrated on recent changes in the patients' subjective experiences, and the results were presented in the form of selected quotations. Typical were the following: 'Things are coming in too fast. I lose my grip of it and get lost. I am attending to everything at once and as a result I do not attend to anything'; 'My thoughts get all jumbled up. I start thinking or talking about something but I never get there.' McGhie and Chapman suggested that the reports indicated that the primary disorder in schizophrenia was a decrease in the selective and inhibitory functions of attention. Many other cognitive, perceptual, affective and behavioural abnormalities were viewed as resulting from this primary attentional deficit.

McGhie's and Chapman's (1961) report was largely substantiated by Freedman and Chapman (1973), who used a standardized questionnaire to interview groups of schizophrenic and non-schizophrenic patients at intake. Among other experiences, the schizophrenic group more frequently reported inability to focus attention, thought blocking which disrupts speech, and impaired perception of speech. About half the schizophrenics described themselves as having an increased difficulty in ignoring irrelevant stimuli. However, only three reported the disorder in the fully developed form described by McGhie and Chapman.

While the above suggests the importance of the study of cognitive impairment for our understanding of schizophrenia, there are several distinct aims to such research (cf. Cromwell, 1978). First, and most prominent, there is the attempt to specify a single cognitive dysfunction, or pattern of dysfunction, from which the various abnormalities resulting in a diagnosis of schizophrenia might be derived. Secondly, cognitive measures have been employed in the search for subgroupings of schizophrenia; it is possible that the relatively coarse concept of schizophrenia may be redefinable as a result of differing cognitive abnormalities shown by such patients. The usefulness of any such definition would, of course, be dependent on the extent of external correlates of the classification. Thirdly, cognitive measures have been prominent in longitudinal studies of high-risk children, that is children having one or both parents diagnosed as schizophrenic, in an attempt to identify factors which might predict later psychiatric breakdown (e.g. Garmezy, 1978). Fourthly, the study of residual impairment in remitted or partially remitted schizophrenics, which might have implications for rehabilitation, and which will be discussed under the heading 'Cognitive impairment and the symptoms of schizophrenia'. Finally, there is the use of cognitive measures to monitor change in response to treatment (e.g. Spohn *et al.*, 1977).

The rationale for an information-processing approach to cognitive impairment

Psychopathology is most usefully considered within the framework of models of normal functioning. In the previous section it was noted that cognitive deficits in schizophrenia remained difficult to interpret; it was hoped that the adoption of the information-processing model of cognitive functioning might enable a precise specification of the disturbance. This was to result from the more explicit relationship between observed task performance and inferred function that was a feature of such models. Research on information processing in schizophrenia was to borrow not only the language and theory of the model, but also many of the experimental procedures.

Information-processing psychology is but one paradigm for studying cognitive psychology, but in recent years has become dominant in research into adult cognitive processes. The major assumption of information-processing approaches is that perceptual and cognitive activities can be construed or represented as a series of transformations of information. The aim of the approach is to 'make explicit the operations, stages, or processes that occur in the time between stimulation and the observed response' (Haber and Hershenson, 1973, p.158) and 'to describe the limits and characteristics of these processes' (Underwood, 1978a, p.2). These stages of processing are not directly observable and their existence must be inferred from performance on a number of tasks and by using the procedure of converging operations. Inherent in the information-processing approach is the need for selectivity within the system, and attention may be viewed as the major control process in the passage of information through the system as a whole. There follows a brief discussion of those aspects of the information-processing paradigm which have been particularly influential in the study of cognitive impairment in schizophrenia, although detailed discussion of the strengths and weaknesses of the models employed is outside the scope of this chapter.

Prominent aspects of the information-processing paradigm in schizophrenia research

Broadbent's (1958) model was the most influential in early studies of schizophrenics' cognitive disturbance; this proposed that a hypothetical filter mechanism screens irrelevant stimuli from a limited-capacity decision channel. The filter was viewed as acting in an all-or-none fashion on the basis of the physical attributes of classes of stimuli. The model resulted in two views as to the nature of the cognitive impairment in schizophrenics; first, that schizophrenics possess a defective filter mechanism (e.g. McGhie and Chapman, 1961); and secondly, that schizophrenics are slow in processing information (Yates, 1966). Broadbent's later probabilistic model of the methods by which the systematic selection of information can take place (Broadbent, 1971, 1977) resembles that of Treisman (1960). Its application to the study of cognitive impairment in schizophrenia has been reviewed by Hemsley (1975). In particular, a distinction is made between stimulus set (filtering) and response set (pigeon-holing).

The concept of a limited-capacity decision channel in Broadbent's (1958) model was influenced by studies indicating a linear relationship between reaction time and the logarithm of the number of equiprobable stimulus alternatives; the slope of this function was regarded as an inverse measure of the capacity of the decision channel. Such models of choice-reaction time, based on communication theory, have required considerable modification. Nevertheless, the quantitative expressions of the theory continue to provide an adequate description of average reaction times in a variety of situations (Audley, 1973), and the model has remained popular with investigators of schizophrenics' choice-reaction-time performance. Closely related to such research is Sternberg's (1969, 1975) development of the stage model of choice-reaction-time performance, variants of which are beginning to be employed in the study of cognitive disturbance in schizophrenia. It has obvious appeal for those attempting to specify the particular stage of processing which is impaired. Sternberg's model assumes that changes in a task may influence the duration of one stage without affecting others. Current studies of schizophrenics' cognitive impairment are increasingly employing the design of the manipulation of a single variable considered to increase the load on a particular stage of processing. If no differential effect on reaction time is found between a schizophrenic and a control group, it is argued that the particular stage is not implicated in schizophrenic cognitive disturbance. Thus, in the main section of this chapter, the review of studies of cognitive impairment, emphasis will be placed on speed of information processing as indicated by various reaction-time procedures and aspects of selective attention.

Before reviewing attempts to specify the locus of the impairment, it is necessary to indicate briefly the problems associated with the establishment of a reliable cognitive deficit in schizophrenia, regardless of its theoretical interpretation.

Problems in the assessment of cognitive deficits in schizophrenia

There are numerous methodological problems associated with the study of cognitive disturbance in schizophrenic patients. They should be seen as indicating a need for caution in the interpretation of the studies discussed on pp.176-90.

Selection of schizophrenic subjects

Until recently the majority of studies of cognitive deficit in schizophrenia have employed hospital diagnoses of unknown reliability to identify their samples. Systematic differences in diagnostic criteria, particularly between the United States and England, the former adopting a broader definition of the disorder, have been particularly troublesome, and these factors have certainly contributed to the widespread failures to replicate in this area of research. The introduction of more specific diagnostic criteria and the use of structured interviews have eased this problem, but are still not employed routinely in the study of cognitive deficits.

Control groups

The majority of investigators have employed normal subjects as controls. However, a psychiatric control group should also be used, otherwise findings may be interpreted as relating only to psychiatric patients rather than specifically to schizophrenics. While a deficit common to two psychiatric groups may be of practical interest, if it is to be argued that certain forms of cognitive disturbance may be causally related to schizophrenic symptomatology (cf. McGhie and Chapman, 1961), the need for the psychiatric control group is apparent.

The assessment of differential deficit

There is increased emphasis on the demonstration of differential deficits, that is a greater deficit on one task than on another. Such studies help to clarify the specific nature of schizophrenics' impairment. However, there remain problems in their interpretation. Chapman and Chapman (1973) have argued that a differential deficit may emerge for purely psychometric reasons, namely the discriminating power of the tests employed, which are in turn dependent on their reliability and difficulty level. Unless tasks are matched on these variables, the attribution of a differential deficit to the diagnostic variable may not be justified.

In contrast, Carbotte (1978) suggests that in the study of cognitive processes the level of difficulty of a task is often an inherent feature which must change as some particular independent variable is manipulated. Attempts to match two conditions on 'discriminative power' could confound two independent variables. As Strauss (1978) notes, the matching of tasks 'may remove the variance that must be studied in order to make valid inferences about the nature of the psychological processes that are involved in task performance' (p.318). Instead, Carbotte argues for an experimental approach to eliminate alternative hypotheses about the specific processes which could account for an observed deficit in schizophrenics.

The effects of anti-psychotic medication

The experimental study of cognitive disturbance in schizophrenia has been greatly complicated by the widespread use of anti-psychotic drugs. Performance on many of the tests employed is modified by drug treatment (e.g. Spohn et al.,1977). While this is generally in the direction of improved cognitive functioning, this cannot be assumed, and the failure to find a difference in performance between a medicated schizophrenic group and controls is particularly difficult to interpret unless drug withdrawal is feasible.

The stage of the disorder

Studies of cognitive impairment frequently omit a discussion of the clinical state of the patient at the time of testing, and in its most extreme form this can result in an investigation of residual cognitive disturbance in asymptomatic patients. The explicit aim of the study may be quite different, namely to describe the pattern of cognitive impairment causally related to the abnormalities which result in a diagnosis of schizophrenia. For this it is obviously highly desirable that only a short time elapses between diagnostic assessment and cognitive testing.

Studies of cognitive impairment in schizophrenia within an information-processing framework

Many of the studies to be considered in this section have employed unspecified groups of schizophrenics. Where subcategories have been assessed, this will be noted, and later in this section there will be presented a brief summary of the few consistent findings to have emerged from the use of the chronicity dimension, the process-reactive scale, and the paranoid/non-paranoid distinction.

Selective attention

As Underwood (1978b) notes: 'attention may be used for selecting information which is to be perceived, and for selecting that which is to be responded to, as well as selecting for any number of intermediate or subordinate processes' (p.242). However, investigations of cognitive impairment have relied heavily on Broadbent's (1958, 1971) formulations as to the mechanisms of selectivity. Both the earlier and later models postulate a filter mechanism, acting on the basis of physical characteristics of the stimulus, to exclude, or in the later model, attenuate, irrelevant information at an early stage of processing.

The studies carried out by McGhie and his colleagues (1965a, 1965b) are often quoted. On psychomotor tasks involving little information processing, a schizophrenic group's basic performance was found to be low relative to a number of control groups, including depressives; when such tests were repeated with distraction, the performance of most groups deteriorated slightly, but this decline was no more evident in the schizophrenic than in any other diagnostic group. However, on tasks requiring the processing, storage and recall of information, the schizopherenics showed a generally greater susceptibility to distraction. It was argued that on tasks with low information-processing requirements a breakdown in the filter mechanism may still not result in overloading of the limited-capacity decision channel. Where more complex decision making is required, such a defect is more likely to lead to a deterioration in performance. However, the groups differed markedly in verbal intelligence, hence one cannot infer that the schizophrenics' inefficient filtering is a specific deficit rather than a reflection of a more general impairment.

The evidence most directly relevant to the possibility of a filter defect arises from studies employing dichotic shadowing tasks. Although some investigations have examined recall following the dichotic presentation of material, this is less easily interpretable. Unfortunately, the results of shadowing experiments are somewhat contradictory. Payne *et al.* (1970) demonstrated that schizophrenics perform more poorly than normal controls when irrelevant distraction is presented; no difference was found in the no-distraction condition, but this may well be an artifact of difficulty level, very few errors being made by any subject in this condition. In addition, no psychiatric control group was employed. A later study (Wishner and Wahl, 1974) found this effect only at a fast rate of presentation. However, they also assessed the recall and recognition of 'distractor' words and found the alcoholic controls to show superior performance. They suggest that, 'the memory data indicate that the controls did not achieve their more differentiated shadowing performance by excluding or "gating out" the material at the input stage' (p.545). This conclusion might be justified if filtering were seen, as in Broadbent's (1958) model, as an all-or-none mechanism. However, his later formulation (1971) views filtering as a process of attenuation, and recall is dependent on many factors other than the strength of the signal passing the filter mechanism. The findings therefore remain ambiguous.

Schneider (1976) found no general performance differences

178   The pathology and psychology of cognition

between schizophrenics and non-schizophrenics using conditions of neutral distraction. He did find that 'delusional' schizophrenics performed significantly more poorly than other groups when material pertaining to the individual's delusion was presented. Schneider concluded that schizophrenic attention is allocated in an unusual way, rather than being disturbed in its selective function. Such a result implicates altered response biases, similar to the effect of hearing one's own name in a dichotic listening task even if it is presented to the unattended ear (Moray, 1959). However, since the control subjects in Schneider's study were not given personalized distraction, his conclusion may be unwarranted. This was further investigated by Straube and Germer (1979), who employed four distraction conditions: (a) no distraction, (b) neutral words, (c) semantically similar words, and (d) affective words. The shadowed stimulus words in the relevant channel were always neutral; newly admitted schizophrenics were compared to both neurotic and normal controls. Shadowing performances did not differ between groups in any condition with or without distraction although all performed better in the no-distraction condition, and significantly better when neutral irrelevant distraction was presented rather than affective material. Similar findings on shadowing performance have been presented by Korboot and Damiani (1976) and Pogue-Geile and Oltmanns (1980). The findings from dichotic listening tasks therefore provide little support for the hypothesis of defective filtering in schizophrenics, relative to other psychiatric patients. The results of comparisons of schizophrenic and normal subjects are mixed.

In an attempt to assess the extent of the schizophrenic filter defect in the visual modality, the present author compared acute schizophrenics and depressives on a choice-reaction-time card-sorting task (Hemsley, 1976a). Stimulus and response uncertainty were varied independently and there were two main conditions, no distraction and distraction; in the latter, there was a further symbol on the corner of each card, different from that in the centre upon which sorting was to be based. Hence, selection was to be on the basis of physical location. Although the schizophrenics were slower overall, they were not significantly more affected by distraction.

In a review of schizophrenics' disturbances of selective attention within the framework of Broadbent's (1971) model, the present author suggested that filtering inefficiency should be reflected in a reduction in the discrepancy of performance on a short-term memory task between the condition of pre-instruction as to the relevant material and that of post-instruction, provided that a clear physical cue separates the relevant and irrelevant items (Hemsley, 1975). Normals showed a clear advantage of pre-instruction (stimulus set) on such a task (Broadbent, 1970). A comparison of normals, depressives and schizophrenics (Hemsley and Zawada, 1976) indicated that while the normals showed a significantly greater improvement with pre-instruction than did the psychiatric groups, the schizophrenics and depressives did not differ. The authors suggest that the filter defect 'may not be specific to schizophrenia, but may rather be related to a "severity of illness" dimension, not important causally in many of the behavioural abnormalities seen in schizophrenia' (p.460).

The above review of defective filtering as an explanation of cognitive impairment in schizophrenia is, of necessity, selective. In particular, it has ignored the numerous studies which have inferred such a defect from performance on a single task. Such deficits are usually open to alternative explanations and almost inevitably reflect multiple sources of variance. Even those dichotic shadowing studies reviewed may be criticized for their failure to equate no-distraction and distraction conditions for discriminating power (cf. Chapman and Chapman, 1973). However, the difficulty level employed in the studies has generally been low for the no-distraction condition, and moderate for the distraction condition. Hence, any generalized deficit would tend to result in a greater group difference on the latter (Chapman and Chapman, 1973, p.88). The consistent failure to find clear evidence for a filter defect when psychiatric controls are employed, despite this potential artifact, is particularly impressive.

The second method of selectivity of information processing within Broadbent's (1971) model, pigeon-holing, relies heavily on semantic cues; the relationship between this and the aetiology of disordered speech is intuitively more appealing. The mechanism is considered to operate not solely within tasks aimed at assessing selectivity, but across the range of cognitive functions. In its role as a bias towards certain categories of response in real-life situations, rather than those biases imposed by the task instructions, it may be viewed as a way of making use of the redundancy and patterning in environmental input to reduce information processing demands. As Broadbent (1977) notes, this 'kind of attention selects some of the possible interpretations that a man may hold about the world and eliminates others as candidates for use in the particular situation.' (p.110). However, when the actual stimulus is unexpected, normal biases may act to impair performance; hence, if there is considered to be a general defect in the pigeon-holing mechanism, one might be able to construct tasks where schizophrenics would be expected to perform better than normals. A recent example of schizophrenics' superior performance to normals when the use of the inherent stimulus organization in a visual display is maladaptive, may reflect a related aspect of functioning (Schwartz Place and Gilmore, 1980). Magaro (1980) reviews earlier work relevant to this, although from a different theoretical position, and suggests that the abnormalities of non-paranoids 'should result in superior performance when stable or dominant conceptual categories are a hindrance to task perfor-mance' (p.217). If a clear pattern of non-paranoid schizophrenics' superior performance on certain types of cognitive tasks were to be established, this would overcome many of the problems of interpreta-tion of schizophrenic functioning considered earlier.

Direct evidence relating to a possible disturbance of pigeon-holing in schizophrenia, as reflected in selective attention tasks, is scarce, but an exception is a recent study by Hemsley and Richardson (1980). Based on an experimental paradigm devised by Treisman (1964), this required subjects to shadow one of two simultaneously presented prose passages. The messages were both presented binaurally, in the same voice, and at the same rate of presentation; the task of distinguishing between them allows no possibility of the operation of the filter mechanism. Successful performance on the task requires subjects to use contextual variables in determining selection of the appropriate response. It is thus dependent on the pigeon-holing mechanism, whereby category-state thresholds may be raised or lowered according to the nature of the evidence derived from the preceding context. The passages to be shadowed were narrative extracts from a novel, and the irrelevant material consisted of technical extracts. Schizophrenics, depressives and normals were tested; these groups did not differ on verbal IQ or shadowing ability without distraction. Two rates of presentation were employed: 60 wpm and 100 wpm. The schizophrenics performed significantly worse than both other groups, consistent with a defect at the pigeon-holing stage, and there was a trend for the normals and depressives to improve with increasing presentation rate and for the schizophrenics to deteriorate. A comparison of the performance of the normals in the present study with that of the subjects in Treisman's (1964) investigation raises the possibility of a non-monotonic relationship between shadowing accuracy and presentation rate. Although comparisons across studies must be treated cautiously, Treisman (personal communication) points out that two factors may limit performance on such a task. At a very slow rate, it may be increasingly difficult to keep the previously shadowed context in mind; at fast rates, performance may be limited by problems in response organization. One might speculate that the limitation factor on normals' performance within the range of conditions examined is availability of context, but the performance of the schizophrenics is beginning to be limited by slowness in response selection. The suggestion is consistent with a recent report by Hammond and Gruzelier (1978), who required subjects to detect longer target tones from a sequence of short tones, and varied the rate of presentation. Normals and non-schizophrenics tended to perform better at the fast rate of presentation, as expected if the correct response depends on a comparison of the current stimulus with a decaying trace of the preceding tone. In contrast, schizophrenics tended to improve at a slow rate of presentation. The authors suggest that performance may have been more limited by response-organization features, and raise the possibility of an impairment at the response-selection stage.

Reaction time

It has been suggested that 'reaction time (RT) studies are the closest thing to a north star in schizophrenic research' (Cancro *et al.*, 1971, p.152). The generalized slowness of schizophrenics over a wide range of tasks is indeed well established.

Simple RT in schizophrenia has been extensively investigated by Shakow and his colleagues for more than forty years (e.g. Shakow, 1971). However, choice RT studies may allow more precise specification of the stages of information processing that are impaired in schizophrenia. The degree of schizophrenic deficit as a function of task complexity is relevant to Yates's (1966) suggestion that schizophrenics show a slowness in processing information. In particular, the prediction is of an increased slope of the function relating RT to variations in the level of a factor seen as influencing the demands on the particular stage of processing considered impaired. Many investigations have involved CRT tasks in which stimulus and response uncertainty are manipulated. As may be seen in Table 7.1, the findings are inconsistent. However, the results may be understood if account is taken of the stimulus-response compatibility of the task, that is the degree of obviousness or naturalness of the response appropriate to a particular stimulus. The effect of prolonged practice in a given task is similar to that of high 'S-R compatibility; both reduce the slope relating RT to the number of S-R alternatives. The idea of the slope as a fixed measure of channel capacity cannot therefore be maintained. Wickens (1974) suggests that with high compatibility or prolonged practice, the response-selection stage is bypassed by a direct stimulus-response association or link. The effect of varying the number of S-R alternatives may then be solely that due to varying stimulus uncertainty.

In Table 7.1 studies of schizophrenics' CRT performance are summarized as a function of stimulus uncertainty, response uncertainty and stimulus-response compatibility (Hemsley, 1976b). The notation employed follows that of Marshall (1973). Thus $S_{\log_2 n}$ represents the degree of stimulus uncertainty, n being the number of equiprobable stimulus alternatives; $R_{\log_2 m}$ represents the level of response uncertainty, m being the number of equiprobable response alternatives. In all the studies the schizophrenics were slower overall than the control groups, attributable to factors common to the conditions employed, e.g. motivation, motor speed; our concern is with the extent to which the slopes relating RT to stimulus and response uncertainty differ across groups. The results may be summarized as follows: the degree of schizophrenic deficit increases mainly as a function of increasing response uncertainty. This is, however, apparent only on tasks with low S-R compatibility. If Wickens's (1974) model is adopted and the response selection mechanism considered bypassed on highly compatible tasks, and if it is further suggested that a disturbance at the level of response selection is of primary importance, the apparently contradictory findings are resolved. Consistent with the view of response complexity as of major importance in determining level of deficit is a review of schizophrenic performance on untimed psychophysical tasks (Levine, 1978). Chronics and normals did not differ in studies using a two or three-choice procedure; however, they were reported to show deficits on tasks involving numerous response alternatives.

In addition to investigations of variations in stimulus and response uncertainty, a number of studies have involved the manipulation of other variables and the measurement of the rate of increase in response latency in schizophrenic and control groups. Two studies have directly applied Sternberg's paradigm to the study of schizophrenia. Checkosky (quoted in Sternberg, 1975) assessed chronic schizophrenics, acute schizophrenics and alcoholic controls; he varied stimulus intactness (implicating the encoding stage), memory set size (implicating the serial comparison stage), and presence v. absence of the stimulus (implicating the decision stage). In all cases there were significant main effects, that is differences in intercepts between the groups, but no differences in slope. Thus, there was no evidence for schizophrenics' impaired functioning in the first three stages of Sternberg's model. Similar findings are reported by Wishner et al. (1974) and Marusarz and Koh (1980).

Russell and his colleagues have carried out a series of studies in an attempt to clarify the stage of processing which is impaired in schizophrenia. Russell and Page (1976) required subjects to identify which of two target letters was embedded in displays of varying numbers of non-targets. The rate of increase in response time with increased numbers of letters displayed was not markedly different for groups of paranoid and non-paranoid schizophrenics and normals; the usual finding of schizophrenics' overall slowness was reported. Of interest is their comparison between subjects' performance on a simple RT task, and the condition of the main search task where non-target letters were absent, but where a response choice was nevertheless involved. The difference in those response times, viewed as an inverse measure of speed of response selection, was significantly greater for the schizophrenic groups; paranoids were the faster patient group. Their most recent report (Russell et al., 1980) is of a hybrid visual and memory-search task requiring subjects to search displays of up to fifteen letters for a target, which in different conditions was drawn from a memorized set of one, three or six letters. Although intercepts and response times of the schizophrenics exceeded those of controls, no differences were found in rates of increase in response time as a function of the number of memorized or displayed items. The pattern of results across these studies indicates a retardation in processes involved in response selection

Table 7.1 Schizophrenics' CRT performances as a function of stimulus uncertainty, response uncertainty and stimulus-response compatibility

Study	Control group	S and R uncertainty variations	Type of task	S–R compatibility	Results
King (1954)	Normals	$S_0 R_0$, $S_1 R_1$	Discrete	Low	Schizophrenics more affected by increasing task complexity
Venables (1958)	Normals	$S_0 R_0 \rightarrow S_3 R_3$*	Discrete	High	No difference in slope function
Benton et al. (1959)	Normals	$S_0 R_0$, $S_1 R_1$	Discrete	High	No difference in slope function
Venables (1965)	Normals	$S_{5.7} R_1 \rightarrow S_{5.7} R_{4.7}$**	Continuous	Low	Schizophrenics more affected by increasing response uncertainty
Karras (1967)	Mixed psychiatric	$S_0 R_0$, $S_1 R_1$	Discrete	High	No difference in slope function
Court and Garwoli (1968)	Normals	$S_0 R_0$, $S_1 R_1$, $S_2 R_2$, $S_3 R_3$	Discrete	High	No difference in slope function
Slade (1971)	Mixed non-psychotic psychiatric patients	$S_1 R_1$, $S_2 R_2$, $S_3 R_3$, $S_4 R_4$	Continuous	Low	Schizophrenics more affected by increasing task complexity

Karras (1973)	Depressives and neurotics	$S_1 R_0, S_1 R_1$	Discrete	High	No group difference in slope function
		$S_1 R_0, S_1 R_1$	Discrete	Low	Depressives and schizophrenics more affected by increasing task complexity than are neurotics
Marshall (1973)	Neurotics and prisoners	$S_1 R_1, S_2 R_1, S_{\approx} R_1,$ $S_2 R_2, S_3 R_2, S_{\leq} R_3$	Continuous	Low	Schizophrenics more affected by increases in both stimulus and response uncertainty Response uncertainty effects greatest
Hemsley (1976a)	Depressives	$S_1 R_1, S_2 R_1, S_{\leq} R_1$ $S_2 R_2, S_3 R_2, S_{\leq} R_3$	Continuous	Low	Schizophrenics more affected by increasing response uncertainty. No difference in the effects of increasing stimulus uncertainty

Source: Hemsley, 1976b, copyright Psychonomic Society Inc. Reprinted with permission cf the publishers.

* Eight conditions

** Seven conditions

and execution, with the additional possibility of a slowness in search initiation.

A number of studies, using a range of techniques, have attempted to establish a schizophrenic impairment at the very earliest stages of processing by means of procedures employing the brief presentation of visual stimuli (cf. Sperling, 1960). The aims have been both to examine the quality of iconic storage in schizophrenia and also to assess the rate of processing of information from the icon into short-term memory.

Neale et al. (1969) and Neale (1971), employing a forced-choice letter-recognition task with brief exposure found that schizophrenics performed as well as controls on single-letter displays but less well when irrelevant or noise letters were introduced, suggesting slow encoding from the icon. However, the findings are also consistent with the suggestion that schizophrenics may require more time to initiate a search. Slowness of encoding from the icon is also indicated by the results from a backward masking study carried out by Saccuzzo et al. (1974). Employing a forced-choice recognition procedure, and both single-letter and eight-letter displays, chronic schizophrenics were found to display longer masking functions. Thus, the control groups processed all the information from the icon in less than 200 milliseconds, whereas the performance of the schizophrenic groups was still improving at a 300-millisecond delay of the mask. The possibility that such slowness is attributable to an unnecessarily exhaustive examination of each stimulus was investigated by Davidson and Neale (1974). The similarity of targets and distractors was manipulated and found to affect acute schizophrenics in the same way as controls, speed increasing with increasing dissimilarity. This is contrary to what might have been expected if under dissimilar conditions schizophrenics were less able to reject the distractor items on the basis of discriminating critical features.

Knight et al. (1977) employed Sperling's post-cueing partial-report condition. Their schizophrenics were classified as overinclusive, middle inclusive or underinclusive on the basis of scores from Payne's (1962) Object Classification Test. The overinclusive group displayed no deficit in comparison with non-psychotic controls and showed all the icon attributes that Sperling (1960) originally described. The other schizophrenic groups neither took advantage of the reduction in output interference in the partial-report condition to perform better than in the full-report condition, nor showed a decay function in partial report. As the authors note, a number of interpretations are possible; these groups may have an inadequately formed iconic image, they may be impaired in their ability to respond to the cue, or they may have difficulty in attending to the cue indicated subset of letters. The present author would agree with their conclusion that 'as far as specifying the particular process underlying the information processing deficit of selected sub-groups of schizophrenics, the present data have produced more questions than answers' (p.253).

In a comprehensive review of span-of-apprehension studies, as they relate to speed of encoding from the icon, Magaro (1980) concluded that 'a slower rate of processing is reported for both schizophrenics and paranoids' (p.183). However, it is not clear that this represents a basic impairment, particularly in view of the negative findings obtained for overinclusive schizophrenics. It may instead represent a learned strategy of slowed processing from the icon due to the schizophrenic requiring greater certainty concerning the identification of a stimulus. It may even be viewed as an adaptive strategy if subsequent stages of processing are impaired.

Memory

A number of studies have employed recognition tasks as a measure of the operation of short-term memory processes in schizophrenia. The majority have not found differences between schizophrenics and control groups (e.g. Bauman and Murray, 1968). In contrast, a schizophrenic recall deficit has been observed across many different kinds of materials and in both manifestly psychotic individuals, and those relatively free of disturbance at the time of testing (e.g. Koh, 1978). Such an impairment has most often been explained by assuming that schizophrenics are lacking in the ability for mnemonic organization. Proponents of such a view argue that items to be recalled are retrieved from the memory store by a search process relying on organizational schemes set up by the subject during acquisition of the material. In recognition tasks, however, the search and retrieval process is considered unnecessary, the memory store being accessed on the basis of the perceptual characteristics of the items presented for recognition. The relationship between normal recall and recognition remains the subject of considerable research, but the above framework has guided many of the investigations into schizophrenic impairment.

An early example is a study by Bauman (1971), who compared schizophrenics and normals on recall and recognition of lists of ten trigrams, the trigrams within each list beginning with sequential letters of the alphabet. Half the subjects in each group were advised that recall could be facilitated by attending to the first letter of each item, and as expected, the groups differed on recall, but not on recognition performance. In addition, the schizophrenics, unlike the normals, failed to benefit from the clues provided. These results and similar findings by Koh and his colleagues (e.g. Koh, 1978) were interpreted in terms of a failure by the schizophrenics to organize the incoming information. This was supported by later research, which not only replicated these findings, but also provided direct indices of subjective organization such as the extent to which the subject employs the conceptual categories supplied by the experimenter as an aid to recall (Koh et al., 1973); this was found to be less in the schizophrenic group. This and similar studies were seen as indicating a disruption in controlled processing, rather than a failure to perceive the stimulus attributes utilized by normals as an aid to recall. The latter possibility was ruled out by studies indicating basically identical clustering by schizophrenics on sorting tasks (e.g. Koh et al., 1974). As Neale and Oltmanns (1980) conclude, 'their [schizophrenics] difficulty lies in actively organizing information once it has reached the level of conscious experience and short term memory . . . they are less consistent in their construction and utilization of memory structures' (p.140).

The initial suggestion of schizophrenics' inefficient organization arose from a comparison of recall and recognition performances. However, as Chapman and Chapman (1973) have pointed out, this may represent solely an artifact due to the tasks not being matched on discriminating power. Subsequent research, comprehensively reviewed by Koh (1978), has employed the strategy of converging operations, as advocated by Carbotte (1978), to clarify the locus and nature of schizophrenics' deficits in recall and mnemonic organization. Future studies may well find it useful to consider the distinction proposed by Hasher and Zachs (1979) between automatic and effortful processes in memory. The former are seen as having minimal attentional requirements and hence not interfering with other ongoing activities; they occur without intention and do not benefit from practice; and these processes encode the fundamental aspects of the flow of information, namely spatial, temporal and frequency-of-occurrence information. Contrasted with these are effortful operations such as rehearsal and elaborative mnemonic activities, which compete with other cognitive activities requiring capacity. This formulation may facilitate the integration of research into schizophrenics' memory functioning with the approaches to the study of their cognitive impairment presented earlier in this section.

Subgroup differences on cognitive tasks

The majority of studies of schizophrenics' cognitive impairment have not included acute – chronic, process – reactive, and paranoid/non-paranoid comparisons. An increasing number are, however, specifying their schizophrenic group in terms of one or more of these dimensions, and this facilitates the comparison of findings from different investigations.

In general, non-paranoids have been found to perform more poorly than paranoids on a wide range of tasks (e.g. Shakow, 1971), chronics more poorly than acutes (e.g. McGhie et al., 1965a), and process patients more poorly than reactives (e.g. Taylor and Hirt, 1975). The majority of such findings are explicable in terms of a severity-of-illness dimension, rather than a specific pattern of cognitive impairment. In addition, there appears to be lowered responsiveness in process and chronic patients. Thus Weinberger and Cermak (1973) compared short-term retention in acute and chronic paranoid schizophrenics; the former tended to make more errors of commission, the latter errors of omission. Similarly, De Wolfe (1974) in reviewing comparisons of process and reactive patients stresses the under-responsiveness of the former to task demands.

Comparisons of acute and chronic patients require particular comment since it is often inferred that such differences may reflect patterns of intra-individual change across time. These in turn could be viewed as indicators of deterioration, institutionalization or adaptation. As Strauss (1973) has pointed out, the inferior performance of chronic patients on many tasks is interpretable not only in terms of such changes, but equally plausibly in terms of sampling biases, those most severely impaired tending to become chronic. Longitudinal investigations are obviously required to clarify this issue. However, there are a few studies where the pattern of chronics' performance differs from acutes, and where the differences are consistent with Broen's (1968) proposal that learned adaptive strategies may increasingly be employed by chronic patients. Thus, a number of findings are suggestive of narrowed cue utilization in chronic patients (Broen and Nakamura, 1972; Cegalis and Tegtmeyer, 1980). This may on occasion result in chronics showing performances superior to those of acute patients (e.g. de Silva and Hemsley, 1977), and an explanation in terms of patient selection is less convincing.

Differences in performance between paranoid and non-paranoid schizophrenics have most often been interpreted in terms of the level of disorganization and/or preferred methods of adaptation. Thus, Shakow (1971) wrote

> the paranoid pattern of response may represent an over-reactive protection against the underlying pressure towards disorganization which characterizes the psychosis. The hebephrenic (non-paranoid) apparently give way to these forces whereas the paranoid attempts to organize his resources to fight these disruptive trends. (p.309)

More recently, however, Magaro (1980) contends that the non-paranoid schizophrenic has difficulty in creating an organization of conceptual material, while the paranoid has problems in performing common perceptual-type tasks. His formulation relies heavily on Schneider and Shiffrin's (1977) distinction between automatic and controlled processing. The non-paranoid is expected to perform adequately when automatic processing is appropriate, and to be deficient in those experimental situations requiring controlled processing. In contrast, controlled processing is seen as most characteristic of the paranoid; however, his categorical set operates so that the controlled processing is a biased search for specific attributes. It would be premature to evaluate this model of the paranoid/non-paranoid distinction. However, it provides clear predictions as to the nature of the deficits expected, and will undoubtedly stimulate considerable research.

The adequacy of the information-processing approach to cognitive impairment

Models of information processing have been influential in determining those variables which might be manipulated in order to specify more precisely the nature of the cognitive impairment in schizophrenia. The usefulness of this approach is dependent on the extent to which it has enabled inferences to be made from task performance to a disturbance at a particular stage of processing; and this necessitates an adequate model of the functional processes involved in the task. Unfortunately, as Rabbitt (1979) points out, a large number of performance models share the asumptions of Sternberg's approach to reaction time, (e.g. Sternberg, 1975), that is of linear, serial and independent processing stages, without these assumptions being tested with the same rigour as has been demonstrated by Sternberg.

Further problems of interpretation arise from disagreement concerning even gross characteristics of the human information-processing system. For example, the question of whether any early selection of information takes place continues to stimulate research (e.g. Johnston and Heinz, 1979); hence, results from experiments attempting to identify a defective filter mechanism in schizophrenia must remain ambiguous. Even research based on Sternberg's (1969) paradigm becomes less easily interpretable in the light of findings indicating the effects of S-R compatibility on the slope of the function relating memory set size to reaction time (Ogden and Alluisi, 1980); and this suggests that the processes identified by stage differentiation research are highly dependent on task demands. Ogden and Alluisi conclude that, 'both the identified stages, and the processes characterising the stages may vary as a function of the specific task requirements and the human resources and strategies brought to bear to satisfy the task requirements' (p.437).

The above quotation is an indication of the growing awareness that a consideration of cognitive activity is incomplete unless it takes into account the variable strategies of information processing applied by the individual; a simple example is the use of ear order or temporal order of recall on split-span tasks. Such variability is apparent not only between individuals but has been clearly demonstrated within individuals over a wide range of experimental tasks (Battig, 1975). Research into cognitive impairment in schizophrenia has sought to specify the structural limitations and capacity restrictions of particular stages of processing. Cognitive psychologists are, however, increasingly interested in the factors affecting the use of these structures to achieve particular goals. Underwood (1978a) argues that the strategies we can isolate, and distinguish from the effects of structure, will be defined in terms of the information used by the subject, the stages of processing which are applied, and of the effects of a given strategy upon behaviour. In part, optimal strategies are dependent on expectancies, built up on the basis of the redundancy and patterning of sensory input, which may be employed to overcome the processing limits of the structural features in the system. Hence, Moray (1978) notes that the study of differences in strategy 'would be more concerned with the criteria for decisions, the placing of decision cut-offs, and the interpretation of biases and pay-offs' (p.302). Moray provides examples of experiments demonstrating the development of optimal response criteria as a result of practice; such techniques may well be of interest in the study of cognitive impairment and could provide a link with the research into inappropriate response biases in schizophrenia considered earlier in this chapter.

It is, therefore, apparent that variations in strategy must be considered when evaluating individual differences in cognitive performance. Indeed, Rabbitt (1979) argues that this is essential for a consideration of the changes in function resulting from practice, stresses and such conditions as old-age and schizophrenia. He notes that as yet we do not even possess a model to explain how simple RT improves with practice, but that it is clear that one cannot assume that practice simply increases the efficiency of one or more of a set of operations, leaving their nature and sequence intact. In similar vein Schneider and Shiffrin (1977), contrasting the controlled processing apparent in novel tasks and the automated processing of the same tasks after extensive practice, argue for a qualitative difference between the two types of processing. This raises the further difficulty that the experiments upon which information-processing approaches to schizophrenia have been based have often employed highly practised normal subjects (e.g. Sperling, 1960), allowing for the development of optimal processing strategies. In contrast, studies of schizophrenic functioning have usually involved only limited practice. Unfortunately, there has been little research into the effects of practice on schizophrenic performance.

Although there is a clear need to investigate strategies employed by schizophrenics on information-processing tasks, it remains possible that structural limitations in processing, specific to the disorder, may themselves influence the likelihood of certain strategies being employed. This point will be elaborated below.

Cognitive impairment and the symptoms of schizophrenia

As was noted in the introduction to this chapter, a number of authors have argued that cognitive impairment may be viewed as causal in relation to schizophrenic symptoms. Two areas of theorizing and related experimentation may usefully be distinguished. First, the suggestion that certain aspects of schizophrenics' functioning may represent attempts to reduce the behavioural disorganization resulting from the cognitive disturbance; such a position is most commonly concerned with the negative symptoms of schizophrenia such as poverty of speech, social withdrawal and retardation (e.g. Hemsley, 1977). The second approach seeks to account for the principal symptoms of schizophrenia, such as hallucinations, delusions and thought disorder, in terms of the cognitive impairment (e.g. Frith, 1979).

The present author argued that the pattern of cognitive deficits shown by schizophrenics might usefully be seen as resulting in a state of information overload, and that the strategies of processing employed by normal subjects in situations of experimenter-induced overload (e.g. Miller, 1960) could be relevant to an understanding of schizophrenic behaviour (Hemsley, 1977). Heilbrun (1977) presents an interesting study of the various strategies which normals may employ to disengage from visual and auditory information. Such strategies would be expected to be learnt over time, and hence to be more prominent in the later stages of the disorder. In contrast, in the acute phase, the predominant pattern would be error responses, the schizophrenic attempting to respond at a rate which would have been error-free prior to the onset of the cognitive disturbance. A summary of possible relationships between clinical phenomena and adaptations to information overload is presented in Table 7.2. While this is inevitably an oversimplification, comparisons of acute and chronic patients, both in terms of symptoms (e.g. Wing and Brown, 1968) and task performance, are broadly consistent with this formulation. Thus Weinberger and Cermak (1973) have reported increased omission errors in chronic patients. Cegalis *et al.* (1980) and de Silva and Hemsley (1977) present data suggestive of a strategy of narrowed attention in chronics, and Koh and Shears (1970) report simplified categorizing, particularly in longer-term patients. However, as noted earlier under the heading 'Subgroup differences on cognitive tasks', there are obvious difficulties in interpreting such studies in terms of intra-individual variation (Strauss 1973).

Factors which might be expected to influence preferred strategies would include severity of cognitive impairment, personality factors independent of the psychosis, and environmental influences. It may well be that the most acceptable methods of adaptation within institutions are those involving withdrawal and under-responding. This has implications for treatment, and will be considered in the following section.

Frith (1979) suggests that hallucinations, delusions and thought disorder may be seen as the result of a defect in the mechanism that controls and limits the contents of consciousness; his formulation relies heavily on the distinction between preconscious and conscious processing of information. It is argued that in schizophrenia certain

Table 7.2 Summary of possible relationships between clinical phenomena and adaptations to information overload

Method of adaptation (Miller, 1960)	Clinical phenomena
Errors Intrustion of associated responses	Inappropriate responding
	Incoherence of speech
Omission Lowered responsiveness	Under-responsiveness *
Raised threshold for response	Poverty of speech *
	Flatness of affect *
Approximation Simplified categorizing system	Undifferentiated responding
Several stimuli elicit the same response rather than there being a differentiated response to each	Delusions
Escape Reduction of exploratory responses	Social withdrawal *
Avoidance of situations of high information load (cf. Broen, 1968)	Catatonic symptoms
Queuing Delayed responding (cf. Hawks and Marshall, 1971)	Retardation *
Filtering Increased attenuation of certain classes of sensory input (cf. Broen, 1968)	Narrowed attention *

Source: Hemsley, 1977, copyright Royal College of Psychiatrists.
Reprinted with permission of the publishers.
* More prominent in chronic patients

aspects of preconscious processing, or the results of this processing, not in themselves abnormal, become conscious. Auditory hallucinations are viewed as an awareness of preconscious incorrect interpretations of auditory stimuli, and are therefore expected to increase in likelihood in conditions of ambiguous sensory input; a recent study confirmed this prediction (Margo *et al.*, 1981). Following earlier authors (e.g. Maher, 1974) Frith considers delusions as attempts to explain and understand the misperceptions resulting from the basic impairment. However, unlike previous formulations, his model can account for the occurrence of delusions in the absence of hallucinations. Percepts may arrive in consciousness abnormally, but give rise to the correct interpretation of an event; the abnormality lies in the fact that normally such an event would not reach awareness. Its registration leads to a search for the reasons for its occurrence. Frith also notes that only certain people might be capable of constructing the complex system necessary to explain all the irrelevant percepts of which they become aware, and that this may relate to such factors as premorbid intelligence. However, as Hemsley (1977) points out, it may also be influenced by the severity of the cognitive abnormality, it being possible to maintain a stable delusional system in the face of limited intrusions of percepts into awareness, but beyond a certain level this may be replaced by the more transient belief system characteristic of the non-paranoid schizophrenic. Thought disorder is seen by Frith as related to a failure to inhibit alternate meanings of ambiguous words from reaching awareness during discourse; his formulation allows the prediction that certain aspects of schizophrenics' performances may be expected to be superior to those of normals (Frith, 1979, p.231). It is at present the most clearly stated position on the relationship between cognitive impairment and the core phenomena of schizophrenia.

Implications for treatment

Despite the increasing use of operant procedures in the modification of abnormalities of schizophrenic behaviour (e.g. Liberman, 1976), there remain a number of limitations of this approach. These include: non-responding, the concurrent deterioration of other aspects of schizophrenic behaviour, and failures of generalization. Hemsley (1978) has argued that these may be understood in terms of the disturbances of cognitive functioning shown by such patients. Thus, it might be expected that for those in whom cognitive impairment remains prominent, and who have reacted by withdrawing from situations requiring complex decision making, any attempt to increase social interaction may result solely in an alternate method of adaptation showing itself as an increase in florid symptomatology. Such ideas also form the basis of a recent critique of milieu therapy for schizophrenia (van Putten and May, 1976), and the importance of considering the level of cognitive functioning of the patient is emphasized. It would, therefore, appear worthwhile to investigate the relationship between rehabilitation outcome and the level of residual cognitive impairment once optimal levels of medication have been achieved. This obviously represents a different research focus to that of establishing the nature of the cognitive impairment, although the measures employed would undoubtedly be influenced by recent research in this area. It is of interest that both Cancro *et al.* (1971) and Zahn and Carpenter (1978) report significant relationships between simple RT and prognosis.

For some patients in whom the cognitive disturbance has largely remitted or been successfully treated, certain behavioural abnormalities resulting from previously adaptive strategies, such as narrowed scanning, slowed responding and social withdrawal, may no longer be serving a useful purpose. In such cases operant procedures might be employed to reverse the deficits. An example is presented by Meiselman (1973), who demonstrated the effectiveness of a training procedure to alleviate narrowed cue utilization in chronic schizophrenia; unfortunately, generalization to another task was not achieved. There is the further possibility that those patients who remain cognitively impaired might be trained to utilize the most appropriate strategies to minimize the behavioural abnormalities demonstrated in a given situation.

A more ambitious approach is suggested by Magaro (1980) and involves training procedures which attempt to reduce the basic information-processing problems of both the paranoid and the non-paranoid schizophrenic. Since the paranoid is seen as only perceiving that which fits his conceptual framework, the programme would aim to extend his perceptual input. In contrast, the focus of treatment for the non-paranoid would be to strengthen his conceptual framework by creating stable associative structures. This approach draws heavily on the literature on remedial programmes for learning-disabled children. As yet there is little evidence for its efficacy; the major problem is likely to be a lack of generalization of the effects of training procedures.

Conclusions

The information-processing approach has enabled the specification of those task variables, such as response uncertainty, which relate clearly to the extent of the schizophrenic deficit. Of equal significance are those manipulations, such as varying memory load, which do not appear differentially to affect schizophrenics and controls. Inferences concerning the localization of the impairment at one or more stages of processing are less precise. This is in part attributable to methodological problems, but also to issues concerning the adequacy of current models of normal cognitive functioning.

The suggestion that schizophrenics fail to establish appropriate response biases, and hence do not make use of temporal and spatial redundancy to reduce information-processing demands, merits further research. As Michon (1978) has argued, the temporal patterning of stimuli helps to reduce the class of possible stimuli to be expected, and thus to decrease the likelihood of overload of the processing channels. The experiments of Garner and his colleagues (Garner, 1974), dealing with the discovery and utilization of temporal patterning in sequences of events, might indicate methods of assessing this aspect of schizophrenic functioning. In addition, this formulation suggests further possibilities for the construction of tasks where schizophrenics would be expected to perform better than normals, due to the latter forming inappropriate expectancies. Such findings would be less open to alternative explanations than are schizophrenic deficits.

If strategies of information processing are seen as inappropriate, attempts might be made to train optimal strategies to normalize task performance (cf. Meiselman, 1973). However, it remains plausible that certain strategies represent attempts at adaptation to basic limitations. Studies of changes in strategy as the disorder progresses, for example narrowed cue utilization, are therefore clearly required. In addition, the level of residual cognitive impairment, and the adequacy of the adaptive strategies attempted by the schizophrenics, may be of considerable importance in relation to rehabilitation outcome.

198   The pathology and psychology of cognition

References

Audley, R. J. (1973) Some observations on theories of choice reaction time: tutorial review. In S. Kornblum (ed.) *Attention and Performance* Vol. IV. New York: Academic Press.

Battig, W. F. (1975) Within individual differences in 'cognitive' processes. In R. L. Solso (ed.) *Information Processing and Cognition: The Loyola Symposium*. Hillsdale, NJ: Lawrence Erlbaum Associates.

Bauman, E. (1971) Schizophrenic short-term memory: a deficit in subjective organization. *Canadian Journal of Behavioural Science 3*: 55-65.

Bauman, E. and Murray, D. J. (1968) Recognition versus recall in schizophrenia. *Canadian Journal of Psychology 22*: 18-25.

Benton, A., Jentsch, R. and Wahler, H. (1959) Simple and choice-reaction time in schizophrenia. *AMA Archives of Neurology and Psychiatry 81*: 373-76.

Bleuler, E. (1950) *Dementia Praecox or the Group of Schizophrenias*. New York: International Universities Press. (Originally published 1911.)

Broadbent, D. E. (1958) *Perception and Communication*. London: Pergamon Press.

Broadbent, D. E. (1970) Stimulus set and response set: two kinds of selective attention. In D. Mostofsky (ed.) *Attention: Contemporary Theories and Analysis*. New York: Appleton-Century-Crofts.

Broadbent, D. E. (1971) *Decision and Stress*. New York: Academic Press.

Broadbent, D. E. (1977) The hidden preattentive processes. *American Psychologist 32*: 109-18.

Broen, W. E. (1968) *Schizophrenia: Research and Theory*. New York and London: Academic Press.

Broen, W. E. and Nakamura, C. Y. (1972) Reduced range of sensory sensitivity in chronic nonparanoid schizophrenics. *Journal of Abnormal Psychology 79*: 106-11.

Cameron, N. (1939) Schizophrenic thinking in a problem solving situation. *Journal of Mental Science 85*: 1012-35.

Cancro, R., Sutton, S., Kerr, J. and Sugerman, A. A. (1971) Reaction time and prognosis in acute schizophrenia. *Journal of Nervous and Mental Disease 153*: 351-9.

Carbotte, R. M. (1978) Converging operations or matched control tasks? *Journal of Psychiatric Research 14*: 313-16.

Cegalis, J. A. and Tegtmeyer, P. F. (1980) Visual selectivity in schizophrenia. *Journal of Nervous and Mental Disease 168*: 229-35.

Chapman, L. J. and Chapman, J. P. (1973) *Disordered Thought in Schizophrenia*. New York: Appleton-Century-Crofts.

Court, J. M. and Garwoli, E. (1968) Schizophrenic performance on a reaction-time task with increasing levels of complexity. *British Journal of Social and Clinical Psychology 7*: 216-23.

Cromwell, R. L. (1978) Conclusion. *Journal of Psychiatric Research 14*: 327-31.

Davidson, G. S. and Neale, J. M. (1974) The effects of signal – noise similarity on the visual information processing of schizophrenics. *Journal of*

Abnormal Psychology 83: 683-6.

de Silva, W. P. and Hemsley, D. R. (1977) The influence of context on language perception in schizophrenia. *British Journal of Social and Clinical Psychology 15*: 337-45.

De Wolfe, A. S. (1974) Are there two kinds of thinking in process and reactive schizophrenics? *Journal of Abnormal Psychology 83*: 285-90.

Freedman, B. and Chapman, L. J. (1973) Early subjective experience in schizophrenic episodes. *Journal of Abnormal Psychology 82*: 46-54.

Frith, C. D. (1979) Consciousness, information processing and schizophrenia *British Journal of Psychiatry 134*: 225-35.

Garmezy, N. (1978) Attentional processes in adult schizophrenia and in children at risk. *Journal of Psychiatric Research 14*: 3-34.

Garner, W. R. (1974) *The Processing of Information and Structure.* Potomac, Md: Lawrence Erlbaum Associates.

Haber, R. N. and Hershenson, M. (1973) *The Psychology of Visual Perception.* New York: Holt, Rinehart & Winston.

Hammond, N. V. and Gruzelier, J. A. (1978) Laterality, attention and rate effects in the auditory temporal discrimination of chronic schizophrenics: the effect of treatment with chlorpromazine. *Quarterly Journal of Experimental Psychology 30*: 91-103.

Hasher, L. and Zacks, R. T. (1979) Automatic and effortful processes in memory. *Journal of Experimental Psychology: General 108*: 356-88.

Heilbrun, A. B. (1977) An analogue study of disattentional strategies in schizophrenia. *Journal of Abnormal Psychology 86*: 135-44.

Hemsley, D. R. (1975) A two-stage model of attention in schizophrenia research. *British Journal of Social and Clinical Psychology 14*: 81-9.

Hemsley, D. R. (1976a) Attention and information processing in schizophrenia. *British Journal of Social and Clinical Psychology 15*: 199-209.

Hemsley, D. R. (1976b) Stimulus uncertainty, response uncertainty and stimulus - response compatibility as determinants of schizophrenic reaction time performance. *Bulletin of the Psychonomic Society 8*: 425-7.

Hemsley, D. R. (1977) What have cognitive deficits to do with schizophrenic symptoms? *British Journal of Psychiatry 130*: 167-73.

Hemsley, D. R. (1978) Limitations of operant procedures in the modification of schizophrenic functioning: the possible relevance of studies of cognitive disturbance. *Behavioural Analysis and Modification 3*: 165-73.

Hemsley, D. R. and Richardson, P. H. (1980) Shadowing by context in schizophrenia. *Journal of Nervous and Mental Disease 168*: 141-5.

Hemsley, D. R. and Zawada, S. L. (1976) 'Filtering' and the cognitive deficit in schizophrenia. *British Journal of Psychiatry 128*: 456-61.

Hunt, J. McV. and Cofer, C. (1944) Psychological deficit in schizophrenia. In J. McV. Hunt (ed.) *Personality and the Behaviour Disorders.* Vol. 2. New York: Ronald Press.

Johnston, W. A. and Heinz, S. P. (1979) Depth of nontarget processing in an attention task. *Journal of Experimental Psychology: Human Perception and Performance 1*: 168-75.

Karras, A. (1967) The effect of stimulus-response complexity on the reaction time of schizophrenics. *Psychonomic Science 7*: 75-6.

Karras, A. (1973) Effects of competing and complex responses on the reaction time of acute psychiatric groups. *Journal of Abnormal Psychology 82*: 134-8.

King, H. E. (1954) *Psychomotor Aspects of Mental Disease*. Cambridge, Mass.: Harvard University Press.

Knight, R., Scherer, M. and Shapiro, J. (1977) Iconic imagery in overinclusive and non-overinclusive schizophrenics. *Journal of Abnormal Psychology 80*: 242-55.

Koh, S. D. (1978) Remembering of verbal material by schizophrenic young adults. In S. Schwartz (ed.) *Language and Cognition in Schizophrenia*. Hillsdale, NJ: Laurence Erlbaum Associates.

Koh, S. D. and Shears, G. (1970) Psychological scaling by schizophrenics and normals: line lengths and music preferences. *Archives of General Psychiatry 23*: 249-59.

Koh, S. D., Kayton, L. and Berry, R. (1973) Mnemonic organization in young nonpsychotic schizophrenics. *Journal of Abnormal Psychology 81*: 299-310.

Koh, S. D., Kayton, L. and Schwarz, G. (1974) The structure of word storage in the permanent memory of non-psychotic schizophrenics. *Journal of Consulting and Clinical Psychology 42*: 879-87.

Korboot, P. J. and Damiani, N. (1976) Auditory processing speed and signal detection in schizophrenia. *Journal of Abnormal Psychology 85*: 287-95.

Kraepelin, E. (1919) *Dementia Praecox and Paraphrenia* (translated by R. M. Barclay). Edinburgh: E. & S. Livingstone.

Levine, R. R. J. (1978) Response complexity and social interaction in the psychophysical testing of chronic and paranoid schizophrenics. *Psychological Bulletin 85*: 284-94.

Liberman, R. P. (1976) Behaviour therapy for schizophrenia. In L. J. West and D. E. Flinn (eds) *Treatment of Schizophrenia: Progress and Prespects*. New York: Grune & Stratton.

McGhie, A. and Chapman, J. (1961) Disorders of attention and perception in early schizophrenia. *British Journal of Medical Psychology 34*: 103-16.

McGhie, A., Chapman, J. and Lawson, J. S. (1965a) The effect of distraction on schizophrenic performance: (1) Perception and immediate memory. *British Journal of Psychiatry 111*: 383-90.

McGhie, A., Chapman, J. and Lawson, J. S. (1965b) The effect of distraction on schizophrenic performance: (2) Psychomotor ability. *British Journal of Psychiatry 111*: 391-8.

Magaro, P. A. (1980) *Cognition in Schizophrenia and Paranoia*. Hillsdale, NJ: Lawrence Erlbaum Associates.

Maher, B. A. (1974) Delusional thinking and perceptual disorder. *Journal of Individual Psychology 30*: 98-113.

Margo, A., Hemsley, D. R. and Slade, P. D. (1981) The effects of varying auditory input on schizophrenic hallucinations. *British Journal of Psychiatry 139*: 122-7.

Marshall, W. L. (1973) Cognitive functioning in schizophrenia. I. Stimulus analyzing and response selection process. *British Journal of Psychiatry 123*: 413-23.

Marusarz, T. Z. and Koh, S. D. (1980) Contextual effects on the short-term memory retrieval of schizophrenic young adults. *Journal of Abnormal Psychology 89*: 683–96.

Meiselman, K. C. (1973) Broadening dual-modality cue utilization in chronic schizophrenics. *Journal of Consulting and Clinical Psychology 41*: 447–53.

Michon, J. A. (1978) The making of the present: a tutorial review. In J. Requin (ed.) *Attention and Performance* Vol. VII. Hillsdale, NJ: Lawrence Erlbaum Associates.

Miller, J. G. (1960) Information input overload and psychopathology. *American Journal of Psychiatry 116*: 695–704.

Moray, N. (1959) Attention in dichotic listening: affective cues and the influence of instructions. *Quarterly Journal of Experimental Psychology 11*: 56–60.

Moray, N. (1978) The strategic control of information processing. In G. Underwood (ed.) *Strategies of Information Processing*. London: Academic Press.

Neale, J. M. (1971) Perceptual span in schizophrenia. *Journal of Abnormal Psychology 77*: 196–204.

Neale, J. M., McIntyre, C. W., Fox, R. and Cromwell, R. L. (1969) Span of apprehension in acute schizophrenics. *Journal of Abnormal Psychology 74*: 593–6.

Neale, J. M. and Oltmanns, T. F. (1980) *Schizophrenia*. New York: Wiley.

Ogden, G. D. and Alluisi, E. A. (1980) Stimulus-response compatibility effects in choice reactions and memory scanning. *Journal of Experimental Psychology: Human Learning and Memory 6*: 430–8.

Oltmanns, T. F. and Neale, J. M. (1978) Abstraction and schizophrenia: problems in psychological deficit research. In B. A. Maher (ed.) *Progress in Experimental Personality Research*. Vol. 8. New York: Academic Press.

Payne, R. W. (1962) An object classification test as a measure of over-inclusive thinking in schizophrenic patients. *British Journal of Social and Clinical Psychology 1*: 213–21.

Payne, R. W., Hochberg, A. C. and Hawks, D. V. (1970) Dichotic stimulation as a method of assessing the disorder of attention in overinclusive schizophrenic patients. *Journal of Abnormal Psychology 76*: 185–93.

Pogue-Geile, M. F. and Oltmanns, T. F. (1980) Sentence perception and distractibility in schizophrenic, manic, and depressed patients. *Journal of Abnormal Psychology 89*: 115–24.

Rabbitt, P. (1979) Current paradigms and models in human information processing. In V. Hamilton and D. M. Warburton (eds) *Human Stress and Cognition: An information-processing Approach*. New York: Wiley.

Russell, P. N. and Page, A. E. (1976) Comparison of schizophrenics and normals on a visual search task. *Perceptual and Motor Skills 42*: 399–402.

Russell, P. N., Consedine, C. E. and Knight, R. G. (1980) Visual and memory search by process schizophrenics. *Journal of Abnormal Psychology* 89: 109-14.

Saccuzzo, D. P., Hirt, N. and Spencer, T. J. (1974) Backward masking as a measure of attention in schizophrenia. *Journal of Abnormal Psychology 83*: 512-22.

Schneider, S. J. (1976) Selective attention in schizophrenia. *Journal of Abnormal Psychology 85*: 167-73.

Schneider, W. and Shiffrin, R. M. (1977) Controlled and automatic human information processing: I. Detection, search and attention. *Psychological Review 84*: 1-66.

Schwartz Place, E. J. and Gilmore, G. C. (1980) Perceptual organization in schizophrenia. *Journal of Abnormal Psychology 89*: 407-18.

Shakow, D. (1971) Some observations on the psychology (and some fewer on the biology) of schizophrenia. *Journal of Nervous and Mental Disease 153*: 300-16.

Slade, P. D. (1971) Rate of information processing in a schizophrenic and a control group: the effect of increasing task complexity. *British Journal of Social and Clinical Psychology 10*: 152-9.

Sperling, G. (1960) The information available in brief visual presentation. *Psychological Monographs 74* (2): whole no.498.

Spohn, H. E., Lacoursiere, R. B., Thompson, K. and Coyne, L. (1977) Phenothiazine effects on psychological and psychophysiological dysfunction in chronic schizophrenics. *Archives of General Psychiatry 34*: 633-44.

Sternberg, S. (1969) The discovery of processing stages: extension of Donders method. *Acta Psychologica 30*: 275-315.

Sternberg, S. (1975) Memory Scanning: new findings and current controversies. *Quarterly Journal of Experimental Psychology 27*: 1-32.

Straube, E. R. and Germer, C. K. (1979) Dichotic shadowing and defective attention to word meaning in schizophrenia. *Journal of Abnormal Psychology 88*: 346-53.

Strauss, M. E. (1973) Behavioural differences between acute and chronic schizophrenics: course of psychosis, effects of institutionalization, or sampling biases. *Psychological Bulletin 79*: 271-9.

Strauss, M. E. (1978) The differential and experimental paradigms in the study of cognition in schizophrenia. *Journal of Psychiatric Research 14*: 316-26.

Taylor, J. F. and Hirt, M. (1975) Irrelevance of retention-interval length and distractor-task similarity to schizophrenic cognitive interference. *Journal of Consulting and Clinical Psychology 43*: 281-5.

Treisman, A. M. (1960) Contextual cues in selective listening. *Quarterly Journal of Experimental Psychology 12*: 242-8.

Treisman, A. M. (1964) Verbal cues, language, and meaning in selective attention. *American Journal of Psychology 77*: 206-19.

Underwood, G. (1978a) Concepts of information-processing theory. In G. Underwood (ed.) *Strategies of Information Processing*. London: Academic Press.

Underwood, G. (1978b) Attentional selectivity and behavioural control. In G. Underwood (ed.) *Strategies of Information Processing*. London: Academic Press.

Van Patten, T. and May, P. R. A. (1976) Milieu therapy of the schizo-phrenias. In L. West and D. F. Flinn (eds) *Treatment of Schizo-phrenia: Progress and Prospects*. New York: Grune & Stratton.

Venables, P. H. (1965) Slowness in schizophrenia. In A. T. Welford and J. E. Birren (eds) *Behaviour, Ageing, and the Nervous System*. Springfield, Ill.: Charles C. Thomas.

Venables, P. H. (1958) Stimulus complexity as a determinant of the reaction time of schizophrenics. *Canadian Journal of Psychology 12*: 187-90.

Weinberger, E. and Cermak, L. S. (1973) Short-term retention in acute and chronic paranoid schizophrenics. *Journal of Abnormal Psychology 82*: 220-5.

Wickens, C. D. (1974) Temporal limits of human information processing: a developmental study. *Psychological Bulletin 81*: 739-55.

Wing, J. K. and Brown, G. W. (1968) *Instiutionalism and Schizo-phrenia. A Comparative Study of Three Mental Hospitals 1960-1968*. Cambridge: Cambridge University Press.

Wishner, J. and Wahl, O. (1974) Dichotic listening in schizophrenia. *Journal of Consulting and Clinical Psychology 42*: 538-46.

Wishner, J., Stein, M. K. and Peastrel, A. L. (1978) Stages of informa-tion processing in schizophrenia: Sternberg's paradigm. In L. C. Wynne, R. L. Comwell and S. Matthysse (eds) *The Nature of Schizophrenia: New Approaches to Research and Treatment*. New York: Wiley.

Yates, A. J. (1966) Data-processing levels and thought disorder in schizophrenia. *Australian Journal of Psychology 18*: 103-17.

Zahn, T. P. and Carpenter, W. T. (1978) Effects of short term outcome and clinical improvement on reaction time in acute schizophrenia. *Journal of Psychiatric Research 14*: 59-68.

8 Drug-induced cognitive and behavioural change

D. J. Sanger and D. E. Blackman

Introduction: the science of psychopharmacology

We are all aware of the profound effects drugs can have on human behaviour. In modern Western society alcohol is probably the most widely used psychoactive drug, but many other chemicals are frequently used for altering human behaviour either for recreational purposes or for medical reasons. Indeed, history shows that man has always had a great enthusiasm for enlisting the aid of chemicals of all kinds to enable him to alter his own or others' psychological state.

Despite the long history and widespread use of psychoactive drugs, the scientific analysis of the ways in which drugs change behaviour really began only in very recent times. It is not surprising that this should be so since the science of psychopharmacology can be considered to lie between the disciplines of psychology and pharmacology, and these are themselves both relatively young areas of scientific endeavour. The development of psychopharmacology had to wait until sufficient pharmacology became known for drugs to be isolated, synthesized and administered systematically; and for psychology to have developed far enough for behaviour to be objectively measured and classified. When these developments had occurred psychopharmacology began in earnest as an objective scientific discipline. Indeed, over the last three decades very many research workers have been actively engaged in analyses of the ways in which human and animal psychological functions can be altered by drugs. In parallel with this scientific development there has also been an increase in the use of drugs by individuals both legally and illicitly for their 'mind-altering' properties, and in the use of psychoactive drugs to treat mental disorders.

We should point out here that even the relatively young science of psychopharmacology has many diverse aspects, and not all researchers would use similar methods of study nor expect similar answers to their experimental questions. Michon (1973) has pointed out that research workers with primary interests in the two parent disciplines of psychology and pharmacology are more than likely to go about the task of acquiring knowledge of psychopharmacology in rather different ways. The pharmacologist who may be interested in a particular class of drugs may wish to know something of their action on a certain psychological process. If he is interested in memory, for example, he will choose an experimental procedure which he believes measures memory and by looking at the ways in which his drugs alter the behaviour of his subjects, as measured with this technique, he will hope to learn more about the properties of his particular drugs. In contrast, a psychologist may wish to know more about the psychological process underlying some particular types of behaviour in which he is especially interested. He might, therefore, choose to study the ways in which these behaviours are modified by a drug whose mode of action at the biochemical level is particularly well understood. If this drug affects in similar ways all the behaviours he is studying, the psychologist may conclude that they all involve a similar underlying psychological process, and he may even wish to speculate on the physiological or biochemical mechanisms underlying this process.

It is possible to characterize crudely these two approaches to the study of psychopharmacology as the use of behaviour as a tool for analysing drugs and the use of drugs as tools for analysing psychological processes. Certainly, both ways of proceeding have been successful in contributing to knowledge in psychopharmacology. However, a strong warning might be sounded here as both approaches can lead to pitfalls. Neither psychology nor pharmacology is sufficiently well developed to provide fully understood experimental tools. Thus, it behoves those who study psychopharmacology to be very cautious in the interpretations which they put on their research findings. Indeed, it may for the present be convenient to consider psychopharmacology simply as the study of interactions between drugs and behaviour, rather than to expect it to provide any breakthrough in understanding the nature of psychological processes or mechanisms of drug action.

The purpose of this chapter is to provide an overview of the way modern science is studying interactions between drugs and psychological processes. It would certainly be impossible even to mention all the drugs which are known to affect behaviour or to review all the ways behaviour can be changed by even a single drug. Therefore, we hope to present a background to current knowledge in psychopharmacology, and will do this by sketching out the methodological and conceptual frameworks within which those who take an information-processing approach to psychology carry out research on the effects of drugs. Having done this we will then describe some selected examples of recent studies which have investigated the actions of drugs on human behaviour. This, we hope, will serve to provide illustrations of the ways in which knowledge is currently developing, and will also demonstrate how research can provide both fascinating insights into human behaviour and also information of great practical utility.

The classification of psychoactive drugs

A psychoactive or psychotropic drug is any drug which will alter psychological processes as defined by changes in behaviour. As in any area of scientific endeavour, psychopharmacology seeks to classify the phenomena it deals with, i.e. drugs, and in this brief section a simple classification will be presented. The reader is recommended to consult more complete works on psychopharmacology (e.g. Ray, 1978) to obtain fuller information on the variety of different drugs which are known. However, consultation of too many texts is quite likely to cause confusion as there are a variety of methods which can be used for categorizing psychoactive drugs (in terms ranging from chemical structure to legal status), and also a great deal of terminological overlap and confusion. For those interested in both drugs and behaviour the most relevant classification is in terms of the major effects of drugs, and this is what we have attempted here. However, as we will point out below, it must not be assumed that because a drug has been categorized as having a particular type of psychological effect under most circumstances it will not have a completely different effect in other conditions.

Table 8.1 provides a simple classification of the major types of psychoactive drugs, but we do not claim that this is exhaustive. Certainly, there may be drugs which will fit into none of these categories, and there are definitely drugs which fit into more than one category. Nevertheless, this classification is a well-accepted one and one which is convenient for most purposes.

It should become immediately apparent from Table 8.1 that these categories of drugs may be considered either as those used for treating psychological disorders, such as depression or anxiety, or as those used to induce abnormal psychological states. It might be said that drugs can either induce cognitive dysfunction or can improve

Table 8.1   Classification of psychoactive drugs

Type of drug	Major effects	Selected examples
Psychomotor stimulants	Increased activity Reduced fatigue Euphoria	Amphetamines, caffeine, nicotine
Hypnotics, sedatives and minor tranquillizers	Induction of sleep Reduction of anxiety	Barbiturates, Benzodiazepines, e.g. diazepam, Alcohol
Antipsychotics	Treatment of schizophrenic symptoms	Chlorpromazine, haloperidol
Antidepressants	Treatment of depression	Imipramine
Major psychedelics	Major alterations in visual perception	LSD, mescaline
Minor psychedelics	Minor alterations in perception and mood	Cannabis
Analgesics	Reduction in pain	Morphine

cognitive disorders produced by other conditions, but it should not be assumed that a particular drug will have only one or other of these two major effects; under differing circumstances the same drug may have very different actions. For example, a minor tranquillizer may be very effective at reducing anxiety in a neurotic patient and may be said to produce significant improvements in cognitive functioning. The same drug, however, may also lead to disruptions in certain psychomotor skills, such as car driving, which would be taken as indicating disrupted information processing.

By making these points we intend only to indicate that the interaction between drugs and behaviour can take a wide variety of forms. Thus, simple generalizations are rarely possible in psychopharmacology, and the temptation of drawing premature general conclusions about the effects of drugs on psychological processes should always be resisted.

The assessment of drug action

The data base of psychology consists of patterns of human and animal behaviour and the way in which behaviour changes with alterations to an organism's environment. Thus, what the psychologist or psychopharmacologist can directly observe and measure are aspects of the environment and aspects of behaviour. The conceptualization of man as an information-processing system, however, allows psychological processes to be categorized with a view to providing a means of understanding the ways in which human behaviour alters.

Figure 8.1 provides a very simple representation of man as an

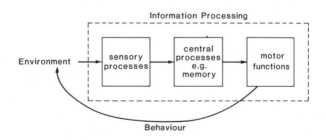

Fig. 8.1　Simplified information-processing model.

information-processing system. Here there are three hypothetical types of psychological processes which may intervene between environmental events and overt behaviour. These are sensory and perceptual processes, which are concerned with the gathering and analysis of sense data; central processes (such as memory) which involve the further analysis and elaboration of perceptual information; and motor mechanisms which involve the organization of complex sequences of overt behaviour.

The importance of this convenient conceptual system for psychopharmacology is that the changes in behaviour induced by drugs may be identified as resulting from actions at any of these three basic levels of information processing. Thus, a drug may have effects predominantly on sensory mechanisms, or on memory or perhaps on motor functions.

In order to use this model to study drug effects it is, of course, necessary to have techniques which will provide measurements of the different aspects of human information processing. In a recent discussion of the methods available for investigating the actions of drugs on human psychomotor performance, Hindmarch (1980) has provided a list, reproduced in Table 8.2, of many of the experimental methods which have been made use of in such research. It should be quite apparent, even to those unfamiliar with the details of many of these test procedures, that a plethora of methods is available to the researcher interested in studying the way drugs affect human performance. The problem, of course, for those interested in learning more about the way drugs alter specific aspects of human information processing is to be able to select tests which are able to give reliable measures of *particular* processes. It is clear that all such psychomotor tests must involve sensory processes, central processing and motor output to varied extents. Thus, if a reaction-time task is used, for example, a light may be presented to a subject who has been told to press a button as quickly as possible on seeing the light. A drug may be found to slow the time the subject takes to react. Although this result may be of interest in its own right, particularly if it is known to predict the drug's action in everyday life, it does not itself tell us very much about how the subject's psychological processes have been altered by the drug. Even the simple act of responding to a light obviously involves sensory, central and motor processing, and thus it is conceivable that the drug may have affected any one, or more, processes.

As Hindmarch and others (e.g. Clayton, 1976) have pointed out, however, by judiciously selecting test procedures it is often possible to draw inferences about the level of information processing at which a drug is acting. In attempts to assess the way drugs alter motor processes tests have been developed which require simple motor co-ordination but which have relatively small contributions made by sensory elements or central processes. A commonly used method is to ask a subject to tap a button as fast as possible for a short period of time. By contrast, in order to assess the action of a drug on sensory or perceptual processes, tasks need to be used which maximize sensory input while minimizing the non-perceptual processing required and also requiring very simple responses. Some experts prefer to use

Table 8.2 List of psychomotor tests and measures which have been used in the assessment of drug effects

Tapping speed	Digit span
Proof reading	Simple response times
Duration of spiral after-effect	Body sway
Low speed car handling	Duration of after images
Card sorting	Serial subtraction of numbers
Car-driving simulation	Purdue pegboard
Symbol copying	Stabilometer
Absolute auditory threshold	Concept identification
Verbal learning	Group vigilance
Short and long-term memory	Cancellation of numbers
Eyelid conditioning	Category clustering
Figural after-effect	Saccadic eye movements
Muscular grip strength	Rudder control test
Adaptive tracking	Multiple limb co-ordination
Beam balancing	Auditory discrimination
Digit symbol substitution	Choice reaction time
Delayed auditory feedback	Simulated night driving
Ocular convergence	Actual car driving
Speed of putting caps on pens	Spontaneous reversals of necker cube
Galvanic skin response	Two handed co-ordination
Hidden word task	Whipple's tracing board
Auditory reaction time	Trigram recognition
Gibson spiral maze	Critical flicker fusion
Time estimation	

Source: Based on the discussion presented in Hindmarch (1980) where references to studies in which all these and other procedures used for studying drug effects will be found.

methods based on traditional psychophysics for this purpose (e.g. Michon, 1973), but many other tasks have important perceptual elements. One measure which has been used in psychopharmaco-logical research is the critical-flicker frequency which is the frequency at which a flickering light appears to a subject as a continuous light. This measure, which presumably provides an indication of sensory processing, is altered by a number of drugs including stimulants and sedatives (Smith and Misiak, 1976).

All the test procedures listed in Table 8.2 involve central processing to greater or lesser extents. The method selected for an experimental study, however, will of course depend upon the interest of the experimenter. If memory processes are being investigated, for example, techniques can be selected or developed which maximize the contribution of memory processes while attempting to minimize sensory and motor elements. In this way the effects of a drug on different aspects of memory can be assessed.

In the following sections we will show how, by careful and often laborious research, psychopharmacologists have recently been able to add to knowledge about the ways human behaviour is altered by drugs. We will first describe some studies of the alterations to sensory and perceptual functioning produced by drugs, and secondly, some studies of the effects of drugs on human memory; and finally, we will give some consideration to the actions of drugs on motor processes. In each of these three sections neither a review of the different ways the particular cognitive process is changed by a certain drug, nor a complete description of the alterations to this process induced by drugs from different classes will be found. Instead, we have selected a small number of recent studies which seem to exemplify many aspects of modern human psychopharmacology. In this way we hope that the reader will acquire an understanding of some of the many ways in which drugs can change human behaviour, and also note some of the complexities and problems involved in carrying out this research.

The effects of drugs on sensory processes

The class of drugs which appears to affect sensory processes is that which we have called psychedelics. These drugs have also been called psychotomimetics and hallucinogens. The term psychotomimetic was used because it was thought that such drugs produced a condition similar to psychosis, but most authorities now believe that this comparison is not entirely appropriate as psychedelic drugs generally induce changes in visual perception which occur relatively infrequently in schizophrenic patients. The use of the term hallucinogen is also not favoured by some workers since it implies that these drugs produce 'true' hallucinations, whereas their primary effects may be to induce distortion of normal perception.

We have chosen the more neutral term psychedelic here, but whatever the name used for these drugs their main characteristic is that users report that they induce very vivid distortions of visual perception. The drugs having the most major action in this respect are mescaline, which is a naturally occurring substance and has been used for many years by North American Indians, and LSD which was first synthesized by Hofmann several decades ago. A variety of other drugs also appear to have effects on sensory and perceptual processes, which justify their being characterized as either major or minor psychedelics. These range from cannabis, whose effects seem relatively mild, to phencyclidine, which produces a number of major effects on perceptual and other psychological processes which have led to its use being considered to produce a major social problem in the USA in recent years (Snyder, 1980).

As we have indicated in a previous section, there are many methods which an experimenter might select to investigate the actions of drugs on sensory and perceptual processing. With drugs such as LSD and mescaline it might be argued, however, that the effects experienced by users are so profound that to demonstrate that these drugs alter sensory thresholds, critical-flicker fusion thresholds or visual acuity might be adding to knowledge of their mode of action in only relatively trivial ways. To attempt to obtain more detailed and meaningful information about the psychopharmaco-logy of psychedelic drugs Siegel, Jarvik and their colleagues carried out a systematic research programme on the action of these drugs, and have reviewed the results of their own and other workers' studies (Siegel and Jarvik, 1975).

Having demonstrated that psychedelic drugs would produce changes in the behaviour of laboratory animals indicative of altered perceptual processing, Siegel and Jarvik went on to study the action of the same drugs in man. In the initial studies subjects were given marihuana or tetrahydrocannabinol (the active constituent of marihuana and cannabis). They were then placed in a dark room where they were instructed to close their eyes and report their visual imagery, paying particular attention to forms, colours and movements. The verbal reports were tape recorded and later analysed by observers, who were able to place the imagery reported by the subjects into a variety of categories of forms (e.g. curve, line, random, etc.), colours, and movements (e.g. vertical, horizontal, rotational, etc.).

The experimenters found that the drugs caused the subjects to provide many more reports of visual images than did subjects in a placebo condition, and Table 8.3 shows some of the results obtained in this study. After smoking the marihuana cigarettes the subjects reported seeing more visual images and the number of images reported increased with increasing doses of THC. Similar effects occurred with all three imagery categories. However, although it was possible to categorize imagery into forms, colours and movements, the subjects often noted that they had difficulty in putting their visual experiences into words. For this reason subsequent studies made use of subjects who, before receiving drugs, were first trained in a kind of concept-identification task.

To do this the experimenters showed their subjects a very large number of slides containing shapes and colours which the subjects were trained to categorize in several ways. The colour categories were black, violet, blue, green, yellow, orange, red and white; the form categories, random, line, curve, web, lattice, tunnel, spiral and kaleidoscope; and the movement categories, aimless, vertical, horizontal, oblique, explosive, concentric, rotational and pulsating.

Table 8.3 Total number of imagery reports after marihuana (n = 14)

Type of Imagery	Placebo	Dose of THC		
		4.25 µg/lb	9.41 µg/lb	40.0 µg/lb
Form	170	248	277	313
Colour	246	248	296	327
Movement	33	67	72	84

Source: Adapted from Siegel and Jarvik, 1975.
Each value is the total number of imagery reports given after placebo and after smoking marihuana containing different doses of THC expressed as µg/lb body weight.

(Apparent movement was produced with the slides by using a method of rotary polarization). When the subjects were thoroughly familiar with these methods of categorizing visual stimuli they were again given drugs and asked to report their visual imagery.

Several drugs were used in this study and it was found that psychedelic drugs (LSD, mescaline, psilocybin and THC) not only increased the frequency with which the subjects reported visual images, but that the relative frequencies reported in different categories were changed substantially. When they had not been given a drug the subjects tended to report random forms, black, violet and white colours and aimless and pulsating movement. The psychedelic drugs, however, produced increases in the reports of lattice and tunnel forms, orange, red and yellow colours and oblique and concentric movements.

Having obtained these findings about the nature of the visual imagery produced by psychedelic drugs, Siegel and Jarvik went on to carry out more complex analyses of the subjects' reports and to draw conclusions and speculate about the mechanisms of action involved. The importance of this research lies in the demonstration that with ingenuity and care, the methods of modern experimental psychology can be successfully applied to the study of drug-induced alteration of perceptual processes.

The effects of drugs on central processes

The information-processing model of human psychological activity puts great emphasis on central cognitive processes which are believed to mediate sensory and motor mechanisms. Such central processing involves the integration of perceptual information with stored information to give rise to complex behaviour. In order to assess the effects of drugs on central processing a variety of techniques have been devised and utilized in psychopharmacological studies. These include measures of accuracy and speed of carrying out mental arithmetic, and the digit symbol substitution test in which a subject is required to replace digits with symbols according to a pre-established code (Hindmarch, 1980).

Information storage and retrieval are important aspects of cognitive activity and it is of considerable interest to know in what ways memory can be altered by drug administration for three reasons. First, it is important to know whether drugs which are used, either clinically or non-clinically, for other purposes might give rise to impaired memory function. Clearly, it would be most undesirable if a drug used to treat anxiety or depression were found to interfere with patients' ability to store or retrieve information. There are, in fact, data to suggest that a variety of common drugs, including alcohol, benzodiazepine tranquillizers and cannabis, can, under certain conditions, interfere with memory.

The second reason for studying drug-induced changes in memory is in the hope that drugs will be discovered which can actually improve human memory. In the past a small number of drugs have been identified which have appeared to enhance either information storage or retrieval. Claims to have demonstrated such effects, however, have generally been controversial, and at present there is no drug or group of drugs which is generally accepted as improving memory in normal man. Recent research, however, has set itself the more realistic aim of searching, not for drugs which improve memory in everyone, but rather to discover drugs which may produce improvements in patients suffering from impaired memory function. There are quite large numbers of individuals suffering from senile or presenile dementia in whom pharmacological agents might be able to produce significant improvements in memory and thus greatly improve the quality of life. At the present time research is being carried out in a number of laboratories, both in universities and in pharmaceutical companies, to identify a drug which would be useful in such patients, and a number of interesting leads have been identified. Squire and Davis (1981) have recently reviewed a large amount of work on the pharmacology of memory.

Alterations to memory processes induced by drug administration are also of interest for the knowledge they may provide about the physiological basis of human memory. Drugs which are known to have certain actions on the biochemistry of the brain may be used in studies of memory either in animals or man. The results of these studies may then be used to draw conclusions about the role of certain biochemical mechanisms in information storage. To provide one example: acetylcholine is believed to act as a transmitter substance, carrying messages between neurones in the brain. Drugs which interfere with the activity of acetylcholine have been reported on a number of occasions (e.g. Caine et al., 1981) to lead to disruptions of memory processes, and this has led many researchers to the view that acetylcholine may play an important role in the physiological substrate of memory.

Of course, as human memory is a complex set of processes complex procedures and experimental designs are necessary to assess the ways it is affected by drugs. Heise (1981) has recently pointed out that we infer that memory consists of three basic processes: learning, retention and retrieval, and drugs may interfere with memory at any of these levels according to when the drug is taken or its mode of action. Thus, if a drug prevents learning from occurring then clearly retention and retrieval also cannot occur. It is also possible, however, that a drug may inhibit or enhance retrieval without learning or retention being affected. It is of great importance in studies of drug effects on memory that conclusions about memory processes are not drawn prematurely when a drug is found to alter behaviour in a memory task. Thus, an apparent failure to learn after taking a drug may indeed be due to impaired learning, retention or retrieval, but might also be caused by interference with sensory, motor or motivational processes.

An example to illustrate this point was provided by a study carried out by Darley and his colleagues (Darley *et al.*, 1973). These researchers were interested in the possibility that marihuana might interfere with the retrieval of information from a short-term memory store. In order to assess this experimentally they used a memory-search paradigm developed by Sternberg (1966). Subjects were given either an oral dose of marihuana extract or a placebo, and on each trial of the memory test they were read a list of words. Following each list a test word was presented and each subject was required to press one of two buttons according to whether the test word was present in the list (called positive and negative responses). The measure of retrieval from memory was the reaction time taken to press a button. Marihuana was found to increase these reaction times and both positive and negative response times increased as is shown in Figure 8.2. However, a detailed analysis of the results led these researchers to conclude that the drug was probably not exerting a specific action on memory processes but rather was having a generalized action on motor mechanisms.

Another factor which needs to be taken into account in considering the way drugs alter memory processes is state-dependent learning. It has been demostrated in many experiments with animals and man that if information is learned in a particular drug state then it may in some circumstances be retrieved only when the organism is again in the same state. The opposite may also be true, that information learned in a non-drug state can only be retrieved in this state. This phenomenon is, of course, of considerable importance as drugs may on occasion appear to be preventing information from being learned when they are, in fact, producing state-dependent learning.

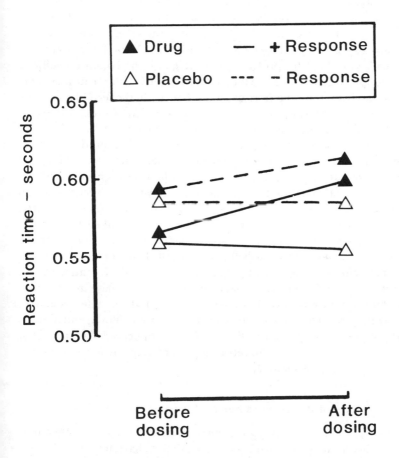

Fig. 8.2   The effects of a dose of THC on reaction times of positive and negative responses in a memory-search procedure.
Source: Darley *et al.* (1973).

A dramatic illustration of state-dependent learning induced by alcohol was provided in a study by Petersen (1977). Petersen was concerned to investigate not only whether state-dependent learning was produced by alcohol, but also whether the occurrence of this phenomenon depended upon the particular learning task used. The experimental design that was necessary for demonstrating state-dependent learning consisted of four conditions. Subjects learned the experimental material after being given either alcohol or placebo (the drug and non-drug states), and were subsequently tested under either the same or opposite conditions, thus producing changes in state in both directions. On the first day the subjects were asked to learn lists of words under four conditions; in two of the conditions recall was aided by providing cues (e.g. in one condition subjects were given lists of words which could be cued with a category label such as 'fruit' for the names of several fruit). On the second day of the experiment the subjects were asked to recall the words; and again cues were provided in the appropriate conditions.

The results of this study showed that alcohol produced state-dependent learning, but only on the two learning tasks where cues were not presented. Thus, subjects who had been given alcohol on the first trial but not the second trial, showed less accurate recall than subjects who had been given alcohol on both trials. Similarly, subjects given alcohol on only the second trial recalled fewer items than subjects who had been tested under placebo on both trials. Under the conditions involving cued recall, however, no such state-dependent learning was apparent, and indeed alcohol appeared to have no effects on either learning or recall. These results thus demonstrated not only that alcohol could produce state-dependent learning, but also that whether or not this occurred depended upon the context in which recall occurred. It appeared, in fact, that providing cues as an aid to retrieval prevented the drug from causing any disruption of memory.

The effects of drugs on motor performance

Changes in information processing produced by drugs can, of course, only be directly observed as changes in behaviour. As all overt behaviour involves motor activity, drug-induced alterations in motor activity could be produced through actions on sensory or central processes. It is also possible though that some drugs may leave sensory and central processing unaffected, but may, nevertheless, produce disruptions of motor performance.

Because psychoactive drugs are used very widely by many individuals, it is of great importance to know how motor performance is affected by different drugs. Many aspects of modern life involve complex motor skills, and decrements in skilled performance could lead to a variety of problems and perhaps dangers. The most widely known example is, of course, car driving, and there has been legislation in force for some years to attempt to prevent individuals from driving at times when their performance is impaired by alcohol or other drugs. In addition to the well known dangers of impaired performance produced by alcohol and other 'social' drugs, it is important to determine whether the many drugs used clinically for treating psychological disorders, and indeed other medical complaints, may also interfere with the ability to drive. It should also be remembered that many other behaviours both at work and in the home involve complex motor skills, and interference with skilled performance by drugs which disrupt motor activity could have significant consequences here also.

Many studies of the decrements in car-driving performance produced by alcohol have been carried out over the last 30 years, and Clayton (1976, 1980) has written two useful reviews of this work. These studies had as their purpose both the search for a better understanding of the psychopharmacology of alcohol and also the rather less academic aim of establishing a legal limit for blood-alcohol levels (as this was considered to be a predictor of impaired performance) and a convenient method for assessing such levels. This, of course, was established some years ago, but it should not be thought that it constituted a threshold below which there was necessarily no impairment of car-driving ability or other types of motor performance. The extent to which an individual's performance is impaired by alcohol or any other drug will depend upon many factors relating both to the particular situation and also to the individual.

The development of appropriate experimental techniques for studying the effects of drugs on driving and other types of motor performance is not an easy matter. Of course, it is possible to study drug effects in a 'naturalistic' setting, and studies have been carried out in which the car driving of subjects who had been given drugs was monitored. Bjerver and Goldberg (1950), for example, found that alcohol increased the length of time required for subjects to complete several driving manoeuvres. It is not always possible to use such a naturalistic setting for assessing drug action, however, and even when it is possible the accurate measurement of performance may present problems. What is necessary is a more convenient test, or set of tests, which can be used in the laboratory, but which will provide a good prediction of performance in everyday skills.

This may be achieved by developing a complex test which simulates many of the aspects of driving, and driving simulators have been used in many research studies. Another approach which has been preferred by some reseachers, involves searching for simple laboratory measures whose impairment by drugs will nevertheless predict the impairment of much more complex motor performance such as car driving. As mentioned earlier, several test procedures have been developed, such as speed of tapping or balancing on a pivot, which attempt to assess motor performance while minimizing the role of sensory or central processing. These tests have been quite widely used and a number of drugs including sedatives and tranquillizers have been found to impair performance (Hindmarch, 1980; Wittenborn, 1979). Such impairments do not necessarily predict decrements in driving and other complex skills, although it is generally to be expected that complex motor performance will be disrupted by drugs more readily than will simpler motor responses (Kleinknecht et al., 1975).

In one recent study Ellinwood and his colleagues (Ellinwood et al., 1981) set out to investigate whether interference with performance in some very simple laboratory tests would provide a prediction of impaired driving ability. These researchers noted that two relatively complex tasks, a tracking task and a task involving divided attention, provided a useful indication of car-driving performance. However, even these two laboratory procedures involved considerable amounts of time and facilities to carry out effectively. For certain purposes, therefore, particularly as practical tests of whether an individual was unfit to drive a car, they were rather inconvenient. Therefore, this group of workers carried out a study in which they correlated the effects of a sedative on measures of tracking ability with the effects of the drug on two much simpler measures: standing steadiness and pendulum eye tracking.

The volunteers who acted as subjects in this study were asked to carry out several tasks after being given a placebo or three doses of pentobarbital. After taking the drug, the volunteers performed the tasks at four time periods to provide measures of the length of action of the drug. At each time period the subjects were given tests of continuous tracking, standing steadiness and pendulum eye tracking. Continuous tracking was measured as a subject sat watching a screen on which a moving bar was projected. By using a steering wheel the subject tried to keep the bar in the centre of the screen, and his skill in doing this was automatically recorded. Standing steadiness was measured simply by asking the subject to stand on a platform facing straight ahead with eyes closed, and the amount of body movement was then recorded. Pendulum eye tracking was also recorded very simply; each subject watched a bar projected on a screen, the bar moving from side to side in a pendulum-like motion, and the accuracy with which the subject's eyes were able to track the bar was recorded with electrodes.

As the experimenters had expected, performance on the complex continuous-tracking task and also on the two simple tests was impaired by the barbiturate. These results are illustrated in Figure 8.3, which shows the time course for the effects of two doses of the barbiturate in impairing performance on the complex tracking task and in the standing-steadiness test. It was clear that there was a strong correlation between these time courses, and a similar correlation was found with measures of pendulum eye tracking. In fact, the correlation between impaired performance on each of the two simple tasks and impaired performance on the complex task was considerably better than the correlation between impaired performance and the concentration of the drug in the blood. This indicates that with this particular drug, blood levels do not necessarily provide an accurate indication of impaired psychomotor performance.

As the authors of this study pointed out, the correlation between the effects of the drug on the complex and the simple tests did not necessarily show that all the tests were measuring the same aspect of human performance. It is possible, though, that the deficit on the complex procedure was produced through mechanisms similar to those producing the deficits in the simple tests. Of greater practical importance, however, was the finding that it was possible to use simple tests to provide an indication of when drugs would lead to impairments of performance in complex skills such as driving.

We should end this section by pointing out yet again that it is not always easy to analyse drug actions in terms of specific aspects of human information processing. As we have tried to indicate, much research, together with individual experience and observation, does seem to suggest that drugs can act directly to interfere with motor

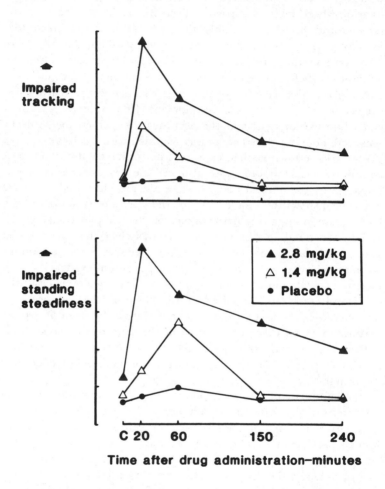

Fig. 8.3   Time courses of the impairment of continuous tracking and standing steadiness produced by two doses of pentobarbital. The data points at C are control values.
Source: adapted from Ellinwood *et al.* (1981).

processes. However, as we noted earlier, even the most simple motor tasks such as standing steady or tapping a key do involve sensory and central, in addition to motor, processing.

Conclusions

Our aim in this chapter has been to provide a brief description of some aspects of contemporary research in psychopharmacology, together with some selected examples of recent studies. We have done this by dealing with human psychopharmacology in terms of an information-processing model of human cognitive function. Such a model suggests that psychological functions can be usefully categorized into several types of process and it is then possible to consider drug action in terms of the effects drugs exert on each of these stages of information processing.

This approach to understanding the ways drugs change behaviour has been used quite explicitly by many research workers in both human (e.g. Hindmarch, 1980) and animal (e.g. Morris and Gebhart, 1981) psychopharmacology. As the examples presented in earlier sections of the chapter show, research of this type has been successful in extending our knowledge. However, one rather basic fact should be always remembered: that psychoactive drugs act directly on physiological and biochemical mechanisms in the brain and other organs to give rise to changes in behaviour. It is these changes in behaviour which the psychopharmacologist is able to measure, and it is from these basic data that information processing and its disruption by drugs is inferred.

All behaviour, however, involves interactions between organisms and their environment, and necessarily involves sensory, motor and central processes. Most drugs also are known to exert a variety of actions on different biochemical mechanisms. Thus, the difficulty of drawing simple conclusions about the mode of action of drugs on particular psychological processes or aspects of information processing should not be underestimated. The consideration of drug action in terms of information processing may provide a convenient and helpful method of organizing data, and may indeed allow for a greater understanding of, and ability to predict, drug action. However, the psychopharmacologist should beware of straying too far from the experimental data.

224 The pathology and psychology of cognition
References

Bjerver, K. and Goldberg, L. (1950) Effects of alcohol ingestion on driving ability: results of practical road tests and laboratory experiments. *Quarterly Journal of Studies of Alcohol 11*: 1-30.

Caine, E. D., Weingartner, H., Ludlow, C. L., Cudahy, E. A. and Wehry, S. (1981) Qualitative analysis of scopolamine-induced amnesia. *Psychopharmacology 74*: 74-80.

Clayton, A. B. (1976) The effects of psychotropic drugs on driving-related skills. *Human Factors 18*: 241-52.

Clayton, A. B. (1980) Effects of alcohol on driving skills. In M. Sandler (ed.) *Psychopharmacology of Alcohol*. New York: Raven Press.

Darley, C. F., Tinklenberg, J. R., Hollister, T. E. and Atkinson, R. C. (1973) Marihuana and retrieval from short-term memory. *Psychopharmacologia 29*: 231-8.

Ellinwood, E. H., Linnoila, M., Angle, H. V., Moore, J. W., Skinner, J. T., Easlier, M. and Molter, D. W. (1981) Use of simple tasks to test for impairment of complex skills by a sedative. *Psychopharmacology 73*: 350-4.

Heise, G. A. (1981) Learning and memory facilitators: experimental definition and current status. *Trends in Pharmacological Sciences* (June): 158-60.

Hindmarch, I. (1980) Psychomotor function and psychoactive drugs. *British Journal of Clinical Pharmacology 10*: 189-209.

Kleinknecht, R. A. and Donaldson, D. (1975) A review of the effects of diazepam on cognitive and psychomotor performance. *Journal of Nervous and Mental Disease 161*: 399-411.

Michon, J. A. (1973) Human information processing - with and without drugs. *Psychiatria Neurologia Neurochirurgia 76*: 163-74.

Morris, M. D. and Gebhart, G. F. (1981) Antianxiety agents and emotional behavior: an information-processing analysis. *Progress in Neuro-Psychopharmacology 5*: 219-40.

Petersen, R. C. (1977) Retrieval in alcohol state-dependent learning. *Psychopharmacology 55*: 141-6.

Ray, O. (1978) *Drugs, Society and Human Behavior*. St Louis: C. V. Mosby.

Siegel, R. K. and Jarvik, M. E. (1975) Drug-induced hallucinations in animals and man. In R. K. Siegel and L. J. West (eds) *Hallucinations: Behavior, Experience and Theory*. New York: Wiley.

Smith, J. M. and Misiak, H. (1976) Critical flicker frequency (CFF) and psychotropic drugs in normal human subjects - a review. *Psychopharmacology 47*: 175-82.

Snyder, S. H. (1980) Phencyclidine. *Nature 285*: 355-6.

Squire, L. R. and Davis, H. P. (1981) The pharmacology of memory: a neurobiological perspective. *Annual Review of Pharmacology and Toxicology 21*: 323-56.

Sternberg, S. (1966) High-speed scanning in human memory. *Science 153*, 652-4.

Wittenborn, J. R. (1979) Effects of benzodiazepines on psychomotor performance. *British Journal of Clinical Pharmacology 7*: 615-75.

9 Cognitive dysfunction following loss of sleep

Ray Meddis

The study of the psychological consequences of prolonged sleep loss has a long and distinguished history. This kind of research is difficult, expensive and exhausting; it requires, and has obtained, investigators of the highest degree of resilience and resourcefulness. As a result of their efforts we now have the benefit of a fine collection of reports detailing with all scientific precision the effects of up to and beyond 200 hours of sleep loss on man's ability to perform at carefully designed batteries of objective psychological tests. Despite these, we still have no generally agreed theory to explain how sleep loss affects man's information-processing ability. This challenge remains as fresh as ever for the next generation of cognitive psychologists.

In this chapter we shall look at the progress made so far and the methodological and conceptual issues which may be impeding this progress, and I shall argue, with the benefit of hindsight, that our problems lie mainly in the unsuitability of the traditional approach to measuring cognitive changes in the presence of stress. Recent research which systematically records spontaneously occurring failures of perceptions and actions, may well be pointing the way forward to a more fruitful style of investigation. We shall look at this possibility in the light of what we already know about the ability of sleep loss to induce hallucinations and inappropriate action.

226 The pathology and psychology of cognition

Throughout the discussion I shall be concerned to discover the reasons why no generally acceptable theory of the psychological effects of sleep deprivation has emerged. In a recent, long and scholarly review of the problem, Kjellberg (1977) summed up the situation as follows:

> The variable results reported during the eighty years of sleep-deprivation research has definitely shown that sleep deprivation does not lead to a state of the organism which can be described by enumerating a number of physiological, behavioural and pheno-menological effects. The futility of a search for the effects of sleep deprivation in itself on any of these levels has been repeatedly demonstrated.

The interested reader is advised to read Kjellberg's detailed account.

Historical perspective

Historically, sleep-deprivation studies are thought to have come of age with an investigation by Patrick and Gilbert (1896) who took three young men, deprived them of sleep for twenty hours, and measured a number of physiological and psychological variables at regular intervals during the vigil. The basic idea was to treat lack of sleep as similar to a physiological deficit such as lack of oxygen. The job of the scientist was to record the ability of the human frame to withstand the stress and to monitor its downward progress. Only two years before, Manaceine (1894) had attempted a similar experiment on dogs, which had died after four or five days. Patrick and Gilbert did not appear to have been put off by the possibility of death in their subjects, and fortunately were rewarded with nothing more danger-ous than extreme sleepiness. Some of their tests, such as choice-reaction time, were not obviously affected by the procedure, but performance decrements were observed for memorization of long digit strings and speed of naming letters in printed text. Speed-of-addition tests yielded equivocal results, however. Their volunteers experienced difficulty in staying awake, showed lapses in memory, reported the intrusion of 'dreams' into their waking thoughts and, on at least one occasion, made a statement which was obviously related to a dream rather than to what was going on at the time.

The basic design of their experiment was simple enough and is typical of almost all studies up to the present. This involves taking a small group of healthy, often carefully selected, volunteers and keeping them in some place where they can be prevented from sleeping for the prescribed duration. At intervals during the vigil the volunteers submit to a battery of tests which are assumed to measure some psychological functions such as perception, vigilance, memory, speed of reaction, problem solving, etc. Other measures of mood, and physiological parameters such as body temperature, muscle tension, heart rate, electrical brain rhythms, etc., might also be made at this time. Usually, a wide range of tests will be chosen, since one of the aims of such studies is to discover which functions, if any, are impaired by sleep loss and which are not.

Kleitman (1963) reviews all of the relevant research literature for the first half of the twentieth century. Surprisingly, he was obliged to report an absence of any consistent psychological deficits. For example, Robinson and Herrman (1922) deprived three men for sixty-five hours and used tests of steadiness, accuracy of aiming, muscular strength, ability to name letters and mental arithmetic. The performance scores 'were not affected by insomnia in any marked or consistent pattern' (see Kleitman, 1963, p.220). Study after study produced an accumulation of contradictory results, so it was not surprising that no coherent and generally accepted theory of sleep loss effects emerged during this period. There was, of course, no doubt that the volunteers were extremely sleepy; they were also often very irritable or dejected, and occasionally experienced hallucinations or misperceptions. The objective test results, however, did not supply any firm ground for pinning down the nature of the deficit.

This was the context in which a sudden blossoming of sleep research occurred during the 1950s and 1960s. These studies emphasized sleep deprivation as a practical problem with applications in industry and the military; and their purpose was to evaluate how sleep affected performance and to devise ways to minimize these effects. They also drew heavily on the current research into psychological processes which were currently being studied in cognitive psychology laboratories (memory, short-term memory, vigilance, signal-detection theory, individual differences as measured by personality inventories, etc.). In addition, investigators showed a new interest in the basic issue of the 'function' of sleep; they were anxious to identify just what was being recovered and how. Sleep deprivation was an obvious tool to use; by observing the difficulties of a man who was starved of sleep they should have been able to collect clues as to what value sleep had for him.

During this renaissance a number of major investigations into the effects of lack of sleep were carried out (e.g. Pasnau *et al.*, 1968; Williams *et al.*, 1959; Berger and Oswald, 1962; Johnson, 1969). These were typically characterized by teams of investigators with skills in many different fields such as psychiatry, physiology, psychology, medicine and biochemistry, collaborating in single, large-scale experiments by taking many measures on a wide range of variables from participants who were expected to stay awake for very long periods – often up to 200 hours. A complementary but contrasting programme was begun in Cambridge, England, by Wilkinson (1970), who used many smaller-scale experiments and concentrated on patiently isolating the variables which were most sensitive to sleep loss. An important additional element in many of these investigations was an interest in the link between the effects of sleep loss and schizophrenia. A number of reports were already available (for example Katz and Landis, 1935; West *et al.*, 1962) which emphasized the possibly psychotic quality of many of the effects of prolonged sleep deprivation. Florid hallucinations had been reported, along with paranoid episodes and general confusion. To some extent, these interests were separate from the issues of forgetfulness and loss of concentration, but they were as much to the fore in terms of public interest.

This new generation of studies did find some performance decrements following sleep loss over a wide range of tasks. A general rule emerged that they were most severe when the test was prolonged or inherently boring, and least severe when the test was short, interesting or supported by incentives. It was confirmed that sleep-deprived volunteers could greatly improve their performance to normal levels by trying harder, (thus showing that the basic mental apparatus was capable of functioning normally for short periods at least), but for some reason they were prone to let matters drift as soon as conscious effort was reduced. Considerable mood swings were observed from dull lifelessness to heightened instability, and all subjects showed signs of the strain from having to make a continuous effort to stay awake. Hallucinations were rare, but still made an occasional appearance. Misperceptions and dreams intruding into waking thoughts were more common.

Selective sleep deprivation

More recently, studies of total sleep deprivation have been supplemented by experiments using selective deprivation of particular kinds of sleep. Human sleep is composed of two types, known loosely as active sleep (AS) and quiet sleep (QS); AS is also known as rapid-eye-movement (REM) sleep and produces the most vivid dream reports if the sleeper is woken from it (Foulkes, 1962). By waking people whenever they show the signs of AS, it is possible to reduce the proportion of time spent in this state from 20 per cent to negligible amounts. It is not possible to deprive people selectively of QS since attempts to do so usually result in no sleep at all. However, QS is made up of discriminable subtypes known as deep, quiet sleep (DQS or stages 3 and 4) and light, quiet sleep (LQS or stage 2). It is possible to deprive people of DQS, but LQS deprivation typically also results in no sleep at all.

Most attention has been given to AS-deprivation studies for various reasons. First, its existence is a recent and surprising discovery which has attracted a considerable research effort; secondly, psychology has traditionally attached considerable importance to the therapeutic and possibly cathartic value of dreaming for the healthy individual. The belief, prevalent two decades ago, that sleep deprivation might lead to psychotic symptoms inevitably encouraged the belief that the sleep-deprived person might be suffering mainly from a 'lack of dreams'. Selective deprivation of AS was an obvious procedure for evaluating this theory. Indeed the earliest attempt (see Dement, 1972) did lead to the conclusion that AS deprivation did lead to 'psychological distress'. Unfortunately, the experiment was flawed by the lack of a control group, and subsequent research produced contradictory and largely negative results (see Cohen, 1979 for review). An ironic twist to this story is that recent research (see e.g. Vogel et al., 1972) has led to the suggestion that some forms of mental illness (such as endogenous depression) may, in fact, be ameliorated by selective deprivation of AS. The demise of the dream-deprivation-leads-to-madness hypothesis has not killed off research in this area, which continues in all vigour. However, its main thrust now is to explore the information-processing activities which may be taking place *during* sleep such as memory consolidation or re-evaluation of recent experiences. Many of the results in this area remain controversial and difficult to evaluate and I shall, therefore, continue to concentrate on the effects of loss of sleep on waking cognitive processes.

The results of these experiments showed quite clearly that sleep deprivation did not necessarily affect any one particular psychological function; what seemed to be most affected was the ability to sustain performance. This simple principle was very useful in explaining many of the contradictions of the past. Volunteers may or may not show a performance deficit according to how hard they were trying or how interested they were in the task. Is this then the final disappointing answer: that volunteers continue to function normally but become less and less inclined to try hard? It seems an unlikely conclusion, but one which might seem inevitable if we restrict our attention too closely to the results of objective performance tests.

Total sleep-deprivation experiment

Before looking in detail at the conceptual issues raised by total sleep-deprivation research in general, it will prove worthwhile to look at a single study in some detail, and this will give the reader an impression of what might actually happen. A good sleep-deprivation study is an enormously complex and expensive operation, fraught with the need for compromises and difficult decisions. It is exhausting for subjects and experimenters alike, and is haunted by the possibility that nothing of real value need result at the end of the day.

Haslam (1981) has recently reported a substantial investigation mounted by the British Army Personnel Research Establishment. The study has benefited by having many previous studies to draw on at the design stage, and is principally distinguished by its efforts to create a realistic combat situation with troops dug into a defensive position in cold weather, repelling attacks by 'enemy' troops and creating their own ambush attacks. Ten soldiers (including two NCOs), formed into a rifle section, were studied under conditions of no sleep for 90 hours (4 days, 3 nights), followed by 6 days with 4 hours sleep per 24 hours. They were dug into a full-section defensive position in open country during November with a typical air temperature of 7°C, but low rainfall, and expected to deal with surprise attacks by 'enemy' troops. In addition, they carried out such routine activities as mine-laying, mine-clearing, first aid, casualty evacuation, marching, patrolling, ambushing, etc. Furthermore, they were subjected daily to a battery of tests to assess shooting, vigilance, cognitive functioning and physical fitness. They were also assessed for military effectiveness.

As the experiment progressed, the soldiers showed a gradual decrement in vigilance-shooting on an electronic target range, logical reasoning and deciphering coded messages. Their performance improved markedly after only one 4-hour session of sleep. However, accuracy of shooting at a stationary target (grouping) was not affected at any time, neither was shooting at moving targets. Both of these tasks were self-paced in the sense that the soldiers could take aim and choose their moment for firing. By contrast, the vigilance-shooting task (which did show a decrement) had offered only brief and unpredictable exposures of the target; it was therefore very sensitive to any weakening of concentration.

All of the soldiers reported some visual misperceptions on the second or third days without sleep, but these misperceptions ceased and did not reappear after the first 4-hour block of sleep. One of the illusions was considered real enough for a sleepy soldier to draw it to the attention of others (an enemy patrol 'ready to move') whereupon the illusion vanished. A number of false alarms occurred in a night-time vigilance observation task when soldiers (alone at the time) reported sightings of enemy movements when no enemy was present. These errors did not occur when the soldiers were working in pairs on the same task.

As the trial progressed, the section became more united and the section commander felt the need to adopt a more relaxed style of leadership. The soldiers' movements, reactions and speech became slower, and towards the end of the vigil they were continually falling asleep and needing to be wakened. This was especially problematic at night. Mood ratings showed a deterioration as sleep loss accumulated. Significantly, however, the biggest drop in ratings for the whole experiment occurred towards the end of the experiment (when they were sleeping 4 hours each day) when there was a change for the worse in the washing facilities!

This experiment confirmed many of the observations raised by three-quarters of a century of sleep-deprivation research:

(1) increased sleepiness and greater mood fluctuations;
(2) occasional misperceptions (especially during quiet conditions when operating alone at night);

(3) poor performance at tasks requiring sustained attention;
(4) good performance on routine tasks or tasks which were self-paced, such as shooting at a target.

Methodological problems

But how many of these effects were due simply to the artificial aspects of being guinea pigs in an experiment? How many were due to the rigours of round-the-clock activity? Could the soldiers not have become irritated and disaffected by the indignity of the continual round of rather pointless-seeming psychological tests? Did they report hallucinations simply because this was expected of them, or did they experience them merely as a consequence of heightened suggestibility? Why was there no control group? What would an appropriate control group look like?

From the earliest days, sleep deprivation experiments have been particularly plagued by problems associated with interpreting their results. Individual studies may have succeeded in dealing with some of these problems, but it would not be unfair to say that the majority of investigations leave a great deal to be desired in this respect. This is not necessarily due to careless experimentation; the problems are such that proper control may always prove elusive. We must pause, then, to examine some of the issues.

The first and easiest difficulty to appreciate arises from the use of repeated measures. Most investigators choose to sleep deprive their volunteers and test them repeatedly using the same or similar tests at intervals throughout the vigil. This means that the sleep-deprived individual inevitably becomes more practised as the experiment proceeds, and as a result his execution of the task should be improving. However, if lack of sleep is depressing his performance, then the two effects may simply cancel out, creating the impression that sleep deprivation does not affect performance at all! More seriously, we must face the possibility of boredom with repeated testing; as we have seen, sleep-deprived volunteers may simply not be trying hard enough. Could this simply be a boredom effect?

We can tackle this problem in various ways, but each solution has its shortcomings. First, we might train participants intensively on a task before embarking on the sleep-deprivation sessions. Unfortunately, the sleep-loss condition is different from training sessions in many ways, and sleep-deprived people need to learn special techniques to combat the debilitating effects of fatigue such as tensing muscles, blinking frequently, etc., so that practice effects do continue. Another complication is that some psychologists like to distinguish between new and over-trained skills, so that training sessions may completely change the nature of the performance being studied from unskilled to skilled.

A second solution involves running a control group in parallel, who are tested as often and at the same times as the experimental group, the only operational difference being that members of the control group are allowed to sleep normally. Of course, this means that tests can only be carried out during the day, and this is a serious limitation since the most dramatic consequences of sleep deprivation are only apparent at night. We might try waking the control group during the night for the purpose of administering the tests, but this would inevitably cause some sleep deprivation in the control group and poor performance may be caused simply by the difficulty of waking up. More seriously, the experimental group are experiencing attitudinal and mood changes which will alter their approach to the experimenters and their tests. They may lose interest in the test or (for different experimenters) look upon the tests as a greater challenge. The control group obviously does not run a parallel emotional course.

A third solution to the problem of repeated measures involves making additional tests after the participants have recovered from their ordeal. The argument goes that any return to approximately baseline levels of performance can be used as proof that a performance decrement during the deprivation period was, in fact, caused by lack of sleep. On reflection, it can be seen that this does not logically follow; a post-recovery subject often has a completely different attitude to the test. He may be coming back to the laboratory after several days and experience a novelty or dishabituation effect, and he is certainly no longer depressed by the thought of repeated future testing under fatigued and irritating conditions. Therefore, how can we separate the effects of reduced information-processing ability and lack of motivation? Haslam (1981) dealt with this problem to some extent by allowing her men 4 hours of sleep per day only while remaining under operational conditions after the completion of the total deprivation days. The 'recovery' testing was carried out during this period, and a considerable improvement was observed that strengthened her assertion that the preceding deficit may have been due directly to sleep deprivation rather than simply to the rigours of the men's situation.

Other methodological problems involve the special circumstances of these experiments. The most obvious problem arises in the logistics of keeping a half-dozen or so young men under constant surveillance for 5 to 9 days. The volunteers are typically confined together within limited accommodation even though they may never have met before. Quite short periods of living cheek-by-jowl with others can lead to tensions, even when the individuals are well known to each other. The problems must be made worse by being unable to choose one's travelling companions, and further compounded by the irritability which is commonly observed in sleepy people. The experimenters must add to the charged atmostphere by being intermittently present, applying constant and unwelcome pressure to keep the participants awake before disappearing to their own beds for refreshing sleep. I know of no study that has run a control group which effectively controlled for the social stresses of this kind. This is worrying, because the frustrations and irritations of the situation could alone be responsible for the observed fall-off in performance. Maybe after 2 or 3 days the volunteer just does not care to try hard any more.

It has often been noted that volunteers expend considerable energy when trying to stay awake; they engage in vigorous exercise and, of course, have to go without the rest which they would normally get during the night when asleep. Bonnet (1980) has recently shown that performance decrements equivalent to 40 hours of sleep loss can be induced in soldiers who have been forced to expend an equivalent amount of energy (but without sleep loss) on a 6½ hour march. This does not mean that the effects of sleep deprivation can always be attributed to energy deficits, but it does highlight an effect which must be compounded in the results of many studies. On the other hand, Webb (1975, pp.121–2) describes an experiment in which subjects were deprived of two nights of sleep while resting in bed. A simple interpretation of Bonnet's results would suggest a reduction in the sleep-deprivation effect; however, the opposite was the case. Subjects found it so difficult to resist sleep without the exercise that a considerable intensification of the effect of sleep loss was observed! It seems unlikely that we will ever be able to disentangle the stimulating effects of present expenditure of energy from the debilitating effect of fatigue.

Conceptual problems

Every study of the effects of sleep loss represents an attempt to solve these methodological problems. In fact, they can never be completely resolved, although we can be sure that some of the contradictions and uncertainties which characterize the scientific literature on this topic are caused simply by these difficulties. However, there are even more serious problems surrounding the concepts we use to interpret the results of our experiments. Concepts like arousal and unconsciousness, which are satisfactory in everyday use, run into difficulties when transplanted into the more demanding context of scientific explanation. Concepts are the building bricks of theories; when they contain unobserved flaws we might expect the theories to prove unsatisfactory. The problem is a general one in contemporary psychology, but it is worth looking at some instances in detail to get a feeling for the difficulty.

Let us, tentatively, accept that most information-processing functions may continue to operate almost normally (at least for short periods) even after considerable sleep loss, and that performance fall-off occurs only when the sleepy volunteer unwittingly disengages from the task in hand. It follows, from what results we already have, that this disengagement is more likely to occur as the vigil proceeds. We now need a theory to explain this effect. Traditionally there have been two main contenders; (a) progressive failure of arousal, and (b) increasing frequency of lapses of attention or microsleeps. I do not wish to argue the case for or against either theory, but to suggest that both suffer from flaws at the conceptual level, which may explain why no one finds either of them generally satisfactory despite the obvious superficial appeal of both. Kjellberg (1977) has recently argued against arousal as the correct explanation for sleep-loss effects; I want to argue more simply that it is simply an illusion of an explanation.

It is very evident (and may even be true by definition) that a sleepy person is less aroused than a person in a more 'normal' condition. The issue now arises as to whether a lack of arousal can be construed as an *explanation* of any performance deficits found in sleepy people. To support such a proposition we need to show that all reductions in arousal (other than those associated with sleepiness) are typically followed by performance deficits of the same kind. This turns out to be surprisingly difficult because we have no generally accepted way of independently measuring psychological arousal. We do have some procedures which we *think* will manipulate arousal, e.g. incentive payments, threat of electric shock, drugs, etc., although we cannot be too sure in the absence of a valid independent measure. In fact, it turns out that these so-called arousing techniques will sometimes improve performance and sometimes make it worse. We attempt to cope with this problem with 'optimum' arousal theory (Corcoran, 1964) (see Figure 9.1). This theory predicts an improvement as we approach the optimum arousal level, either by increasing or decreasing arousal from some previous level. Unfortunately, this optimum level is different for each task and for each person. It is thought to be a function of the difficulty of the task, but difficulty is itself not an easily measured quantity and changes for each subject as the result of practise.

Many attempts have been made to break out of this endless chain of difficulties by giving arousal the status of a joint psycho-

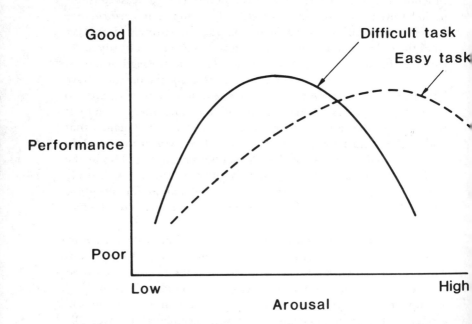

Fig. 9.1   The supposed 'inverted U' relationship between arousal and performance.

logical/physiological concept, thus allowing physiological indicators such as heart rate, muscle tension, body temperature, etc. to be used as objective measures of arousal. Unfortunately, these measures do not always agree, and may even contradict one another, and the attempts have largely been abandoned by psychologists (Claridge, 1981). We therefore still do not have a useful objective indicator of arousal, and as a result a performance decrement can be attributed either to an increase or to a decrease in arousal and, with sufficient ingenuity, it can usually be argued either way. If all else fails, we can retire behind the knowledge that a failure to observe a performance decrement in a sleepy subject is caused by an (arousing) effort of will on the part of the sleep-deprived volunteer! We do not need to argue whether arousal theory is the right or the wrong theory to explain sleep-loss effects. The whole concept is structurally unsafe; we merely need to post a large sign saying 'Danger! Quicksand'.

The attention-lapse hypothesis does not appear to be anywhere nearly so treacherous, but there is still good reason to be wary. It is certainly often observed that sleep-deprived individuals are prone to periods of inattention both brief and prolonged. Bills (1931) made a detailed study of individual responses in such continuous tasks as colour naming, adding digit pairs, naming opposites, code substitution, etc. The performances of normal subjects were characterized by brief pauses or gaps in responding, and these gaps became more frequent as the task continued. Bills proposed that these pauses (later sometimes called 'microsleeps') were caused by a blocking mechanism which served a recuperative purpose, and allowed a man to 'soldier on' and even improve his flagging efforts.

Williams et al., (1959) proposed that the effects of SD could be explained in terms of an increase in the frequency and duration of these lapses. There is no doubt that pauses in responding do occur, and it seems reasonable to assume that these pauses may explain some of the observed performance deficits over a wide range of tasks such as vigilance, tracking and problem solving. I cannot imagine, however, that we could ever prove that they were responsible for all observed performance deficits. Even if we were partly successful, the idea of attentional lapse would never be anything more than a unifying principle for a type of deficit: we would still need to explain why attention did lapse intermittently following sleep loss.

Bills's suggestion that the lapse is caused by microsleeps or periods of unconsciousness is, however, merely a hopeful guess, since we have no means of identifying or measuring such events. In any case, a failure to attend to the task in hand may merely indicate a wandering of attention to other foci. Blocks (pauses or lapses) seem well established as phenomena, but as explanations they appear to fail; attention is too subtle a process to be simply characterized as 'on' or 'off'. Nor are we helped by the knowledge that there are changes in electrical brain rhythms at the time at which these pauses occur (see, for example, Williams *et al.*, 1959), and since we do not yet understand the role of these electrical brain rhythms, they can hardly *explain* the lapses. It may be that these brain rhythm changes have some similarity to changes which occur when we fall asleep. However, introspective reports of people in these transition stages indicate that people are alert and thinking about things at this time.

The microsleep issue raises the general question of whether many of the symptoms of sleep deprivation are manifestations of regular sleep processes now intruding into waking life. Is memory failure in the sleep deprived qualitatively the same as failure to recall the mentations of sleep? Are misperceptions to be explained in terms of the dreaming process? Are the terrifying hallucinations of some subjects, the same as the night terrors (*pavor nocturnus*) which cause some people to wake screaming and kicking? Do the mood fluctuations, the temper flare-ups and the paranoid delusions reflect the vicissitudes of life in dreams?

Variations of these ideas have been proposed by many observers since Gilbert and Patrick, and their attractiveness cannot be denied. However, the usefulness of such explanations is limited, since we have only the vaguest idea of what these sleep processes are and how they operate. Even though considerable exploration has been carried out into the territory of sleep psychology, none would claim that we have produced anything more than sketch maps of the area. Now that it is clear that cognitive psychologists have mining rights, we might reasonably look forward to considerably more detailed investigation. Only then will the comparisons of sleep-deprivation symptoms with sleep processes acquire explanatory status. In the meantime they must remain merely possible lines of investigation.

I have used the arousal hypothesis and the attention-lapse hypothesis simply as examples of the general difficulty of finding useful theories to account for the performance decrements observed in experiments following sleep loss. These difficulties must be added to the collection of methodological issues already presented; and they raise the question of whether we should seek to solve the problems with ever greater feats of ingenuity and scientific cunning, or whether we might have approached the problem incorrectly from the start. Perhaps our basic investigatory tool – the deprive and test paradigm – is at fault, and may need to be replaced by an alternative strategy.

Paradigmatic problems

It is my view that the history of sleep-deprivation investigations has provided us with an object lesson of how science can become imprisoned by its own techniques. It has long been evident that sleep-deprived people become very sleepy, suffer from lapses of attention, show reduced interest in obligatory tasks and are therefore often less able to sustain a high level of performance at such tasks. It is also clear that by an 'effort of will' participants can temporarily compensate for these tendencies and turn in normal or even superior performances. Here lies the paradox; by asking volunteers to 'do their best' we were ignoring the main effect of sleep deprivation, which is a disinclination to do anything!

An important characteristic of psychological testing is that the subject does whatever the experimenter asks him to do, however odd this may seem, and however uncharacteristic this may be of normal human behaviour. Therefore, the more helpful the subject and the more supportive the experimenter, the less likely it was that any interpretable pattern of results would emerge! This is true even though it was obvious to all investigators that the subject needed to make an ever greater effort as the vigil wore on. One of the problems of the experimental paradigm in use was that the only *usable* observations were the results of the performance tests (e.g. mean reaction times). To base a theory on the incidental observation of an extra effort requirement was to step outside the paradigm. Moreover 'effort' as a concept was not operationally defined, and attempts to use it (e.g. Tyler *et al.*, 1947; Kleitman, 1963; Corcoran, 1964) in this context are obviously intended as general rather than 'scientific' statements. After all, how can we measure how much extra effort was required by a sleep-deprived volunteer to turn in exactly the same performance?

The difficulty of pinning down performance deficits following sleep loss was widely accepted in the sixties. So much so that a symposium/discussion chaired by Webb (see Chase, 1972, p.323) and involving many leading researchers in this field, had about it the air of a crisis meeting. Webb challenged the group:

> What impresses me so about listening to you gentlemen who have done so many sleep-deprivation studies, is how hard you have to struggle to find something devastating about losing a lot of sleep. Doesn't that strike you as rather peculiar?

Wilkinson's (1969) solution to the problem was to make tests so boring and so long in duration that he was able to defeat this 'effort-of-will' factor. His tasks involve sheets and sheets of simple addition tests, 20 to 30 minutes of listening for faint noises against a white noise background, or cancelling every instance of a particular letter in many pages of type. His idea that the tests should be long and repetitve, and should be seen as unimportant by the individual (see Chase, 1972, pp.340-2), has proved useful as a basis for devising tests which are sensitive to moderate amounts of sleep loss. Poulton (1978), for example, has recently shown how valuable this principle can be by asking hospital doctors to complete a simple, but routine card-sorting task (which required careful attention to the grammar of statements on the cards) when leaving the ward at the end of their spells of duty. By taking care not to imbue the test with any great significance, he found that it was very sensitive to sleep debts *as small as 3 hours* despite its shortness and simplicity.

By making the tasks very boring and very long, Wilkinson (1970) has solved the problem of producing reliable performance deficits following sleep loss. In doing so he has won the gratitude of the sleep-research community, which was having difficulty in finding any reliable results in a situation where even an untrained observer could easily see that the sleep-deprived man was behaving abnormally in many respects. In addition, his work might be used as the basis for a generalization to the effect that performance drop-off is not restricted specifically to certain kinds of tasks such as vigilance, memory and decision making, but is dependent upon such qualities as duration and interest. It is valuable to have the matter formulated so clearly, but it would be misleading to suggest that we have discovered something new here. Most people would claim to know that very boring tasks are best avoided at times of extreme sleepiness.

Perhaps, instead, we might claim that the use of controlled experimentation has led to more certain knowledge than could be acquired from casual observation of everyday life. Undoubtedly, it is a fine thing to seek to control experiments as carefully as possible, but this has its penalties. Every control that we introduce and each new variable that we seek to measure threatens to reduce the 'naturalness' of the phenomenon under study. It is not unusual for people to stay awake at night for parties, to complete some pressing work, when travelling, when danger threatens, during illness or severe insomnia. In such cases people adopt particular strategies to minimize the effects of sleepiness; for example, by resting whenever they notice a fall off in performance and by taking the first reasonable opportunity to go to sleep. In sleep-loss experiments we lose track of the natural history of sleepy behaviour; volunteers do tests which they would never otherwise consider doing, simply because the experimenter asks them to do so. Moreover, they continue at the tasks long after the point when they would normally desist. We end up with the study of the *unnatural* history of sleep deprivation.

Such conditions may be natural in a military context, so it is not surprising that many of the major experiments in this area have been carried out either by the armed forces directly or, indirectly, by agencies which have their interests in mind. We have, therefore, a large body of evidence of considerable practical value concerning the kind of behaviour we might expect from sleep-deprived people under orders from superiors to carry out tasks which they otherwise are unlikely to do. But this represents only one aspect of life. The nearest to my ideal study is Dement's (1972) account of the case of Randy Gardiner, the sleep-deprived disc jockey on a publicity stunt. Equally revealing are the accounts of what happened to participants in more formal experiments *between* the periods of testing; see for example, Pasnau (1968), Oswald (1974, pp.56-9). However, the dominant tradition in this area has been to make people sleepy and then see what happens when they are *prevented* from doing what comes naturally.

I am arguing, with the benefit of hindsight, that sleep-deprivation research has relied too heavily on the deprive-and-test paradigm, which only generates reliable effects when the sleepy person is restrained by the need to complete long and boring tests in situations representative of only a limited range of typical human experience. The consequence of this strategem is a collection of results which are often unreliable and difficult to generalize to the unrestrained behaviour of people. They are also restricted to a very narrow range of performance measures. They ignore the subtler aspects of experience and changes in spontaneous behaviour. When a sleepy subject tracks a dim spot of light while sitting alone in a darkened laboratory in the early hours of the morning, he resembles, in many ways, a lightly anaesthetized cat fixed in a restraining cradle with lights shone into his eyes while recordings are made from electrodes implanted in his brain. In the case of the cat, we record only the electrical activity of individual brain cells or fibres; in the case of our volunteer, we record only the amount of time he is 'off-target'. The information is useful and collected for a good reason, but it is a special kind of information, and we must bear this firmly in mind when reviewing what we know about the overall effects of sleep loss on cognition.

Alternative approaches

My own biases and preferences in this area have clearly influenced this account, and my main departure from orthodoxy is that I do not believe that sleep has a restorative function (Meddis, 1975, 1977; Webb, 1975). If this view holds, then sleep-deprivation studies are doomed to frustration whenever their prime purpose is to reveal the psychological functions which are most impaired by the lack of this restorative process. I do not believe that such effects as are observed result from the lack of a repair process, since some individuals naturally operate quite effectively on very little sleep (Meddis, 1977, Chapter 3).

My view is that sleep is primarily a part of a behaviour-scheduling mechanism which restricts an animal's activities to limited and pre-ordained periods of the circadian cycle. It therefore interests me how this mechanism alters psychological functioning in such a way as to facilitate the cessation of regular activities and promote withdrawal to a safe and comfortable sleep site. The specification of such a mechanism must be complex. It must be flexible enough to permit continued functioning if we are prevented from reaching the sleep site or if danger threatens. It must also be insistent; otherwise the mechanism would be disregarded on any pretext, and we know that this is not the case. People always eventually fall asleep.

Starting from such a viewpoint, I would prefer to see a more global characterization of the effects of sleep deprivation before attempting a detailed theory of how the mechanism brings these effects about. In this respect the existing research literature is disappointing. It is common for authors to allow one paragraph, or maybe two, for a description of subjects' general condition, but the rush is soon on to present the facts and figures of the specific detailed measures featured in that study. We lack a good natural history of sleep deprivation which lists and classifies the behaviours, attitudes and propensities of people who lack sleep. This requires observation and description first before testing. Would we ever try to investigate sexual behaviour by inducing sexual frenzy and then testing for choice-reaction time and short-term memory deficits?

It would also be welcome if more attention were paid to the pleasanter aspects of mild amounts of sleep loss; relaxation, creativity, camaraderie and other loosening-up effects which modern man typically looks to drugs, such as alcohol, to induce. Anecdotally, many creative musicians and authors claim to work best during the night when the circadian performance cycle is held by scientists to be at its lowest ebb. Katz and Landis (1935) report the following (shortened) poem written by their volunteer after 9 days without sleep. The basic theme is that women can prove a mixed blessing to a man.

> Functions that hamper and gifts that requite
> Must by their nature in women unite
>
> . . . .
> New fashions go leering, old modesties blare
> I come in the springtime, their tortoise shell dare:
> Over insistence, and collect what you may
> Evoke pleasures of night to sustain in the day.
> Northward the lust and the yearning conspire
> Sweet south, how delightful sensed form to attire. (p.314)

By any standards this is a fine piece in the modern idiom; at the very least it indicates 'mental integration and integrity even at this period of sleepiness'.

I am conscious of my own past failure to adopt a global perspective. My wife and I (and later an Australian student friend) lived for a while on a 48 hour regime which involved sleeping only on alternate nights (Meddis, 1968). At that time we came to know sleepiness very well; the problems of concentration, forgetfulness, the difficulties of reading even very interesting books, the nausea of fighting sleep at difficult times, irritability and the moments of uninhibited levity in public like the feeling of being drunk. We resorted to simple tasks like decorating and household chores, which we preferred in the dark, early hours of the morning. However, I kept no diary and, wishing to be a good scientist, merely recorded body temperature, number of hours slept and the results of simple and pointless (so it now seems) psychomotor tests and mood-rating scale assessments. In retrospect they told me very little, but were thought scientific enough to be accepted for publication in one of Britain's most reputable scientific journals.

Misperceptions

\ Hallucinations (and misperceptions (following sleep loss are a good example of a cognitive dysfunction which is not readily studied using objective performance tests. Their ephemeral nature has meant that spontaneous occurrences of these essentially private experiences have been exposed to very little systematic investigation. They are sometimes reported if the investigators are made aware of their occurrence, but few attempts have been made to classify them, time their occurrence or isolate any reliable precipitating factors. I do not know of any study which began with a set of detailed hypotheses concerning the misperceptions which investigators sought to test.

The reasons for this are partly historical. Misperceptions are a common feature of sleep-loss experiments but various authors (e.g. Tyler et al., 1947; West et al., 1962; Katz and Landis, 1935 and Berger and Oswald, 1962) had likened such effects to psychosis or some aspects of schizophrenia. As a result, the central controversy of the time was, put crudely, whether 'sleep deprivation led to medness'. ¶ Researchers were then at pains to point out that hallucinations were rare, that they were short lasting, and that they were typically milder than the occasional florid hallucinations which attracted media interest. Doubt was occasionally cast on the prior mental health of those who reported hallucinations during sleep deprivation. The prevalence of perceptual anomalies might therefore be explained away in terms of the strangeness of the people who were likely to volunteer for this kind of experiment. The general message from the sleep-research community was that sleep loss did not induce psychosis, and that healthy well-balanced individuals had little to fear from the experience. Whilst this may be true, the desire to play down the phenomenon (see, for example, Johnson and Naitoh, 1974, p.12) may have proved unfortunate.

It is possible to distinguish a number of different kinds of perceptual breakdown. At one end of the scale we have the full-blown hallucination where highly unlikely events are experienced as real along with considerable emotional upheaval, and Pasnau *et al.*, (1968) describe one participant who, after 168 hours of sleeplessness, 'went berserk during the psychomotor tracking task. He screamed in terror and pulled his electrodes off and fell to the floor sobbing and muttering incoherently about a gorilla and repeatedly asking to be taken off the experiment' (p.501). The condition was purely temporary; after some reassurance he was able to continue the experiment.

Alternatively, we hear of misperceptions which are clear enough for someone to attempt to draw the attention of another to it, although no emotional significance is attached to it. Haslam (1981) reports one occasion, referred to above, when a soldier (who was alone at the time of the illusion) 'took the corporal to see a "patrol ready to move", whereupon the illusion vanished'. In that study nine out of the ten subjects reported at least one illusion when observing alone at night; fourteen were reported in all. On at least five occasions soldiers reported spotting people moving about during the night-time vigilance task when there were none there. These experiences are distinguished by the fact that the misperception is confused with reality.

Other failures of perception may be less dramatic, but still intrude into the subjects' actions. Patrick and Gilbert (1896) reported an incident where the sleep-deprived participant was lifting two pails to decide which was the heavier: 'instead of saying that No. 1 or No. 2 was the heavier he said "trimmings", evidently having fallen asleep as he was lifting or setting down the pails and dreamed that they contained trimmings' (p.480). The intrusion of 'dreams' which are clearly recognized as such by subjects are very commonly reported. Gilbert and Patrick again reported, 'another subject, standing with eyes open, reflectively gazing at a piece of apparatus upon which there were some pieces of rope, suddenly reported that he had had a dream about a man being hung'.

Sometimes the illusions involve simple distortions of perception. Collins (1977) reported on the performance of volunteers at an aviation tracking task under sleep deprivation conditions: 'By day 3 some visual hallucinations were reported, for example, the localiser needle appeared to be "dripping", the needle took on the appearance of a man, and visual scenes appeared to be superimposed on the tracking instrument'.

Quite a different kind of misperception occurs when the delusions build up in a series one upon another to create a substantial transformation of the sleep-deprived person's interpretation of what is happening around him. These often resemble paranoid confabulations and can prove embarrassing and difficult to handle for the experimenters. Oswald (1974, p.56 ff) offers a startling description of a paranoid episode in an experiment carried out with Ralph Berger. They were sleep depriving two volunteers when, on the fourth day without sleeping, one of them began to build up an elaborate series of delusions: 'Arthur felt frightened, for Berger was questioning Sandy about his dreams and slowly the realisation dawned that Berger was taking Sandy away to lock him up after first hypnotising him'. Such episodes are apparently not uncommon (see, for example, Katz and Landis, 1935).

Because misperceptions are not believed to be a *necessary* consequence of sleep deprivation, they have been presented by sleep researchers mainly as incidental effects. Because their primary interest lies in the sleep process rather than cognitive structure, little systematic observation or analysis of these phenomena has been attempted. Nevertheless, the phenomenon seems to offer a golden opportunity to those who wish to study the anatomy of perception through its pathology, an opportunity which has yet to be taken seriously. The sleep-deprived volunteer seems to be an infinitely more manageable object of study than the schizophrenic patient, the amphetamine narcosis sufferer or the LSD consumer. Misperceptions followng sleep loss may even be more common than is assumed; both Pasnau *et al.* (1968) and Oswald (1974) indicate that their subjects had originally not intended to reveal what was happening to them.

Action failures

At the other end of the information-processing chain we may observe a variety of inappropriate actions following sleep loss. Once again, these are typically reported only as asides in the literature, mainly because investigators are closely focused on a limited range of measures of such things as reaction time, mental arithmetic, target spotting, etc. From what little we do know, it seems that a rich vein is there for mining by the adventurous pioneer.

Some errors involve a sudden switch to a different line of thought: 'While reciting the alphabet a subject may suddenly interject a comment about his wife or, during a conversation, lose his train of thought completely' (Webb, 1975, p.124). Katz and Landis (1935) reported one occasion when their volunteer

> arose suddenly and walked to a desk which he mistook for a drinking fountain. On still another occasion he arose suddenly and walked down a corridor trying every door as he passed. He explained this by saying that he thought he was on a different floor and was hunting for the room to which he had been assigned. (p.313)

Oswald (1974) describes the errors made by sleep-deprived men when they were asked to help out in the sleep laboratory by writing down the time every two minutes on the brainwave tracings which were emerging from the EEG machine.

> Many mistakes were made and there was evidence that multiple attempts were occasionally made to do this simple job. Sometimes, instead of times, senseless words or phrases were found to have been written, such as 'story burden', 'batting by one', 'cormial brier', 'a dorable', 'SBT' and '12.81D Cuba here we commerce'. (p.56)

It is understandable that investigators should have felt less happy with miscellaneous stories of such slips and bizarre acts than with neat tables of reaction times, numbers of nonsense syllables recalled or speed of letter-cancellation performance. The latter are more readily marshalled, presented, analyzed and applied to tightly formulated theories; the former simply stand around looking interesting. However, techniques have emerged recently (Reason, 1979; Norman, 1981) which allow us to gather data on spontaneous errors and to subject such data to analysis. These 'actions not as planned' offer a most valuable stimulus to the generation of theories concerning control systems which guide human action, and it seems likely that sleep-deprived people will generate a large crop of such action errors and slips of the tongue.

The important contributions of Reason and Norman consist of showing that observation of naturally occurring events can be just as productive of useful theories of cognitive functioning as controlled observation of structured laboratory situations. They used a diary technique where participants recorded spontaneous occurrences of silly mistakes in their own behaviour and the behaviour of others. When a large collection of such accounts is available, they can be categorized and systematized. For example, some errors result from a memory failure (e.g. going into a room but forgetting why you went in); others involve side-tracking along habitual grooves (e.g. driving to work on Saturday morning when meaning to drive to the country); and yet others may involve inappropriate classification of objects (e.g. putting the teapot lid on the marmalade jar). We might reasonably ask whether sleep loss potentiates all kinds of error or whether particular types of error such as memory failure are more likely to be affected. The advantages of the diary technique are that they are unobtrusive and easily applied to real-life examples of sleep loss. The technique is not without its problems; it can easily descend to the level of the merely anecdotal. However, the available research in this area suggests that, in the hands of competent professionals, it can lead to many valuable insights.

One of the advantages of techniques which rely upon unrestricted observation of the effects of sleep loss, is that events are allowed to speak for themselves. This compares favourably with controlled observation when only a very limited set of hypotheses are addressed. What do we expect these spontaneous slips and misperceptions to tell us about the underlying processes at work in the minds of sleepy people? It is, of course, difficult to say in advance, but we do already know some things about the behaviour of sleepy people, and this knowledge does influence the way we think about sleep loss. I am not aware that any of these approaches have been formulated as explicit hypotheses, but the view to be discussed below is present informally in the writings of many sleep researchers.

Sleepiness as a change in priorities

This view is simply that a sleepy man assigns an increasing priority to the need to go to sleep, and that all behaviour changes are a consequence of this. Two analogies might be a man in love or a student preoccupied by thoughts of an impending examination. All three conditions produce inattention and inappropriate behaviour, and any task unrelated to the motivational focus receives reduced priority and suffers performance deficits. The focal topic (sleep, the loved one, the examination) continues to assert its influence over behaviour at the expense of an integrated approach to other matters. A continuous conscious effort is the only way of coping with essential matters; and this is an effort which proves increasingly difficult to maintain. In the case of sleep, the aim of this change is to disengage the individual from any task which will delay the onset of sleep.

This change in priorities is not to be confused with Murray's (1965) suggestion that sleep loss leads to a general reduction in motivation. This impression is given by sleepy people, but mainly because they are unable to maintain interest in the tests supplied by the experimenter, although they are very interested in going to sleep. Kjellberg (1977) has explicitly endorsed a similar position in terms of reinforcement theory in that he feels that anything which gets the sleepy person nearer to the point of going to sleep is reinforcing. Withdrawing from the task is a reasonable first step from the subject's point of view; only the experimenter's priorities keep our volunteer on the job. However, as Kjellberg (1975) has shown, the subject will always give up if he is allowed to do so with honour.

At the detailed level of psychological mechanism we are clearly talking about control of attention. By attention I mean that faculty whereby the organism directs its perceptions and actions towards the achievement of a single objective at the expense of other objectives. Attention facilitates perception of objects and events which are relevant to our goal at the expense of all other possible perceptions; it regulates our thoughts and prevents irrelevant intrusive ideas; and it guides our actions through a maze of choice points when an infinity of alternative actions is continuously present. For some reason the firmness of this guide is weakened in sleepy people; the essential divide between the appropriate and the inappropriate is narrowed at these times. This may, of course, be of benefit where people are required to generate novel or surprising ideas, but for many routine tasks it will produce a degradation of performance.

Some detailed laboratory evidence does exist (Hockey, 1970; Fisher, 1980) that attention is less tightly focused in sleep-deprived subjects. The point is well illustrated by Norton's (1970) card-sorting investigation where volunteers were expected to sort a deck of cards into piles according to what was on the cards. Some of the cues on the cards were irrelevant to the sorting task. These 'distractor' cues slow down the sorting process for all subjects, but are particularly disruptive for sleep-deprived volunteers.

The failure to regulate perceptual processes in the case of

250   The pathology and psychology of cognition

misperceptions, and full hallucinations may be further examples of
this process. Any perception can be thought of as a final unconscious
decision following analysis of the evidence of the senses; a correct
decision involves inhibiting a range of alternatives which have been
suggested by the same sense data as well as by current expectations
and preoccupations. A misperception is an example of a false
decision; if sleep loss weakens those regulatory processes which
exclude the irrelevant and the inappropriate, then misperceptions
are more likely to occur. |Full hallucinations |with their emotional
content appear to call for a more elaborate explanation, but these
may also result from some simple analogous process whereby
inappropriate emotional preoccupations are allowed to control
perceptual decision making.|

This view is not strictly formulated and it is not new; I think that it
is implied in the writing of many researchers. However, the explicit
goal of most experiments has been to explore the effects of sleep loss
in a range of restricted conditions using a limited range of objective
tests. As a consequence, we have missed the opportunity to explore
the wider aspects of sleep loss which involve changes in the
experiences of the individual and spontaneous alterations in his style
of behaviour. These are additional to the spontaneous failures of
perception and action. My attempt to paint a broader picture of the
effects of sleep loss is not a wholesale rejection of past research;
rather it is an attempt to highlight the restrictions of the deprive-
and-test paradigm and encourage the possibilities of more profitable
approaches. So far they remain only untried possibilities, but they do
already provide a conceptual framework for reappraising the
difficult and slow progress which has characterized sleep-deprivation
research up to the present.

References

Berger, R. J. and Oswald, I. (1962) Effects of sleep deprivation on be-
    haviour, subsequent sleep and dreaming. *Journal of Mental
    Science 108*: 457-65.
Bills, A. G. (1931) Blocking: a new principle of mental fatigue. *American
    Journal of Psychology 43*: 230-45.
Bonnet, M. H. (1980) Sleep, performance and mood after the energy-
    expenditure equivalent of 40 hours of sleep deprivation. *Psychophysiology
    17*: 56-63.

Chase, M. H. (1972) *The Sleeping Brain*. Los Angeles: Brain Information Service.

Claridge G. (1981) Arousal. In G. Underwood and R. Stevens (eds) *Aspects of Consciousness*. Vol. 2. London: Academic Press.

Cohen, D. B. (1979) *Sleep and Dreaming*. Oxford: Pergamon.

Collins, W. E. (1977) Some effects of sleep deprivation on tracking performance in static and dynamic environments. *Journal of Applied psychology 62*: 567-73.

Corcoran, D. W. J. (1964) Changes in heart rate and performance as a result of loss of sleep. *British Journal of Psychology 55*: 307-14.

Dement, W. C. (1972) *Some Must Watch While Some Must Sleep*. Stanford, Calif.: Stanford Alumni Association.

Fisher, S. (1980) The micro-structure of dual-task interaction. 4. Sleep deprivation and the control of attention. *Perception 9*: 327-37.

Foulkes, D. (1962) Dream reports from different stages of sleep. *Journal of Abnormal and Social Psychology 65*: 14-25.

Haslam, D. R. (1981) The military performance of soldiers in continuous operation. In L. C. Johnson *et al.* (eds) *Biological Rhythms and Shift Work (Advances in Sleep Research 7)*. New York: Spectrum Publications.

Hockey, G. R. J. (1970) Changes in attention-allocation in a multi-component task under loss of sleep. *British Journal of Psychology 61*: 473-80.

Johnson, L. C. (1969) Psychological and physiological changes following total sleep deprivation. In E. Kales (ed.) *Sleep: Physiology and Pathology*. Philadelphia: Lippincott.

Johnson, L. C. and Naitoh, P. (1974) *The Operational Consequences of Sleep Deprivation and Sleep Deficit*. AGARDograph no. 193. NATO Advisory Group for Aerospace Research and Development.

Katz, S. E. and Landis, C. (1935) Psychologic and physiologic phenomena during a prolonged vigil. *Archives of Neurological Psychiatry 34*: 307-16.

Kjellberg, A. (1975) Effects of sleep deprivation on performance of a problem-solving task. *Psychological Reports 37*: 479-85.

Kjellberg, A. (1977) Sleep deprivation and some aspects of performance. *Waking and Sleeping 1*: 139-54.

Kleitman, N. (1963) *Sleep and Wakefulness*. Chicago: University of Chicago Press.

Manaceine, M. de (1894) Quelques observations experimentales sur l'influence de l'insomnie absolue. *Archives Italiennes de Biologie 21*: 322-5.

Meddis, R. (1968) Human circadian rhythms and the 48-hour day. *Nature 218*: 964-5.

Meddis, R. (1975) On the function of sleep. *Animal Behaviour 23*: 676-91.

Meddis, R. (1977) *The Sleep Instinct*. London: Routledge & Kegan Paul.

Murray, E. J. (1965) *Sleep Dreams and Arousal*. New York: Appleton-Century-Crofts.

Norman, D. A. (1981) Categorisation of action slips. *Psychological Review 88*: 1-15.

Norton, R. (1970) The effects of acute sleep deprivation on selective attention. *British Journal of Psychology 61*: 157-62.

Oswald, I. (1974) *Sleep* (3rd ed). Hammondsworth: Penguin.

252   The pathology and psychology of cognition

Pasnau, R. O., Naitoh, P., Stier, S. and Kollar, E. J. (1968) The psychological effect of 205 hours of sleep deprivation. *Archives of General Psychiatry 18*: 496–505.

Patrick, G. T. W. and Gilbert, J. A. (1896) On the effects of loss of sleep. *Psychological Review 5*: 496–83.

Poulton, E. C., Hunt, G., Carpenter, A. and Edwards, R. S. (1978) The performance of junior hospital doctors following reduced sleep and long hours of work. *Ergonomics 21*: 279–95.

Reason, J. T. (1979) Actions not as planned. In G. Underwood and R. Stevens (eds) *Aspects of Consciousness*. New York: Academic Press.

Robinson, E. S. and Herrmann, S. O. (1922) Effects of loss of sleep. *Journal of Experimental Psychology 5*: 19–32.

Tyler, D. B., Goodman, J. and Rothman, T. (1947) The effect of experimental insomnia on the rate of potential changes in the brain. *American Journal of Physiology 149*: 185–93.

Vogel, G. W., Thompson, F. C., Thurmond, A., Geisler, D. and Barrowclough, B. (1972) The effect of REM deprivation on depressive syndromes. *Sleep Research 1*: 167.

Webb, W. B. (1975) *Sleep the Gentle Tyrant*. Englewood Cliffs, NJ: Prentice-Hall.

West, L. J., Janszen, H. H., Boyd, K. L., Floyd, S. and Cornelisoon, Jr., (1962) The psychosis of sleep deprivation. *Annals of the New York Academy of Sciences 96*: 66–70.

Wilkinson, R. T. (1969) Sleep deprivation: performance tests for partial and selective sleep deprivation. In L. E. Abt and B. F. Riess (eds) *Progress in Clinical Psychology*. Vol. 8. New York: Grune & Stratton.

Wilkinson, R. T. (1970) Methods for research on sleep deprivation and sleep function. In E. Hartmann (ed.) *Sleep and Dreaming*. Boston: Little, Brown.

Williams, H. L., Lubin, A. and Goodman, J. J. (1959) Impaired performance with acute sleep loss. *Psychological Monographs 73*: 14 (whole no. 484).

10 Information processing and redevelopment: towards a science of neuropsychological rehabilitation

**Anthony W. H. Buffery
and Andrew Burton**

Throughout this book an effort has been made to determine how far the examination of cognitive disturbance can inform our understanding of the mechanisms of information extraction, analysis and organization in the control of behaviour, especially as these activities are embodied in systems of processing within the human brain. Many of the data under scrutiny have come from the field of clinical neuropsychology, for it is here that possibly the richest variety of theoretically interesting examples of cognitive impairment are to be found.

However, as Lishman commented in 1975, after asserting his belief that neuropsychology had traditionally lacked a therapeutic emphasis, 'It is a fascinating subject of enormous theoretical importance, but it seems often to be oriented in directions other than helping people to get better'.

This is a provocative challenge and one which cannot be ignored, for it is surely important that what we have to say about information processing in the brain should not only be interesting, but also useful. In this final chapter, therefore, without attempting a comprehensive review of the topic, we propose to examine the applications, actual and potential, of contemporary cognitive psychology to the rehabilitation of patients in whom cognitive processes have been disrupted as a result of brain damage.

In practice, rehabilitation represents a point of convergence for several distinct professional skills, including neurology and speech therapy, as well as psychology and related disciplines. Our perspective, essentially that of experimental cognitive psychology, has yet to make a major impact on the strategies of rehabilitation. Yet current textbooks concerned with cognitive psychology contain a world rich in relevant material: for example, models of word recognition, reading and selective attention; the organization of concepts in memory; forgetting; theories of motor skill; and studies of problem solving. The value of the information-processing perspective in describing and interpreting neuropsychological dysfunction opens up the prospect of applying such topics to neuropsychological rehabilitation.

The venture is an attractive one for several reasons. Information-processing psychology has already been applied successfully to many practical problems (see for example, Baddeley, 1981). This is partly because it offers a set of common principles through which a wide range of disparate phenomena can be systematically described. The information-processing perspective therefore offers some hope of bringing together the bewildering variety of often highly specific impairments found in clinical neuropsychology. In turn this should favour the evolution of an integrated research base which rehabilitation has generally lacked, arguably to its detriment.

Information-processing models also provide established laboratory paradigms and measurement techniques which can be used to isolate particular stages and structures of processing and representation. The precise nature of a breakdown, therefore, may be accurately defined, and remedial work focused on the defective processes by selecting appropriate tasks; and changes in performance may also be reliably monitored. Cognitive psychologists generally are becoming increasingly concerned with the need for their work to give a proper account of individual differences in information processing (e.g. Hunt, 1978), which ought to stimulate the development of rehabilitation methods matched to the needs of individual patients. In addition, the observation that the performance of many patients appears to fall short of their real potential finds expression in the distinction acknowledged by information-processing psychology between *competence* and *performance*. The recognition of this distinction should encourage a search for factors likely to aid the translation of unused potential into actual achievement. Finally, from many points of view, cognitive processes are best regarded as complex *skills*, suggesting that in principle they are capable of being relearned after being lost or disrupted; and according to the particular viewpoint of the 'systems' approach to information processing, any complex skill is seen as a dynamic interaction among various contributory activities operating at different levels. No stage of processing occupies a fixed position, and the same ends may be achieved through different means. Such flexibility would suggest that disordered functions might be re-established by using intact processes to 'bridge' defective ones.

Certainly, there are some solid arguments for developing a neuropsychological science of functional restoration based on information-processing psychology. However, the enterprise is founded on an assumption – that the brain has some capacity for functional recovery.

Recovery of cerebral function

Any attempt to re-establish or stimulate the recovery of cognitive skills disrupted as a consequence of brain damage, rests on the belief that the brain is capable, in some sense, of reorganizing how it processes information and controls behaviour, or possibly that any capacity the brain may have for 'self-repair' or regeneration can be nurtured and augmented. Many lines of research feed into and inform this general topic of *cerebral plasticity*.

For example, developmental neurology is concerned with basic research into the growth and plasticity of neural tissue, and with the influence of the environment and experience upon the development of the brain's structural and functional efficiency. Knowledge of this area is important for the creation of neuropsychologically based techniques to promote recovery after varieties of central nervous system damage. Findings from research into the development and regeneration of the nervous systems in various species have been reviewed by Stein, Rosen and Butters (1974), and more recently by Lund (1978). In particular, work on the development of feature-extracting neurons, on visual prosthesis, and on changes in the pattern of neural growth with changes in the pattern of sensory input, have clear relevance to the role of the clinical neuro-psychologist as therapist. Theoretical evaluation of this research has been made by Le Vere (1975) and Isaacson (1975, 1976). St James-

Roberts (1979) reviewed this whole area whilst focusing upon its implications for the handicapped child; and Finger (1978) has reviewed recovery from brain damage, a topic to which we now turn.

The observation that, with time, there is virtually always some degree of recovery of functions lost or severely impaired as a result of a brain lesion is itself uncontroversial. What the return of such abilities signifies in terms of functional arrangements in the brain, however, is not well understood, and has been a subject of considerable argument. Terms commonly used to describe the phenomenon of recovery, such as 'sparing', 'restitution', 'compensation' - even 'recovery' itself - often imply a particular mechanism of underlying brain processes. The importance of understanding the mechanism of recovery is not merely academic, since one's model of the underlying changes will influence asssumptions on which systematic intervention procedures are based, and therefore the nature of the therapeutic programme. In order to clarify the various possible changes which might underlie recovery and the factors thought to influence this process, an analogy will be used.

Suppose that you are the manager of a famous symphony orchestra (*Sinfonia hemispherica* perhaps) currently enjoying a successful European concert tour. Everything is going smoothly until late one afternoon half your violins succumb to a bout of food poisoning from which they never recover. The concert is due to start in less than two hours. You stare wildly at the queues forming outside the concert hall, run your hands distractedly through your hair and decide that the show must go on.

How will the orchestra play? This, of course, depends on many things - just as there are many factors which will affect how well the brain will perform when part of it is suddenly wiped out. To begin with, there is the size of the region of damage to consider - the more violinists who succumb, the worse the consequences. It is also widely recognized that the type of lesion, e.g. whether it is focal or diffuse, exerts a strong influence - imagine what would happen if the illness were to strike down members of the orchestra indiscriminately rather than being confined to the violins. For the concert, drastic revisions to the programme may be required; and the depleted ranks of violinists will surely mean a reduction in the orchestra's repertoire. It may not be possible to perform works in which violin parts are prominent, though some solo pieces may be feasible. Similarly, the effect of a localized brain lesion will be to create more difficulty in the execution of some skills (those that depend heavily on the damaged areas) compared with others.

On the first night there may well be chaos: not only is there a big hole in the violin section, but the entire orchestra, numbed by the sudden demise of its colleagues, is in a state of shock. Not surprisingly, none play well, but the orchestra's performance is far worse than it would have been, had, for example, the late-lamented violinists simply been held up in a traffic jam. Such an effect is embodied in the concept of 'diaschisis', a term originally coined by Von Monakow (1911), who suggested that damaged or diseased brain tissue actually depresses the activity of healthy tissue, even at some distance from the area of the lesion. On this view, recovery would be, at least partly, the result of a recession of this inhibitory activity - just as eventually the members of the orchestra would adjust to the departure of their colleagues and begin to play normally again. Support for the idea comes from various sources, notably the observation that retrograde amnesia following trauma 'shrinks' over time, many once-inaccessible memories gradually returning to the patient.

What are the orchestra's prospects? Obviously, in the long term, new recruits might be obtained to replace those who have been so tragically struck down. The possibility that recovery of cerebral function might be due in part to neural regrowth or to other permanent physical changes in the central nervous system, has often been discussed. For example, simple regeneration - a process by which damaged neurones regrow to form new connexions with areas they originally innervated - is frequently observed in the peripheral motor and sensory systems. Another phenomenon, collateral sprouting, by which, for example, intact nerve fibres adjacent to lesioned ones send out fresh 'shoots' to sites previously occupied by the damaged ones, has also been demonstrated. The literature on this subject is extensive and highly specialized, and we shall not pursue it any further. Authorities such as Finger (1978), Hécaen and Albert (1978) and Kolb and Whishaw (1980), to whom the reader is referred for detailed consideration of the relevant studies, seem to agree that while the potential importance of such mechanisms is enormous, it is necessary to remember, first, that the data may have only limited application to recovery processes in the *central* (as opposed to peripheral) nervous systems of *higher* animals; and secondly, that even where genuine neural changes can be reliably shown, there is no guarantee that they have any real adaptive value – by making wrong connexions they may simply cause confusion.

So, suppose that it is not possible to recruit new players. What organizational changes might be made within the orchestra? Roughly speaking, three courses of action are available. First, you could make no real changes at all, but just try to extract the best from the orchestra as it is, leaving things more or less as they are. The remaining violinists will just have to play more loudly – intact brain tissue might be able to work harder to compensate for the damaged region. A second possibility is that since violin passages are so important, you could ask some of the other players to play the relevant passages on their own instruments. Note that this would not necessitate any alterations to the basic orchestral roles: 'cellists still play 'cellos, oboists, oboes and so on; players would simply be allocated new musical parts. The idea that brain processing systems might be flexible enough to allow the same *ends* to be reached through different *means* appears to have been suggested originally by Flourens (1824) following some work on cockerels. A good example is the increased use that blind children make of auditory cues to find their way around. Its most notable recent champion has been Luria (e.g. 1969) who describes, for example, the retraining of articulation following motor cortex lesions by a progressive shaping of spontaneously produced movements of the speech organs in order to create sounds which are approximately correct. Pursing the lips to blow out a match, for example, resembles the correct position for a 'p' sound. The process of articulation is thus reconstructed using such new functional systems for producing sounds. Musically, the result might not sound quite right – purists, of course, argue that transcriptions never do – and resource limitations might make certain forms of functional reorganization extremely demanding. It would be difficult, if not impossible, to play flute parts on a 'cello, for example. Nevertheless, the potential scope of such functional adaptation is considerable.

A third possibility would be to persuade some of your players to take up the violin. It ought to be possible for accomplished musicians to learn to play a different instrument, just as undamaged areas of the brain might, conceivably, take on entirely new information-processing functions, i.e. those formerly carried out by the damaged regions. Clearly, taken literally, this model of recovery would entail considerable reorganization and redistribution of processing activities in the brain. The overall quality of the orchestra's playing is likely to suffer too, since the number of violinists has been increased at the expense of other instruments. Traditionally, however, the model (first apparently alluded to by Munk, 1881) has been associated with the idea that there are portions of the brain, not committed to any particular functions, which are only pressed into service in emergencies. On this 'spare tyre' view, no reallocation of existing players to new instruments would be involved; it is as if the orchestra actually included a number of reserves who could be asked to step in when required.

However, excluding for the moment the possibility of surplus processing capacity, it is easy to see that there are potential limitations to the orchestra's power to adapt in the way envisaged. Much depends on the flexibility of the players; as musicians they all share *general* skills, such as being able to read music, but at the same time they have a highly specific knowledge of a particular instrument. The opportunities for re-education might be quite limited and, just as a viola player would probably find it a struggle to switch to the tuba, to expect adequate transfer of skills from one part of the brain to another might be unduly optimistic.

One of the most frequently studied and debated factors influencing the likelihood of recovery from brain damage and, by implication, the brain's capacity for functional rearrangements, is the age at which a lesion is sustained. The idea, sometimes referred to as the 'Kennard principle' (after the work of M. A. Kennard, a major figure in a long tradition of animal experimental work comparing early, with late lesions) that the earlier the damage, the less severe its effects, has been an influential one. A popular clinical generalization is quoted by McFie (1975): 'if the speech centre is damaged before the age of ten, the child will recover his speech'. Systematic reports broadly support such a clinical impression: Alajouanine and L'Hermitte (1965) found that 24 of 32 children (age range 6–15 years) with childhood aphasia, had normal or virtually normal language when examined one year after the injury. Hécaen (1976) studied the course of a number of language disturbances in fifteen cases of childhood brain injury (age range 3–15 years) and reported a marked improvement in almost all and a total recovery in five of the cases within 2 years or so. These data contrast sharply with figures presented by Teuber (1975) for improvement in dysphasia resulting (mainly) from combat wounds sustained at ages from 17

260   The pathology and psychology of cognition

years onwards. In a 20 year follow-up study less than 25 per cent were thought to have improved. Though one would need to take into account important differences between the types of population and lesions involved, and the methods of assessing language functions, the more favourable outcome following childhood lesions is very clear.

Less attention has been given to abilities other than those involving specific language disturbance, but the studies of Kohn and Dennis (1974) suggest that a broadly similar rule may apply. Adult patients who had undergone right hemispherectomy (a radical form of surgery in which an entire hemisphere is removed to control chronic and potentially fatal seizures) at various ages during childhood, were found not to be impaired compared with a left-hemisphere lesion sample on a number of visuospatial tasks on which deficits typically occur in patients who have sustained right-hemisphere brain injury as adults (see Chapter 4). On other similar tasks, however, impairments were found, suggesting that although there may be compensatory processes at work, there are limits on the ultimate level of achievement.

This conclusion is strengthened and the argument carried a stage further by the observations of Woods and Teuber (1973; see also Teuber, 1975). In this study patients with either left or right-hemisphere lesions sustained at ages ranging from birth to 15 years were compared on the Wechsler Adult Intelligence Scale (WAIS),

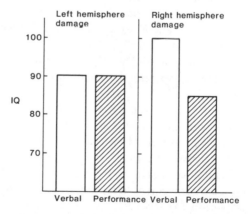

Fig. 10.1   IQ scores (Wechsler) of adults who had sustained right- or left-hemisphere lesions in infancy.

with one another, and with sibling controls, at least 5 years after the lesion. The findings (see Figure 10.1) suggest a clear hemispheric asymmetry in the effects of early lesions, left-sided damage depressing both 'verbal' and 'performance' measures, and right-sided damage affecting only performance scores.

The interpretation of these results favoured by Teuber, is that there has been a shift of language from the left to the right hemisphere in the left-damaged group, resulting in interference with those visuospatial (right-hemisphere) processing activities which are considered vital to success on the performance subtests of the WAIS. When there is damage to the right side, however, no equivalent transfer of visuospatial functions to the left hemisphere occurs (or if it does, there is no apparent interference with language functions). The overall implication, therefore, is that in early development the left hemisphere of the brain is relatively more committed to its various language functions than is the right hemisphere to those functions which it will eventually serve. The more plastic right hemisphere is potentially capable of mediating some functions of the damaged left hemisphere, but the reciprocal process occurs only in a more reduced fashion, if at all. The data are persuasive, though an alternative hypothesis might be that the performance subtests of the WAIS are, to some extent, also dependent on verbal processing, and that deficits in such cases are a likely consequence of left-side damage. On the other hand, it is difficult to see how one could explain, on this basis alone, the lower performance scores in the right hemisphere compared with the left-hemisphere group since, presumably, the former group suffered minimal interference to verbal functions.

Cerebral plasticity, therefore, appears to depend both on age and on the functions being considered, at least in so far as plasticity is defined in terms of an inferred inter-hemispheric shift of functional representation. Language and language-related activities seem more capable of transplantation than do other information-processing activities. According to Smith (1981), this is because although each hemisphere of the brain contains structures that are, in principle, capable of compensating for impaired functions resulting from lateralized lesions, there are both developmental and evolutionary pressures favouring the survival of language and verbal skills over many non-verbal ones. To accommodate such age-related phenomena within our orchestral model of brain function, one could introduce the assumption that, generally speaking, the longer someone has been playing a particular instrument, the harder it will be to switch to another; and even where shifts occur, the result may be imperfect – bassoonists, for example, might not make very good violinists. In addition, Smith's 'language primacy' hypothesis would entail the supposition that there would be strong pressure to retain certain sections of the orchestra. Clarinets make an important contribution to an orchestra, but without violins it is difficult to see how it could function at all; so, violins must take precedence. Of course, these arguments assume that the preservation of particular cognitive abilities might be achieved after brain injury by a process of interhemispheric transfer of function. This is a reasonable enough hypothesis when considering hemispherectomy cases, and it is broadly the model of language recovery favoured by authorities such as Lenneberg (1967). In practice, however, the majority of brain lesions are less extensive and an intra- rather than inter-hemispheric shift might be more probable. In fact Rasmussen and Milner (1975) reported that only 12 per cent of adult patients who had sustained early left-hemisphere damage had *right*-hemisphere speech representation (determined using the sodium amytal technique), compared with 4 per cent for undamaged controls. An orchestral parallel might be that it is likely that you would first try to persuade other *string* players to take the place of missing violins before asking say, the percussion or wind section to have a shot, since string players at least have a working knowledge of the relevant variety of instrument.

There is a second sense in which one could conceive of the right hemisphere replacing, or at least assisting, a damaged left hemisphere in carrying out language functions. This entails the idea, somewhat resembling Hughlings Jackson's concept of multiple re-presentation of function at different points in the brain, that in early development language is learned with both hemispheres, but that at some point – according to Moscovitch (see e.g. 1979) possibly around the age of five – inhibitory processes are brought into play which prevent further involvement of the right hemisphere. Subsequent language abilities are, as it were, channelled (normally) to the left hemisphere, though the earlier acquired functions remain unused in the right. Without introducing the idea of disinhibition or reactivation of latent language structures in the right hemisphere, the rapid rate of recovery from childhood aphasia cannot, in the view of Geschwind (1974), be satisfactorily explained. Geschwind also believes that good recovery from aphasia in adults may be attributable to the revival of right-hemisphere language functions. Conceivably, he argues, it may be possible to stimulate recovery by resuscitating this dormant language base, assuming, of course, it still exists. This intriguing possibility we discuss in more detail later, under the heading 'Language and brain-function therapy'. There is no obvious counterpart to an inhibitory process in a symphony orchestra, proof that all analogies have their limits. However, for a possible parallel, imagine that two children (cerebral hemispheres) start to learn the piano (language). Gradually one child (left hemisphere) begins to monopolize the keyboard, forcing the second child (right hemisphere) to switch to another instrument (visuospatial processing). In this example, one child eventually specializes in piano playing, but the other nevertheless retains some of the basic elements of the skill.

This brief and highly selective examination of various lines of evidence concerning the process of recovery has focused deliberately on the recovery of cognitive functions, and has been limited to the effects of cortical lesions. Our aim has been to outline the general topic of plasticity and also to delineate the various possible means by which restoration of function might be achieved. Certain functions appear more 'plastic' than others. Language may be preserved in preference to other skills, though it is difficult to isolate the reasons for this. Lesions sustained earlier in life are, generally speaking, associated with larger amounts of recovery, apparently due to the greater opportunity for cerebral reorganization in less mature subjects. Recovery in adults can be remarkably impressive in individual cases, as Burklund and Smith (1977) have shown (see also Smith, 1981) in their studies of hemispherectomy. One patient, for example, who had undergone total removal of left-hemisphere tissue nevertheless showed a consistent pattern of general improvement on a wide range of verbal and non-verbal tests until death occurred as a result of tumour recurrence eighteen months later. The WAIS performance IQ reached 99 at one point during the post-operative period. According to Teuber (1975) there may also be a weak effect of age within adult populations, since in his study younger patients were observed to have improved more compared with older ones over a 20 year period. This may indicate that plasticity of function is not confined to childhood.

Thus, that recovery occurs is not generally disputed. Part of this may be regarded as a natural process of (structural) self-repair. How much of it, if any, is due to functional reorganization through which impaired activities are genuinely re-established in some sense, is not known. In fact, opinion is divided as to whether the central nervous system has any real capacity for this sort of flexible, long-term adaptation at all. A damaged brain is a damaged brain, and improvement a relative concept. Whatever the mechanisms underlying recovery, they are only partially effective. There are commonly persistent residual deficits, many of which, according to Teuber (1975), are not detected with conventional psychometric instruments. Recovery may occur at a price; for example, language at the expense of non-verbal functions. Thus, the possibility of actually enhancing or initiating recovery by intervention is hedged about with uncertainties. Any effort to capitalize on a natural process of spontaneous recovery must be viewed in the context of the reality that the reorganizational powers of the brain are limited.

Cognitive retraining

Though it is not possible to make a firm choice between the various models of recovery discussed earlier, the data on plasticity are encouraging, and have helped to stimulate a general interest in the possibility of promoting recovery from cognitive disturbances by systematic retraining. There are several promising lines of research, though as yet the involvement of psychology in this field has not been extensive. We shall consider selected examples of strategies which have been used, and propose to examine them in relation to the area of functional impairment concerned.

Memory

Memory disturbances are one of the most frequent effects of brain damage. As we have seen in Chapter 3, a variety of problems can occur, the majority reflecting an underlying difficulty in acquiring new information. By and large, attempts to alleviate such problems seem to have developed from one of two starting points.

First, there have been efforts to train patients in the use of mnemonic techniques known to be effective with normal subjects. Following the repeated laboratory demonstration that visual-imagery mediation facilitates retention in normals (Bower, 1972; Paivio, 1971), the principle focus of much of this research has been the use of visual imagery to aid memory. Patten (1972) reported great improvements in the memory performance of four amnesic patients following careful instruction in the use of the well-known 'conceptual peg' system. In this technique a list of common words ('peg' words, e.g. cup) is learned in advance, and each of the to-be-remembered items (e.g. city) is then linked with one of these. Emphasis is laid on the creation of a vivid, even bizarre image of the associated terms (e.g. Manchester City winning the FA Cup). The obvious application of this method (and the main test of it in this study) is to the learning of specific items of information such as names, addresses, appointments and so on. Though the method is therefore limited in scope, memory for such relatively simple pieces of information is commonly disturbed, and the beneficial effects of such improvements on self-esteem and morale could be considerable. No 'untreated' control group was used in this study, nor was any attempt made to investigate other mnemonic strategies; thus, it is not possible to attribute the reported improvements directly to the use of visual imagery.

A better controlled study is reported by Jones (1974), who studied paired-associate learning in groups of patients with right, left or bilateral temporal lobe damage. All patients were instructed in the use of visual imagery, and their performance was compared with those of a group of normal controls, half of whom were given identical imagery instructions and half asked merely to learn. Immediate and delayed (2 hours) recall was measured. All subjects, except those with bilateral damage, were found to improve compared with their baseline scores after being instructed to use imagery, but the effect was fairly small and limited mainly to the immediate recall condition. Similar though more encouraging findings were reported by Lewinsohn et al. (1977), in whose investigation brain-damaged subjects were allocated at random to imagery or control conditions. Patients in the imagery condition were then given detailed instructions and practice in the use of visual imagery. The performance of both groups was then compared with a normal control group (who were also divided into imagery and no-imagery groups) on a paired-associate learning task and a task requiring names to be linked to faces. Imagery training improved the performance of both brain-damaged and control subjects, both at acquisition and when recall was examined 30 minutes later, but the superiority was lost when retention was tested one week later. For the advantage of imagery mediation to be maintained, further rehearsal may be necessary, a conclusion which may also be drawn from Jones's study. In view of the frequency with which such patients fail to remember peoples' names and faces, this is a somewhat disappointing result. However, the particular technique used may have been partly responsible, since subjects had particular images suggested to them rather than producing their own.

A second starting point for memory rehabilitation research has been to identify experimental variables which improve the performance of patients with memory problems, and then to construct methods of intervention in which the use of these is maximised. As we have seen in Chapter 3, many factors have been found to benefit such patients, and of these, the 'partial information' effect (Warrington and Weiskrantz, 1970) has been used for therapeutic purposes by Jaffe and Katz (1975). They taught a severely amnesic Korsakoff patient to remember the names of members of the hospital staff by using an individual's initials as cues for the full name, e.g. 'This person's name is Paul Doty; try to remember the initials P and D'. The patient was later asked 'This is Paul D. What is his full name?' Over a period of two weeks these cues were eliminated until the patient could identify the people by name. A similar method of alphabetical cueing was used to help the patient to remember the location of his locker and some of its contents. Though modest, such improvements are not inconsiderable in a patient who was reported never to have learned a single name in five years of hospitalization.

A different approach to memory rehabilitation has stemmed from the hypothesis (e.g. Cermak et al., 1974) that memory deficits in Korsakoff patients result from incoming information being encoded at only a superficial (e.g. phonemic) level. According to this suggestion, encouraging such patients to analyse to-be-remembered material for its meaning should result in superior learning, a prediction upheld by Cermak and Reale (1978) using a simple recognition task. The therapeutic potential of this finding was tested by Kapur (1978), who described a patient with a left-hemisphere aneurysm who, in a classification task, showed a strong tendency to analyse words for their sound or appearance rather than their meaning. Though there was no evidence of the amnesic syndrome (see Chapter 3), the patient's verbal memory was impaired, and he suffered from a moderately severe repetition deficit (a difficulty in the spoken reproduction of short phrases or single words given orally by the examiner). An attempt was made therefore to encourage him to process stimuli semantically by giving practice in a picture - word matching task over a period of three days. The patient was found to make satisfactory and regular use of a semantic strategy. When retested on the original classification task, there was a definite increase in the number of 'semantic' responses. However, on a task of verbal memory, which allowed semantic to be distinguished from rhyming classifications, the amount of semantic processing was found to be very small. Thus, increasing the patient's sensitivity to the semantic characteristics of words did not improve his verbal memory, suggesting that the problem may be more one of how to encourage the generalization of the semantic classification strategy to other relevant situations.

Though these investigations are often limited to single cases and the improvements reported are moderate, they do at least illustrate the feasibility of developing practical rehabilitation measures. Many factors have been found to affect the performance of patients with memory disturbances in laboratory investigations, but there has been little effort to exploit this knowledge in a therapeutic context. Miller (1978) reminds us that amelioration rather than restitution should be the goal of memory remediation. Even when judged by this criterion, however, there is very little to show so far for what are, in practice, extremely time-consuming exercises, though, of course, the research is still at an exploratory stage of development. It is surprising how many abilities appear absent in the unprompted, spontaneous performance of amnesic subjects, yet may be demonstrated under the right sorts of conditions. It is very often more accurate to say of such patients that they *do not* employ this or that strategy rather than that they *cannot*. Cermak (1976) was able to teach a severely amnesic patient to retain a list of simple facts, including a number of routine domestic 'rules' such as that he, the patient, should put on a sweater when he entered the house. Though perfectly capable of reciting this catalogue, the patient never actually acted on it. For example, when asked what he should do when he came into the house he would reply 'put on a sweater', but he seemed unable to use such rules to 'program' his own behaviour. The task of psychology, therefore, is arguably not only to discover what is lacking in the typical performance of patients with memory impairments (and not just those groups that have been more frequently studied, such as

Korsakoff patients), but also to suggest means by which such patients can be induced to make spontaneous use of knowledge which they undoubtedly possess.

Perception

As described in Chapter 4, patients with brain injuries can experience a variety of perceptual problems ranging from sensory inattention or neglect, to complex disturbances of recognition and perceptual organization. According to Diller *et al.* (1974), such impairments are one of the principal causes of the failure of many patients with brain injuries to return to full employment. Although the study of perception is one of psychology's most flourishing and long-established traditions, very little effort has been directed at developing rehabilitation methods for patients with perceptual difficulties. There is, however, one study reported by Diller *et al.* (1974) in which a systematic perceptual retraining programme was used, with encouraging results (see also Diller and Gordon, 1981).

Diller's project stemmed from the observation that performance on the Block Design subtest of the Wechsler Adult Intelligence Scale (WAIS) is a reliable predictor of the eventual capacity for self-care and ambulation in stroke patients. The Block Design test requires subjects to reproduce a series of increasingly complex patterns with a number of small wooden cubes. It is a test on which brain-injured patients often perform poorly, and requires many skills of perceptual organization including the analysis of whole stimuli into parts, synthesis of parts into wholes as well as powers of spatial visualization and rotation. Since the test lends itself to a systematic analysis of its components it was thought worthwhile to construct a small-scale perceptual rehabilitation procedure aimed at training subjects to improve their performances on the test. The intention was then to look for evidence of transfer to (a) other measures of perceptual abilities; (b) selected neurological and psychometric tests; (c) functional skills of everyday life and assessments provided by occupational therapists.

The construction of the actual Block Design training programme was a complex procedure and would take too long to explain in detail. Broadly, the aim was to produce an alternative series of Block Design forms equal in difficulty to the WAIS series. The rationale of the training was to identify the simplest design in the WAIS series on which failure occurred, and to begin training at the equivalent point in the alternative series, gradually working up through the more difficult forms. Retest scores on the standard WAIS forms were obtained at predetermined points during the hourly sessions, which were held over a ten-day training period. An important feature of the procedure was that patients were allocated randomly to either the experimental (trained) or control (untrained) group. The control group apparently received an equivalent amount of routine occupational therapy during periods when the experimental group was given training.

The mean number of standard designs passed by subjects at the end of the ten-day period is shown in Table 10.1.

Table 10.1   Mean numbers of correctly reproduced Block Designs

Side of Lesion	Baseline	Control
Right hemisphere (experimental)	4	7.9
Right hemisphere (control)	4	3.9
Left hemisphere (experimental)	4	8.5
Left hemisphere (control)	4	4.0

Source: Diller *et al* , 1974.

Thus, training on the alternate Block Design form clearly improves performance on the standard versions.

After training the experimental group also showed a significantly greater improvement than the control group on three perceptual measures: Object Assembly (a test requiring jig-saw parts of familiar objects to be assembled); Bender-Gestalt (a test requiring a number of semi-abstract shapes to be copied); and Purdue Pegboard Test (a test of motor dexterity, although only patients with left-hemisphere lesions improved). Improvement on one neurological measure (motor impersistence - a combined score reflecting the ability to maintain fixation and to sustain specified types of movement) was also noted.

Finally, occupational therapists were asked to supply a general assessment of each patient in areas such as ability to maintain attention, amount of assistance needed in self-care and proficiency in eye-hand co-ordination. These observations were then used to compute an overall 'occupational therapy-gain index'. This measure was found to be significantly higher in the experimental group.

Whatever was acquired during the Block Design training, therefore, seems to have generalized to the standard form of a task thought to tap complex perceptual and organizational skills, to other independently derived though related perceptual measures (and one standard neurological test), and also to aspects of general day-to-day activities.

It is possible to criticize this study on the grounds that morale and general motivation may have been higher in the experimental group since, unlike those in the control group, for whom the daily routine presumably followed a familiar pattern, each group member experienced daily periods of one-to-one interaction with an individual therapist. In addition, the significant differences between experimental and control groups were limited to a relatively small proportion of all the tests actually used. Finally, the therapists' ratings were not carried out 'blind'; they knew which group each patient belonged to (though it is stated that various steps were taken to reduce biased judgements). Nevertheless, Diller's results represent a major advance in work on perceptual training in particular and cognitive rehabilitation in general.

Review

Cognitive rehabilitation research is very much in its preliminary stages; yet from this brief examination it is clear that increasing efforts are being applied to the task of functional retraining in various areas of psychological impairment and that modest, though significant, gains may be achieved with a number of techiques. Research of this kind raises as many questions as it answers; and before embarking on the final section on brain-function therapy for cerebral dysfunction, we should like to make a number of general comments on the material covered so far.

In the work we have considered, the major involvement is arguably that of *psychologists* as distinct from *psychology*. In particular, there has been, as yet, comparatively little direct input from the contemporary literature on experimental cognitive psychology. Approaches have tended to be intuitive and pragmatic and, though associated with the relevant conceptual and theoretical background, they are not obviously deeply rooted in it. Diller's Block Design training programme, for example, is not explicitly based on any clear hypothesis as to what particular processes need rehabilitating in patients with perceptual difficulties. In practice, of course, the technique was encouragingly successful, but nevertheless, the best approach to remediation generally may not necessarily be to train on those specific tasks on which deficits are found. Work could be more explicitly guided by what is known of how a particular impaired process occurs in normals. As an example, consider disturbances of face recognition, which is a fairly common and widely debated problem found particularly in posterior right-cerebral damage. We know from laboratory studies (e.g. Reed, 1972) that subjects learn to discriminate faces by using *prototypes* – essentially general abstract images formed by averaging the characteristics of individual faces. A possible therapeutic strategy might therefore be to determine whether such processes are impaired in patients with face-recognition difficulties, and to train on tasks requiring prototype formation.

In memory retraining the predominant approach has been to give practice in, and to encourage the use of, visual imagery mediation. The explanatory value of mental imagery, however, is now seen as generally more restricted (see Chapter 3), and other approaches should be considered. An increasingly influential view, which can be traced to F. C. Bartlett, is that memory is a reconstructive activity. According to this position, memory for specific stimuli or events is tied to many contextual features – such as the place and time at which events occurred and other, essentially redundant, aspects – which we use to help reconstruct the information originally committed to memory. The power of such effects is considerable, and extends to emotional associations and to complex relations between items or events which actually occur, and others which, though not present, are implied. If you are told that someone dropped a lighted cigarette in a forest and the forest was destroyed by fire, it is a reasonable assumption that the fire was started by the cigarette. Bransford *et al.* (1972) have shown that such inferences do occur during the comprehension of short factual sentences. The idea that poor memory might be due to a lack of this type of elaborative process has been applied to Korsakoff patients by, for example, Huppert and Piercy (1976). They argue that such patients fail to encode the temporal context of events, and consequently have great difficulty in discriminating their relative recency of occurrence.

Training in the effective use of contextual and implicit features in order to enrich what is learned might, therefore, be considered for patients with memory problems. To some extent this approach is embodied in Cermak's depth-of-processing perspective, but, so far, the notion of 'deeper' (more elaborated?) levels of processing seems to have been restricted to verbal – semantic features (Craik and Lockhart, 1972).

Thus, as yet, the heavy artillery of experimental psychology has still to be brought to bear on problems of cognitive rehabilitation. Nevertheless, successful links exist between various theoretical and laboratory-based areas of psychology and practical applied fields, and the future may be viewed with some optimism.

As well as an increased involvement in generating possible rehabilitation strategies, another important role for psychologists is in evaluating their outcome. Of all the questions which may be asked of any form of therapeutic intervention, one is critical. Are observed improvements produced *specifically* by the therapy, or are they due perhaps to spontaneous recovery, or perhaps to non-specific effects such as generally improved morale or increased motivation? The only completely adequate attack on this type of problem is by means of fully controlled studies. Ideally, matched groups of patients should be allocated at random to a 'treatment' group, a 'sham treatment' group (who have comparable amounts and forms of interaction with therapists but do not receive the actual treatment), and an 'untreated' control group. Other procedures such as 'blind' assessment of patients' performance by therapists are also desirable. A common objection to this approach is that it is unethical to withhold from patients forms of treatment which are believed to be effective. This is a powerful constraint, but should be balanced against the ethics of continuing to administer a particular treatment when other, more beneficial, ones may exist. Some attempt should also be made, as in Diller's study, to assess the extent to which improvements transfer to other measures, ideally of behaviour in settings outside the clinic or laboratory. Stated in such broad terms, the process sounds commendably uncomplicated, but in practice, of course, quite the reverse is true, and few, if any, studies meet such rigorous standards. Nevertheless, psychologists can help research come as close as possible to satisfying these requirements by offering expertise at all stages, including the evolution of the method of retraining, the selection of tasks, choice of what to measure and of how to evaluate the outcome. Though these skills are not the exclusive property of psychology, this is arguably one of the ways in which experimental psychology in general, and cognitive psychology in particular, can make an important contribution.

Language and brain function therapy

Probably the longest-established tradition of rehabilitation work is concerned with language disturbance and is, principally, the domain of speech therapists. Speech therapy is a highly specialized professional field, and for this reason we are unable to pursue its methods here. However, collaborative research involving speech therapists and psychologists is beginning to develop and seems likely to increase. In order to exemplify a novel application of modern experimental cognitive psychology to language impairment, brain function therapy (BFT) is to be described in the context of a single case study - that of an intelligent middle-aged male, left-brain damaged, aphasic stroke patient.

The aim of BFT is to influence the course of relearning within the cerebrum itself. Training is involved, but by making use of techniques for lateralized stimulus presentation (especially by means of dichotic listening and tachistoscopic viewing) the intention is to focus the learning process in one or other of the cerebral hemispheres.

The acquisition of language as a form of social communication is a gradual and continuous learning process which begins at birth (Waterson, 1978). However, the usually clearly lateralized brain structures necessary to subserve the perception and production of speech are present not only in the adult brain (Geschwind and Levitsky, 1968), but also at birth (Witelson and Pallie, 1973) and even as early as the eighteenth gestational week (Wada, Clarke and Hamm, 1975). That is to say, in the human brain cerebral asymmetry of structure apparently precedes cerebral asymmetry of function, even though evoked potential studies (Molfese, 1972, 1977; Molfese, Freeman and Palermo, 1975) and dichotic listening studies with infants suggest that some lateralization of 'language' function may be present shortly after birth. Buffery (1970, 1971a) proposed that the usually left-sided cerebral predominance for language function in adulthood is acquired through the interaction of primarily audio-verbal stimuli with innate, species-specific, lateralized and linguistically predisposed neural structures (what Studdert-

Kennedy and Shankweiler in 1970 termed a 'linguistic device'). This proposal was developed by Buffery and Gray (1972) and later revised (Buffery, 1976, 1978). Any approach to the promotion of recovery of function following cerebral trauma must consider the implications of such innate structural asymmetries of the brain.

Measures of recovery from varieties of difficulties in language comprehension and expression following brain damage include the time taken to reach a plateau in post-traumatic performance and the relationship of this to the pre-traumatic asymptotic level (see also Kertesz and McCabe, 1977). To simplify the popular current belief, in younger patients post-traumatic aphasias are quick to recover and do so to a relatively high asymptotic level, whilst in older patients post-traumatic aphasias are slow to recover and do so to a relatively low asymptotic level. However, as mentioned earlier, the precise nature and history of the brain damage together with certain idiosyncratic characteristics of the patient, such as sex and hand preference (Buffery, 1974; Zangwill, 1960), complicate the story. BFT was designed (a) to monitor the damaged brain's ongoing patterns of functional recovery (BFT as 'probe'), and (b) to accelerate the rate of the damaged brain's functional recovery towards a higher asymptotic level of post-traumatic performance than would otherwise be expected (BFT as 'bombardment').

The patient was a university-educated, right-handed gentleman who had suffered extensive damage to his left and language-predominant cerebral hemisphere from strokes in his mid-forties. BFT was started two years *after* his last cerebral trauma, i.e. in his late forties. According to the more widely held views on restoration of cerebral function, a patient of such an age and with such a severe language disability should have reached an asymptotic level of post-traumatic recovery prior to commencement of BFT and, in consequence, no significant improvement would be expected. Indeed, some initial right-sided paresis (slight paralysis) and a slight, right visual-field defect had virtually disappeared by the time BFT was introduced, and yet at the time both language expression and comprehension, together with performance on psychometric tests of verbal skill, all remained severely impaired. The description of this case study will work back from what the patient finally achieved to the details of BFT and the rationale behind it. The BFT was conducted at the Maudsley Hospital and the Institute of Psychiatry, University of London.

Figure 10.2 illustrates one trial of BFT taken from the most advanced task that the patient experienced. The printed word LAD is presented by tachistoscope exposure for 150 msec. to the left visual hemifield, the plastic word BOY is presented for dichaptic perception by the left hand in conflict with the right hand's palpation of a neutral stimulus, i.e. a sponge, and the spoken word

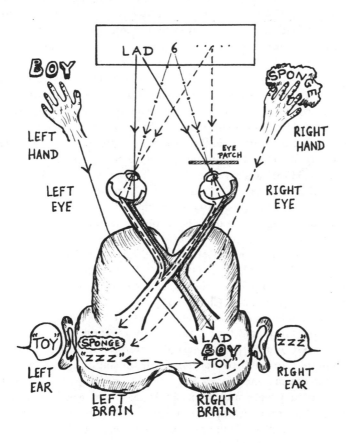

CORRECT RESPONSE = "6 TOY"

Fig. 10.2 Brain Function Therapy (BFT) Lateralized cross-tri-modal semantic discrimination task. Semantic discrimination of 'odd word out' in meaning from works presented simultaneously to the auditory, visual and tactile (haptic i.e., active exploration by touch) modalities. This figure shows a one trial attempt to 'bombard' the patient's functionally less appropriate, though structurally sound, right cerebral hemisphere, rather than 'probe' the functionally more appropriate, though damaged left cerebral hemisphere. Correct answer = '6 Toy'.

TOY by dichotic presentation to the left ear in conflict with the right ear's reception of a neutral stimulus, i.e. 'white noise'. The correct vocal response is '6 TOY', the word TOY being the correct semantic discrimination as the 'odd-word-out' in meaning, and the figure 6 indicating that the patient had fixated the central point of the display during the tachistoscopic exposure. This ensured that the word in the left visual field had been received by the left eye's nasal hemi-retina and the right eye's temporal hemi-retina, and thence transmitted via the crossing nasal and the non-crossing temporal visual pathways, for initial reception by the contralateral right cerebral hemisphere (see Chapter 2). This latter effect can be accentuated by covering the patient's right eye with a patch, and using only the crossing pathway of the left eye's nasal hemi-retina. This is because there is evidence that crossing or contralateral pathways may transmit a clearer signal to the target cerebral hemisphere than do non-crossing or ipsilateral pathways (Hubel and Wiesel, 1959). The simultaneously presented and conflicting dichaptic and dichotic neutral stimulation also accentuate the signal quality from the left hand and ear to the contralateral right cerebral hemisphere (Lehmann, 1968). The precise details of similar apparatus and procedures have been reported elsewhere, e.g. Geffen, Bradshaw and Nettleton (1973), Witelson (1974) and Buffery (1971b, 1976); and there exist thorough reviews of techniques for lateralized stimulation (Bryden, 1978; Witelson, 1977; see also Chapter 2).

In the present study the first tasks of BFT worked through one sensory modality at a time (visual, auditory and then tactile) with progressively more difficult verbal material for recognition (from single letters through to words). Then the simultaneous pairing of different sensory modalities was introduced (V/A, V/T and then A/T), again progressing from single letters to words within each pairing, but then asking for a same/different judgement as to meaning, regardless of whether upper or lower-case letters were used in the visual and tactile displays. Finally, the simultaneous cross-*tri*-modal condition shown in Figure 10.2 was achieved, and a semantic discrimination of one of the three words was required, i.e. to decide which word was the 'odd one out' in meaning. In this cross-tri-modal semantic discrimination task different words were used for each of thirty-six trials, with each sensory modality having the 'odd word out' in meaning on twelve occasions at random. Each of the single fixation numbers from 1 to 9 were used on four occasions, also at random. Throughout BFT a trial was discounted, and repeated towards the end of the session if the visual-fixation number was incorrectly reported. The cross-modal conditions were thought to be important and relevant goals for which to aim because of the evidence concerning the relationship between the development of cross-modal skills and the development of language skills (reviewed by Chapanis, 1977; Davenport, 1977; O'Connor and Hermelin, 1978). There were three or four sessions per week, each of approximately one-hour duration. Why should 'bombardment' by cross-modal verbal stimuli of a functionally less appropriate, though structurally sound, right cerebral hemisphere accelerate any ongoing compensation for a damaged left cerebral hemisphere's impaired language skill, and, as was also the intention, raise the final asymptotic level of such post-traumatic performance? The idea was to promote a structural change in the linguistically naive right cerebral hemisphere – a structural change that would subserve language skill. It was hypothesized that the characteristics of verbal stimuli and the requirement for cross-modal 'serial processing' could modify the usually 'spatial holistic' processing capacity of the right cerebral hemisphere to produce a more appropriate neural substrate for language skill, i.e. the demand for verbal function to create a verbal structure. Evidence supporting the suggestion that the pattern of stimulus input contributes to the pattern of neural dendritic growth (Buffery and Gray, 1972), derives from the research of developmental neurologists and others (e.g. Stein, Rosen and Butters, 1974).

To summarize, in the trial shown in Figure 10.2 the intention is to 'bombard' the right cerebral hemisphere with a cross-tri-modal verbal question, the vocalized answer to which requires a semantic discrimination (i.e. 6 TOY), rather than the sort of acoustic discrimination (i.e. 6 LAD) so commonly made by aphasic patients in early stages of recovery. Thus, a semantic question is posed to a functionally less appropriate, though structurally sound, cerebral hemisphere in an attempt to accelerate and promote the restoration of language skills, i.e. to 'persuade' the right brain to perform a left-brain function or, to paraphrase Wilder Penfield (1965), 'conditioning the uncommitted cortex for language'.

Figure 10.3 summarizes the patient's performance on the most advanced BFT and on parallel psychometric assessments from February 1976 until August 1978. It is clear that performance on the cross-tri-modal verbal task improved progressively over thirty months when the stimulus words were presented to the patient's right cerebral hemisphere, but not when they were presented to the left. In February 1976 the functionally more appropriate, but structurally damaged, left cerebral hemisphere and the functionally less appropriate, though sound, right cerebral hemisphere, were 'probed' by the cross-tri-modal verbal task, and were both found to be performing at around a 33 per cent level of accuracy, i.e. chance level

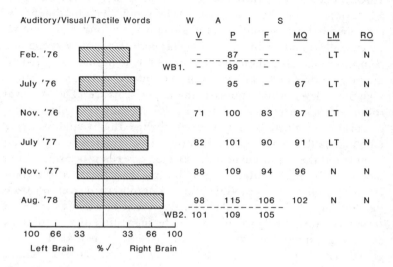

Fig. 10.3 Percentage correct cross-tri-modal semantic discrimination responses for left and right brain stimulus presentation, together with parallel psychometric scores. Correct cross-tri-modal semantic discrimination responses averaged for three days within one week of a month: psychometric scores obtained on one of those same three days.

Key	WAIS	Wechsler Adult Intelligence Scale
	V	verbal IQ
	P	performance IQ
	F	full scale IQ
	WB1 and 2	Wechsler Bellevue 1 and 2 (intelligence scales)
	MQ	memory quotient (Wechsler)
	LM	logical memory (immediate and delayed memory for prose)
	RO	Rey Osterrieth (copying and delayed recall of design)
	LT	performance characteristic of left temporal damage
	N	normal performance

for a task with three equiprobable alternatives. In August 1978 the left cerebral hemisphere was still at chance level, but the right was around an 80 per cent level of accuracy. The patient's scores on various standardized psychometric tests (reviewed by Lezak, 1976) also improved from Feburary 1976 up to August 1978, particularly on those tests with a strong verbal component, e.g. WAIS Verbal Scale subtests (V), the Memory Quotient, and the Logical Memory Task. However, this improvement in verbal skill was not at the expense of scores on the more spatial tasks, e.g. WAIS Performance Scale (P) subtests and the Rey Osterrieth task, and this pattern held true for other neuropsychological tests not shown in Figure 10.3, such as the Serial Learning Task (verbal) and the Raven's Progressive Matrices (spatial). Thus, the improvement in this patient's 'serial-processing' skill, which would normally be predominantly subserved by the left cerebral hemisphere, was not at the expense of the 'spatial-holistic' processing capacity of the right cerebral hemisphere.

Perhaps the most interesting improvement in the psychometric measures was that shown for the Wechsler Bellevue IQ scores. Forms WB1 (February 1976) and WB2 (August 1978) are equated, but different measures of intelligence, and improvement cannot be explained simply in terms of a practice effect. In February 1976 the WB1 Verbal IQ was too poor for measurement, whereas by August 1978 the WB2 Verbal IQ was at the normal average level (101). Such an improvement is rarely, if ever, found to occur spontaneously in a patient in his late forties, and at a time between 2 and 4 years post-cerebral trauma (Kertesz and McCabe, 1977). Further, over the 30-month period the WB and WAIS Performance Scale measures of IQ improved significantly, though clearly less than those of the Verbal Scale. However, there is a considerable verbal factor in these so-called 'Performance' Scale subtests (Guilford, 1967), so consequently one should not assume that the patient's cognitive improvement generalizes to skills other than verbal.

It is as yet not possible to say whether the apparent progressive commitment of the right brain to cross-tri-modal semantic discrimination is related to the progressive improvement in psychometric measures of verbal skill, but it seems a sufficiently likely and worthwhile hypothesis to warrant further investigation. The present data are being examined in the light of applying BFT to more patients with similar problems to those described in the present case study, and to other patients with different loci and causes of cerebral damage, e.g. presenting cross-modal 'spatial holistic' tasks to the functionally less appropriate, though structurally sound, left cerebral hemisphere after right cerebral trauma.

Another single case study of BFT is reported by Code (1980, 1982). The patient was a right-handed, 37-year-old male who developed language-comprehension difficulties after suffering a cerebrovascular accident approximately 4 years before the study began. To treat this, special dichotically presented tasks were devised which required phonemic discrimination (e.g. 'pa' and 'da'), auditory verbal retention (of digits) and recognition (of meaningful words such as 'bat'). Throughout, the subject was asked to report stimuli arriving at his left ear in an effort to maximize the involvement of the right hemisphere in the tasks, which were administered twice weekly in sessions of approximately 35 minutes over a period of 6½ months.

Code's study is especially noteworthy, first, because the patient had apparently ceased to respond to conventional speech therapy (therefore presumably ruling out any further spontaneous recovery); and secondly, because his progress was assessed using formal tests of language function. Pre-test and post-test comparisons of the Porch Index of Communicative Ability (PICA) and *Token Test* scores showed that there was a statistically significant improvement in the former, though not the latter. Measures of post-test, left-ear performance also showed significant gains, especially in the area of digit retention where the improvement was very pronounced. Such a trend is consistent with increased right-hemisphere involvement.

BFT may be seen as a method of re-energizing and, in some sense, developing dormant language structures which, as noted earlier, some authorities have suggested are present in the right hemisphere. These results clearly shed some light on this possibility, but further investigations are needed before they can be properly assessed. For example, we have no grounds for assuming that language recovery in either case is more likely to occur via a shift of language representation to the right hemisphere since, according to Rasmussen and Milner (1975), most 'natural' recovery appears to be mediated by intact portions of the left. However, many of the dichaptic and tachistoscopic as well as dichotic 'laterality' measures in Code's study suggested a right-hemisphere superiority for verbal processing both at the *outset* of the retraining and at its completion, when the effect was even stronger. These results agree with Johnson's (1977) observations of patients recovering from aphasia. Castro-Caldas and Botelho

(1980), on the other hand, report this trend only in *non-fluent* aphasics, fluent aphasics showing the more usual left-hemisphere advantage. Clearly, this is an important issue, since both the patients we have considered suffered significant difficulties in language *comprehension*. It is also very difficult to judge whether the observed changes in the laterality measures are truly a reflection of increased right-hemisphere processing, or alternatively, merely various forms of practice effect, of no genuine 'neurological' significance. There are few clues in the literature because there has been little interest in practice effects, though they undoubtedly occur, and may affect the performance of patients with brain lesions (Sparks and Geschwind, 1968). After more experience of the technique with a variety of patients has been gained, however, BFT should make a significant contribution to the rehabilitation of brain-damaged adults and children (Buffery and Waterson, 1978).

Prospect

Clinical neuropsychology is an applied behavioural science that contributes to the diagnosis, assessment and treatment of patients who suffer from various malfunctionings of the central nervous system (CNS) and, in particular, where such malfunctionings produce changes in intelligence, perception, motor skill or personality. Clinical *developmental* neuropsychology plays a similar role, but is more concerned with younger patients and with either congenital abnormalities of the CNS or with those occurring during pre-natal, perinatal or early post-natal development (reviewed by Denckla, 1979 and by Taylor, 1959).

Clinical neuropsychology has a unique and specialized contribution to make towards the *treatment* of patients with CNS dysfunction. In recent years clinical psychology has become more involved with varieties of therapeutic intervention (Wolpe, 1958; Feldman and Broadhurst, 1976); and less with psychometrics (Cronbach, 1970). Indeed, some would argue that the administration of standardized tests is best left either to trained technicians or to computerized self-assessment modules. Clinical neuropsychology is beginning to make a similar shift in emphasis away from patient assessment and towards patient assistance. Diagnosis and description of cerebral dysfunction alone does not provide a strong argument for the existence of clinical neuropsychology as a separate profession.

Indeed, the skills required for the administration and interpretation of neuropsychological tests should be incorporated into the training of both clinical psychologist and clinical neurologist, and could be done with little difficulty. Similarly, interviewing skills and other methods of examining the person rather than the lesion should be incorporated into the training of the clinical neuropsychologist. The unique, specialized and above all most worthwhile role of the clinical neuropsychologist should be that of therapist; the behavioural scientist drawing together relevant findings and expertise from such disciplines as developmental neurology and experimental psychology, and through research creating patient-specific programmes for the promotion of recovery from CNS damage.

Clinical developmental neuropsychology, concerned as it is with the growing CNS of childhood and with the possibilities of regrowth in the CNS of adulthood, is that aspect of neuropsychological science in which therapeutic research should be pre-eminent, dealing as it does with the relationship of the recovery of damaged neural structures and to the recovery of impaired psychological functions. An example of such clinical developmental neuropsychological research has been described in the previous section dealing with brain function therapy. Clinical developmental neuropsychology should continue to contribute to the diagnosis of CNS damage and to the descriptions of the related impairment, but above all it should promote and accelerate recovery from impairment through strategies of re-education and techniques of rehabilitation.

In the past, however, the emphasis has been very much on diagnosis and description. In fact the relatively recent emergence of clinical developmental neuropsychology could be misperceived as merely an epiphenomenon of the Halstead and the Reitan-Indiana Neuropsychological Test for Children. However, whilst the important contribution of these batteries is recognized, the discipline is certainly more than the sum of their sub tests. The test batteries themselves, which have been described in detail in Reitan and Davison (1974), and by Baron (1978), are derived from the original Halstead Neuropsychological Test Battery for Adults (Halstead, 1947). They attempt to discriminate three forms of brain dysfunction using four methods of inference. The three forms are (a) brain-damaged v. non-brain-damaged patients (Reitan, 1955a); (b) static v. rapidly growing lesions (Fitzhugh, Fitzhugh and Reitan, 1961); (c) right v. left cerebral hemisphere involvement (Reitan,

1955b). The four methods of inference are (i) level of performance; (ii) differential scores and patterns of ability; (iii) specific deficits of pathognomic significance; (iv) functional efficiency of the left v. right side of the body.

At the time of their conception the Halstead and Reitan batteries represented a considerable advance upon tests designed to probe simply for the presence or absence of 'organicity' (Goldstein, 1952). However, these batteries, like others (e.g. Russell, Neuringer and Goldstein, 1970), have themselves now been overtaken by the advances in neuropsychology over the past decade, and have become relatively blunt instruments both for the delineation of the degree and nature of the brain's functional impairment and for the elucidation of the idiosyncratic characteristics of a particular patient's functional recovery. As Townes, Priest and Bourke (1979) point out, the use of a multiphasic assessment battery, such as the Halstead-Reitan, with its intra-individual design and measurements across a standard sample of behaviours, does not exclude an inductive – deductive approach from being introduced, such as that described by Shapiro (1973) and Walsh (1978), in which hypotheses are generated and sequentially tested. The goal of this latter qualitative method is to answer the question *how* rather than the question *how much* a particular function is impaired (Luria and Majovski, 1977). However, such concern over the precise nature of assessment methodology seems somewhat premature when the tests themselves are relatively insensitive, and the ambiguities of the described data are open to a range of interpretations. Clinical neuropsychology has few standardized measures, and at present depends more upon the experienced 'eye' of the clinician than upon any discriminative criteria intrinsic to the procedures. It will perhaps be seen as fortunate for the growth of clinical neuropsychology that the 'experienced clinician's eye' cannot be taught and that, for example, despite the attempts by Christensen (1975) and by Golden, Hammeke and Purisch (1978) and Lewis et al. (1979) to 'package' the clinical expertise of 'the Master', Luria's lasting influence remains his neuropsychological theory. Undue emphasis upon assessment may only confirm the long-established stereotype of the clinical neuropsychologist as being the 'test basher of the brain-damaged', who scrutinizes the pattern of IQ subtest scores with as much fervour as he does the pattern of Rorschach ink-blots for hints of this or that, in keeping, of course, with the effects of any known structural pathology, and even when the differences between the scores are within their own standard error! Clinical neuropsychology may claim that the advent of the Computerized Tomography Scan does not undermine the contribution of the discipline, because localization of cerebral pathology was never the focus of concern, but rather the delineation of the 'dysfunctional topography'. This could sound like the desperate plea of the upstaged acrobat who, on being forced to relinquish the trapeze, directs the attention of the paying customer to the grace and timing of dropping into the safety net. The contribution of the clinical developmental neuropsychologist should, therefore, be weighted towards treatment and the design of patient-specific programmes for education or re-education (Buffery, 1974, 1977, 1978). There is also a need for the discipline to encompass the stroke patient and other such adults suffering from varieties of CNS damage, where the primary problem is that of rehabilitation.

Clinical neurology is a necessary and welcome influence upon neuropsychology because this discipline is the source of a large proportion of referrals, and because of the highly developed diagnostic and interviewing skills of the practitioners. The clinical neurologist and clinical neuropsychologist should share a professional language and nomenclature to a considerable degree, and certainly some aspects of the one discipline should be included in the training curriculum of the other. There are impressive precedents for liaison in neuropsychological research between the medical and behavioural scientists, e.g. Whitty and Zangwill (1977), Gazzaniga, Bogen and Sperry (1965) and Penfield and Milner (1958). There is certainly room for more fruitful communication between such disciplines than simply by sending unintelligible figures in reply to the request for (and this is a quote) 'a spot of psychometry please'. Bladin (1978) has expressed similar concern for improving the dialogue between neurologist and neuropsychologist.

There are areas of experimental psychology that could contribute to the research and conceptualizations of the neuropsychologist; for example, that of information theory to 'quantify' the 'quality' of memory, such as the relative familiarity of events, and Garner in 1962 touched upon this possibility. Corsi's tests of left v. right frontal or temporal lobe dysfunction, as reported by Milner (1971), would certainly lend themselves to such finer-grained analysis, whilst the application of decision theory (Green and Swets, 1966) to the analysis of false - positive and false - negative error rates in discrimination or memory tasks, as suggested by Cutting (1978), may help to distinguish between different types of dementias and memory disorders. Many aspects of assessment in clinical neuropsychology, and indeed in clinical psychology, would gain sensitivity from a more precise measure and appropriate analysis of the temporal dimensions of stimulus and response, (reviewed by Rabbitt, 1978).

Neuropsychological rehabilitation is an interdisciplinary area of research into clinically relevant techniques and strategies for the promotion of functional recovery after CNS damage, and is made possible by the coming together of scientific and professional skills. It is at this point of convergence (i.e. where the academic becomes practical, the pure the applied, and there is a shift from measuring impairment to promoting recovery) that the disciplines of neurology, psychology, of the speech, occupational and physio- therapies, and of nursing and social work converge upon the patient's healing process. Within the University of Melbourne's neuropsychological team, the work of Stanley (1979) on learning disorders, of Vowles (1979) on multiple sclerosis, of Kinsella (1979) on aphasic patients, of Molloy (1978) on amnesia, and of Walsh (1978) on test sensitivity and analysis for early signs of various brain dysfunctions, all emphasize what can be *done for* the patient's *well being* and not merely what can be *said about* the patient's *disability*.

Conclusions

Patients with cognitive disturbances produced by brain damage can suffer profound personal and social problems, and their difficulties present a major practical challenge. Some recovery of function occurs spontaneously, but how much more is possible through effective intervention is not known. The results of cognitive-rehabilitation research have so far been encouraging rather than spectacular, but this is a field suffering immense practical difficulties and many basic issues remain unsettled. For example, should the aims of therapy be to restore skills that are lost or to use those which remain as a 'bridge'? In short, should we speak of 'training' or 'retraining'? In many ways what has emerged from much research on cognitive impairment is that patients often fail to make spontaneous use of knowledge and skills which they actually possess. In Weiskrantz's (1980) words, patients may possess 'varieties of residual experience'. One of the aims of research should, therefore, be to discover how to make the most effective use of intact skills; real progress may depend as much on new ways of thinking as on the emergence of new methods.

At the close of the symposium *Outcome of Severe Damage to the Central Nervous System* (1975), Plum concluded that there were no 'immediate hints of promising methods that could enhance a tendency of the human nervous system for self-repair'. Today there is a growing sense that, provided wider social factors are properly recognized, experimental cognitive psychology can make a significant contribution by clarifying the conditions for relearning which are necessary or optimal.

Acknowledgement

The authors wish to thank Christine Buffery and Esme Burton for their assistance in preparing this chapter.

References

Alajouanine, T. and L'Hermitte, F. (1965) Acquired aphasia in children. *Brain 88*: 653–62.

Albert, M. L., Sparks, R. W. and Helm, N. A. (1973) Melodic Intonation Therapy for aphasia. *Archives of Neurology 29*: 130–1.

Baddeley, A. D. (1981) The cognitive psychology of everyday life. *British Journal of Psychology 72*: 257–69.

Baron, I. S. (1978) Neuropsychological assessment of neurological conditions. In P. Magrab (ed.) *Psychological Management of Pediatric Problems*. Baltimore: University Park Press.

Bladin, P. F. (1978) Localization in the epilepsies. In G. V. Stanley and K. W. Walsh (eds) *Proceedings of the 1976 Brain Impairment Workshop*. Published by the Neuropsychology Group, University of Melbourne.

Bower, G. H. (1972) Mental imagery and associative learning. In L. Gregg (ed.) *Cognition in Learning and Memory*. New York: Wiley.

Bransford, J. D., Barclay, J. R. and Franks, J. J. (1972) Sentence memory: a constructive versus interpretative approach. *Cognitive Psychology 3*: 193–209.

Bryden, M. P. (1978) Strategy effects in the assessment of hemispheric asymmetry. In G. Underwood (ed.) *Strategies of Information Processing*. London: Academic Press.

Buffery, A. W. H. (1970) Sex differences in the development of hand preference, cerebral dominance for speech and cognitive skill. *Bulletin of the British Psychological Society 23*: 233.

Buffery, A. W. H. (1971a) Sex differences in the development of hemispheric asymmetry of function in the human brain. *Brain Research 31*: 364–5.

Buffery, A. W. H. (1971b) Sex differences in cerebral dominance for speech: a theoretical contribution towards a neuropsychology of intellectual development. *Bulletin of the British Psychological Society 24*: 53.

Buffery, A. W. H. (1974) Asymmetrical lateralization of cerebral functions and the effects of unilateral surgery in epileptic patients. In S. J. Dimond and J. G. Beaumont (eds) *Hemisphere Function in the Human Brain.* London: Elek Science.

Buffery, A. W. H. (1976) Sex differences in the neuropsychological development of verbal and spatial skills. In R. Knight and D. J. Bakker (eds) *The Neuropsychology of Learning Disorders: Theoretical Approaches.* Baltimore: University Park Press.

Buffery, A. W. H. (1977) Clinical neuropsychology: review and preview. In S. J. Rachman (ed.) *Contributions to Medical Psychology.* Oxford: Pergamon Press.

Buffery, A. W. H. (1978) Neuropsychological aspects of language development: an essay on cerebral dominance. In N. Waterson and C. E. Snow (eds) *The Development of Communication.* Chichester: Wiley.

Buffery, A. W. H. and Gray, J. A. (1972) Sex differences in the development of spatial and linguistic skills. In C. Ounsted and D. C. Taylor (eds) *Gender Differences: Their Ontogeny and Significance.* Edinburgh: Churchill Livingstone.

Buffery, A. W. H. and Waterson, N. (1978) Neuropsychological assessment and modification of cerebral asymmetry: implications of Brain Function Therapy (BFT) for clinical psychology and developmental neurolinguistics. *Proceedings of 1st International Congress for the Study of a Child Language.* Tokyo, Japan.

Burklund, C. W. and Smith, A. (1977) Language and the cerebral hemispheres. *Neurology 27*: 627, 633.

Castro-Caldas, A. and Botelho, M. A. S. (1980) Dichotic listening in the recovery of aphasia after stroke. *Brain and Language 10*: 145-51.

Cermak, L. (1976) The encoding capacity of a patient with amnesia due to encephalitis. *Neuropsychologia 14*: 311-26.

Cermak, L. S. and Reale, L. (1978) Depth of processing and retention of words by alcoholic Korsakoff patients. *Journal of Experimental Psychology (Human Learning and Memory) 4*: 165-74.

Cermak, L. S., Butters, N. and Moreines, J. (1974) Some analyses of the verbal encoding deficit of alcoholic Korsakoff patients. *Brain and Language 1*: 141-50.

Chapanis, L. (1977) Language deficits and cross-modal sensory perception. In S. J. Segalowitz and F. A. Gruber (eds) *Language Development and Neurological Theory.* New York: Academic Press.

Christensen, A. L. (1975) *Luria's Neuropsychological Investigation.* New York: Spectrum Publications.

Code, C. (1980) Hemispheric specialization retraining in aphasia with dichotic listening. Paper presented at Aphasia Therapy Summer Conference, Cardiff School of Speech Therapy, Cardiff, UK.

Code, C. (1982) Hemisphere specialization retraining in aphasia: possibilities and problems. In C. Code and D. Müller (eds) *Aphasia Therapy.* London:

Edward Arnold.

Craik, F. I. M. and Lockhart, R. S. (1972) Levels of processing: a framework for memory research. *Journal of Verbal Learning and Verbal Behavior 11*: 671–84.

Cronbach, L. J. (1970) *Essentials of Psychological Testing* (3rd edn). New York: Harper & Row.

Cutting, J. (1978) Patterns of performance in amnesic subjects. *Journal of Neurology, Neurosurgery and Psychiatry 41*: 278–82.

Davenport, R. K. (1977) Cross-modal perception: a basis for language? In D. M. Rumbaugh (ed.) *Language Learning by a Chimpanzee: The Lana Project*. New York: Academic Press.

Denckla, M. B. (1979) Childhood learning disorders. In K. M. Heilman and E. Valenstein (eds) *Clinical Neuropsychology*. New York and Oxford: Oxford University Press.

Diller, L., Ben-Yishay, Y., Gerstman, L., Goodkin, R., Gordon, W. and Weinberg, M. (1974) *Studies in Cognition and Rehabilitation in Hemiplegia*. Rehabilitation Monograph no. 50. Institute of Rehabilitation Medicine, New York University Medical Center.

Diller, L. and Gordon, W. A. (1981) Rehabilitation and clinical neuropsychology. In S. B. Filskov and T. J. Boll (eds) *Handbook of Clinical Neuropsychology*. New YorK: Wiley.

Feldman, M. P. and Broadhurst, A. (eds) (1976) *Theoretical and Experimental Bases of the Behaviour Therapies*. London: Wiley.

Finger, S. (ed.) (1978) *Recovery from Brain Damage*. New York: Plenum Press.

Fitzhugh, K. B., Fitzhugh, L. C. and Reitan, R. M. (1961) Psychological deficits in relation to acuteness of brain dysfunction. *Journal of Consulting Psychology 25*: 61–6.

Flourens, P. (1824) *Recherches experimentales sur les propriétés et les fonctions du système nerveux dans les animaux vertébrés*. Paris: Crevot.

Garner, W. R. (1962) *Uncertainty and Structure as Psychological Concepts*. New York: Wiley.

Gazzaniga, M. S., Bogen, J. E. and Sperry, R. W. (1965) Observations on visual perception after disconnection of the cerebral hemispheres in man. *Brain 88*: 221–36.

Geffen, G., Bradshaw, J. L. and Nettleton, N. C. (1973). Attention and hemispheric differences in reaction time during simultaneous audio-visual tasks. *Quarterly Journal of Experimental Psychology 25*, (3): 404–12.

Geschwind, N. (1974) Late changes in the nervous system: an overview. In D. G. Stein, J. J. Rosen and N. Butters (eds) *Plasticity and Recovery of Function in the Central Nervous System*. New York: Academic Press.

Geschwind, N. and Levitsky, W. (1968) Human brain: left – right asymmetries in temporal speech region. *Science 161*: 186–7.

Golden, C. J., Hemmeke, T. A. and Purisch, A. D. (1978) Diagnostic validity of a standardized neuropsychological battery derived from Luria's neuropsychological tests. *Journal of Consulting and Clinical Psychology 46*: 1258–65.

Goldstein, K. (1952) The effects of brain damage on the personality. *Psychiatry*: 246–60.

Green, D. M. and Swets, J. A. (1966) *Signal Detection Theory and Psychophysics*. New York: Wiley.

Guilford, J. P. (1967) *The Nature of Human Intelligence*. New York: McGraw-Hill.

Halstead, W. C. (1947) *Brain and Intelligence: A Quantitative Study of the Frontal Lobes*. Chicago: University of Chicago Press.

Hécaen, H. (1969) Aphasic, apraxic and agnosic syndromes in right and left-hemisphere lesions. In P. J. Vinken and G. W. Bruyn (eds) *Handbook of Clinical Neurology*. Vol. 4. Amsterdam: North Holland.

Hécaen, H. (1976) Acquired aphasia in children and the ontogenesis of hemispheric functional specialization. *Brain and Language 3*: 114-34.

Hécaen, H. and Albert, M. L. (1978) *Human Neuropsychology*. New York: Wiley.

Hubel, D. H. and Wiesel, T. N. (1959) Receptive fields of single neurons in the cat's striate cortex. *Journal of Physiology 148*: 574-91.

Hunt, E. B. (1978) Mechanics of verbal ability. *Psychological Review 85*: 109-30.

Huppert, F. A. and Piercy, M. (1976) Recognition memory in amnesic patients: effect of temporal context and familiarity of material. *Cortex 12*: 3-20.

Isaacson, R. L. (1975) The myth of recovery from early brain damage. In N. E. Ellis (ed.) *Aberrant Development in Infancy*. London: Wiley.

Isaacson, R. L. (1976) 'Recovery' (?) from early brain damage. In T. D. Tjossem (ed.) *Intervention Strategies for High Risk Infants and Young Children*. London: University Park Press.

Jaffé, P. G. and Katz, A. N. (1975) Attenuating anterograde amnesia in Korsakoff's psychosis. *Journal of Abnormal Psychology 84*· 559-62.

Johnson, J. P., Sommers, R. K. and Weidner, W. E. (1977) Dichotic ear preference in aphasia. *Journal of Speech and Hearing Research 20*: 116-29.

Jones, M. K. (1974) Imagery as a mnemonic aid after left temporal lobectomy: contrast between material specific and generalized memory disorders. *Neuropsychologia 12*: 20-30.

Kapur, N. (1978) Neuropsychological retraining paradigms as a tool to study human memory. In M. M. Gruneberg, P. E. Morris and R. N. Sykes (eds) *Practical Aspects of Memory*. London: Academic Press.

Kertesz, A. and McCabe, P. (1977) Recovery patterns and prognosis in aphasia. *Brain 100*: 1-18.

Kinsella, G. (1979) Psychological and social re-adjustment in families of stroke patients. In M. Molloy, G. V. Stanley and K. W. Walsh (eds) *Proceedings of the 1978 Brain Impairment Workshop*. Published by the Neuropsychology Group, University of Melbourne.

Kohn, B. and Dennis, M. (1974) Patterns of hemispheric specialization after hemidecortication for infantile hemiplegia. In M. Kinsbourne and W. L. Smith (eds) *Hemispheric Disconnection and Cerebral Function*. Springfield, Ill.: Charles C. Thomas.

Kolb, B. and Whishaw, L. O. (1980) *Fundamentals of Human Neuro-psychology*. San Francisco: W. H. Freeman.

Lehmann, R. A. (1968) Motor co-ordination and hand preference after lesions of the visual pathway and *corpus collosum*. *Brain 91*, 525-38.

Lenneberg, E. H. (1967) *Biological Foundations of Language*. New York: Wiley.

Le Vere, T. E. (1975) Neural stability, sparing and behavioural recovery, following brain damage. *Psychological Review 82*: 344-58.

Lewis, G. P., Golden, C. J., Moses, J. A., Osman, D. C., Purisch, A. D. and Hammeke, T. A. (1979) Localization of cerebral dysfunction with a standardized version of Luria's neuropsychological battery. *Journal of Consulting and Clinical Psychology 47*: 1003-19.

Lewinsohn, P. M., Glasgow, R. E. and Kikel, S. (1977) Visual imagery as a mnemonic aid for brain-injured persons. *Journal of Consulting and Clinical Psychology 45*: 717-23.

Lezak, M. D. (1976) *Neuropsychological Assessment*. New York: Oxford University Press.

Lishman, W. A. (1975) In *Outcome of Severe Damage to the Nervous System*. CIBA Foundation Symposium no. 34. Amsterdam: Elsevier - North Holland.

Lund, R. D. (1978) *Development and Plasticity of the Brain: an Introduction*. New York: Oxford University Press.

Luria, A. R. and Majovski, L. V. (1977) Basic approaches used in American and Soviet clinical neuropsychology. *American Psychologist 32*: 959-68.

Luria, A. R., Naydin, V. L., Tsvetkova, L. S. and Vinarskaya, F. N. (1969) Restoration of higher cortical function following local brain damage. In R. J. Vinken and G. W. Bruyn (eds) *Handbook of Clinical Neurology*. Vol. 3. Amsterdam: North Holland.

McFie, J. (1975) *Assessment of Organic Intellectual Impairment*. London: Academic Press.

Miller, E. (1978) Is amnesia remediable? In M. M. Gruneberg, P. E. Morris and R. N. Sykes (eds) *Practical Aspects of Memory*. London: Academic Press.

Milner, B. (1971) Interhemispheric differences and psychological processes. *British Medical Bulletin 27*: 272-7.

Molfese, D. L. (1972) Cerebral asymmetry in infants, children and adults: auditory evoked responses to speech and music stimuli. Unpublished doctoral dissertation, Pennsylvania State University.

Molfese, D. L. (1977) Infant cerebral asymmetry. In W. J. Segalowitz and F. S. Gruber (eds) *Language Development and Neurological Theory*. New York: Academic Press.

Molfese, D. L., Freeman, R. B. and Palermo, D. S. (1975) The ontogeny of brain lateralization for speech and nonspeech stimuli. *Brain and Language 2*: 356-68.

Molloy, M. (1978) Memory disorders - helping the patient. In G. V. Stanley and K. W. Walsh (eds) *Proceedings of the 1977 Impairment Workshop*. Published by the Neuropsychology Group, University of Melbourne.

Moscovitch, M. (1979) Information processing and the cerebral hemispheres. In M. Gazzaniga (ed.) *Handbook of Behavioural Neurobiology*. Vol. II: *Neuropsychology*. New York: Plenum Press.

Munk, H. (1881) Über die funktionen der Grosshirnrinde. *Gesammelte Mitteilungen aus den Jahren 1877-80*. Berlin: August Hirshwald.

O'Connor, N. and Hermelin, B. (1978) *Seeing and Hearing and Space and Time*. London: Academic Press.

Paivio, A. (1971) *Imagery and Verbal Processes*. New York: Holt, Rinehart & Winston.

Patten, B. M. (1972) The ancient art of memory. *Archives of Neurology 26*: 25-31.

Penfield, W. (1965) Conditioning the uncommitted cortex for language. *Brain 88*: 787-98.

Penfield, W. and Milner, B. (1958) The memory deficit produced by bilateral lesions of the hippocampal zone. *Archives of Neurology and Psychiatry 79*: 475-97.

Rabbitt, P. (1978) Visual selective attention. In B. M. Foss (ed.) *Psychology Survey No. 1*. London: George Allen & Unwin.

Rasmussen, T. and Milner, B. (1975) Clinical and surgical studies of the cerebral speech areas in men. In K. Zulch, O. Creutzfeldt and G. C. Galbraith (eds) *Cerebral Localization*. Berlin: Springer-Verlag.

Reed, S. K. (1972) Pattern recognition and categorization. *Cognitive Psychology 3*: 382-407.

Reitan, R. M. (1955a) An investigation of the validity of Halstead's measures of biological intelligence. *Archives of Neurology and Psychiatry 73*: 28-35.

Reitan, R. M. (1955b) Certain differential effects of left and right cerebral lesions in human adults. *Journal of Comparative and Physiological Psychology 18*: 474-7

Reitan, R. M and Davison, L. A. (eds) (1974) *Clinical Neuropsychology: Current Status and Applications*. Washington, DC: V. H Winston & Sons.

Russell, E. W., Neuringer, C. and Goldstein, G. (1970) *Assessment of Brain Damage: A Neuropsychological Key Approach*. New York: Wiley Interscience.

Shapiro, M. B. (1973) Intensive assessment of the single case: an inductive deductive approach. In P. E. Mittler (ed.) *The Psychological Assessment of Mental and Physical Handicaps*. London: Tavistock Publications.

Smith, A. (1981) Principles underlying human brain functions in neuropsychological sequelae of different neuropathological processes. In S. B. Filskov and T. J. Boll (eds) *Handbook of Clinical Neuropsychology*. New York: Wiley.

Sparks, R. and Geschwind, N. (1968) Dichotic listening in man after section of the neocortical commissures. *Cortex 4*: 3-16.

Stanley, G. V. (1979) The concept of developmental lag in developmental neuropsychology. In M. Molloy, G. V. Stanley and K. W. Walsh (eds) *Proceedings of the 1978 Brain Impairment Workshop*. Published by the Neuropsychology Group, University of Melbourne.

Stein, D. G., Rosen, J. J. and Butters, N. (eds) (1974) *Plasticity and Recovery of Function in the Central Nervous system*. New York: Academic Press.

St James-Roberts, I. (1979) Neurological plasticity: recovery from brain insult and child development. In H. W. Reese (ed.) *Advances in Child Development and Behaviour 14*. New York: Academic Press.

Taylor, E. M. (1959) *Psychological Appraisal of Children with Cerebral Defects*. Cambridge, Mass.: Harvard University Press.

Teuber, H. L. (1975) Recovery of function after brain injury in man. In *Outcome of Severe Damage to the Nervous System*. CIBA Foundation Symposium, no. 34. Amsterdam: Elsevier-North Holland.

Townes, B. D., Priest, S. R. and Bourke, V. M. (1979) Clinical neuropsychology: an evolving field. *Australian Psychologist 14* (2): 169-74.

Von Monakow, C. V. (1911) Lokalization der Hirnfunktionen. *Journal für Psychologie und Neurologie 17*: 185-200.

Vowles, L. M. (1979) Memory impairment in multiple sclerosis. In M. Molloy, G. V. Stanley and K. W. Walsh (eds) *Proceedings of the 1978 Brain Impairment Workshop*. Published by the Neuropsychology Group, University of Melbourne.

Wada, J. A., Clarke, R. and Hamm. A. (1975) Cerebral hemispheric asymmetry in humans. *Archives of Neurology 32*: 239-46.

Walsh, K. W. (1978) *Neuropsychology: A Clinical Approach*. Edinburgh: Churchill-Livingstone.

Warrington, E. K. and Weiskrantz, L. (1970) Amnesic syndrome: consolidation or retrieval? *Nature 228*: 628-30.

Waterson, N. (1978) Language acquisition: a learning process. *Revue de Phonétique Appliquée 46-7*: 183-92.

Weiskrantz, L. (1980) Varieties of residual experience. *Quarterly Journal of Experimental Psychology 32*: 365-86.

Whitty, C. W. M. and Zangwill, O. L. (eds) (1977) *Amnesia* (2nd edn). London: Butterworth.

Witelson, S. F. (1974) Hemispheric specialization for linguistic and non-linguistic tactile perception using a dichotomous stimulation technique. *Cortex 10*: 3-17.

Witelson, S. F. (1977) Early hemisphere specialization and inter-hemisphere plasticity: an empirical and theoretical review. In S. J. Segalowitz and F. A. Gruber (eds) *Language Development and Neurological Theory*. New York: Academic Press.

Witelson, S. F. and Paillie, W. (1973) Left-hemisphere specialization for language in the newborn: neuroanatomical evidence of asymmetry. *Brain 96*: 641-46.

Wolpe, J. (1958) *Psychotherapy by Reciprocal Inhibition*. Stanford: Stanford University Press.

Woods, B. T. and Teuber, H.-L. (1973) Early onset of complementary specialization of cerebral hemispheres in man. *Transactions of the American Neurological Association 98*: 113-17.

Zangwill, O. L. (1960) *Cerebral Dominance and its Relation to Psychological Function*. Edinburgh: Oliver & Boyd.

Name index

Subject index

acetylcholine, 69, 215
achromatopsia, 81
active sleep, 229
age, 48, 57, 58, 59, 60, 61, 64, 65, 68, 71, 259, 263
aggrammatism, 115, 116, 117, 118
agnosia: apperceptive vs associative, 87; auditory, 106, 107; colour, 82-5; object, 85, 90; tactile, 86 (*see also* prosopagnosia)
alexia, 98, 109
alexia without agraphia, 84
amnesia, global, 63 (*see also* memory disorders)
anomia, 101, 102, 103, 110
aphasia, 90, 259, 274; Broca's, 101, 108ff; conduction, 101, 102, 123; global, 105, 115; jargon, 102, 113ff; semantic, 118; transcortical motor and sensory, 101, 102; Wernicke's 101ff
attention, disorders of, 92ff (*see also* schizophrenia)

Balint's syndrome, 85
blind, studies of, 135, 152-64

block design, 268
bottom-up/top-down processing, 92, 94, 99, 100, 125, 126, 137, 152, 164
braille, 107, 162
brain-function therapy, 273ff
brain scan, 102

cannabis, 212
car driving, 208, 219
cerebral plasticity, 19, 20, 255ff (*see also* compensation, diaschis, etc.)
coding: dactylic, 150; dual 89, 90; semantic 57, 112; tactual 160; verbal vs non verbal, 25, 28, 29
cognitive retraining, 264ff (*see also* rehabilitation, brain-function therapy)
collateral sprouting, 257
colour vision, 81, 82, 86
compensation, 19, 256
competence/performance, 144, 153, 254
computerized axial tomography, 60, 284 (*see also* brain scan)
conservation, 144, 145